li... ...d...h... ...nd hundreds ... I wa... ...op ...les... ...elp... ...y Mike Shooter's profound, careful and utterly conv... ...g insights. He combines all the clinical and scientific expertise of a physician with the understanding, patience and openness of the best therapists. But he has something else too – his own very special gifts of wisdom, warmth, humour and kindness, which shine through on every page . . . I urge you to read it now.'

Stephen Fry

'This is a unique book which combines the wisdom of a psychiatrist who has helped heal the minds of young people in crisis for over four decades and his own experience of a damaged childhood and subsequent depression. The stories he tells are poignant and powerful testimonies to the resilience of the human spirit and will fascinate all of us who struggle to make sense of our own and other people's lives.'

Marjorie Wallace CBE
CEO, Sane

'Brilliant book. Mike Shooter has through the lens of his own lived experience of depression given us a truly 3D picture of the struggles of growing up. This is the first book I've read that bridges the gap between evidence-based texts and what all of us privileged to work with children need – intelligent kindness, emotional intelligence and a listening, non-judgmental ear.'

Professor Dame Sue Bailey
Chair, Academy of Medical Royal Colleges

'Provocative, engrossing and engaging. Compulsive reading and should be compulsory reading for all who have children and those who look after and deal with children and young people. Lessons from a life time of learning and sharing.'

Dinesh Bhugra CBE
Association

'Mike Shooter's book is full of humanity. Following the journey through the stories of people he has seen during his career, we learn so much about the stresses and pains of young people's lives. We also learn about the ways in which thoughtful therapy can make a real difference. Mike places himself by the side of the young people he works with not least by sharing his own life challenges. A wise and ultimately uplifting book.'

Jenny Edwards CBE
CEO, Mental Health Foundation

'In his engaging and informative book, Dr Mike Shooter's wisdom and insight are significant as he works in some of the toughest areas of child and adolescent mental health problems.'

Dr Hadyn Williams
CEO, British Association for Counselling & Psychotherapy (BACP)

'How can we offer advice to others if we don't recognise our own flaws and weaknesses? Mike Shooter reflects on his own journey and the challenges of depression to draw from many a gentle message of hope that things can be better. I have never read a book where turning the page I found myself in tears. A book that was difficult to put down.'

Mike Greenaway
Director, Play Wales

'A highly readable book for families as well as carers and professionals to help to understand the experience of growing up – and a valuable contribution towards better outcomes for many young people experiencing difficulties today.'

Catriona Williams OBE
CEO, Children in Wales

'Reads like a compelling novel with complex characters and challenging plots . . . Inspiring . . . Growing Pains is a book I look forward to re-reading. I highly recommend it . . . It will be one of only a few that live on the shelf above my desk for easy reference.'

Augene Nanning, *BACP Children and Young People*

GROWING PAINS

DR MIKE SHOOTER

Making Sense of Childhood
A Psychiatrist's Story

HODDER

First published in Great Britain in 2018 by Hodder & Stoughton
An Hachette UK company

This paperback edition published in 2019

1

A CIP catalogue record for this title is
available from the British Library

Paperback ISBN 978 1 473 64325 3
eBook ISBN 978 1 473 64324 6

Typeset in Bembo Std by Palimpsest Book Production Limited,
Falkirk, Stirlingshire
Printed and bound by Clays Ltd, Elcograf S.p.A

Hodder & Stoughton policy is to use papers that are natural,
renewable and recyclable products and made from wood grown in
sustainable forests. The logging and manufacturing processes are expected
to conform to the environmental regulations of the country of origin.

Hodder & Stoughton Ltd
Carmelite House
50 Victoria Embankment
London EC4Y 0DZ

www.hodder.co.uk

To the children, young people, their families and carers, from whom I have learnt so much.

CONTENTS

Prologue   1

1. The Death of Mr Dobbs: 9
   Physician, Heal Thyself

2. The Bene't Street Lady: 19
   It's The Relationship That Counts

3. Wayne, Children and Power: 29
   Whose Body is it Anyway?

4. Bernie: Intimacy and Trust   37

5. Bryn and Sian: 47
   Identity and the Danger of Labels

6. Gavin: 57
   Finding a Common Language with Young Children

7. Liam: The Nature of Adolescence   69

8. Cameron and Cheryl: 81
   The Problem of Personality

9. Gwen and Ryan: 93
   Anorexia and Family Dynamics

10. Nathan and Christine: 105
    Tales of Pride and Prejudice

11. Abdi, Hassan and Hijab: Cultural Differences   117

12. Becky: Handling Risk 127

13. Lizzie: A Child's Best Interests 139

14. Will: Recognising an Emergency 151

15. The Drum Majorettes: Peer Group Pressure 163

16. Ricky and Harry: Managing Expectations 177

17. David: 187

 The Mythology and Stigma of Mental Illness

18. Simon and Keri: Dealing with Aggressive Children 201

19. Freddie and Ellie: 211

 Extreme Behaviour and the Concept of Evil

20. Oliver, Jamie, Loc and Ofure: 223

 Giving Children Their Autonomy

21. Little Peety: 235

 Seeing the Problem from All Sides

22. Max and Laura: Children and Loss 245

23. Queenie and Leanne: Cycles of Harm 257

24. Billy: The Nature of Hope 267

25. Robert: The Meaning of Separation 277

Epilogue: Sorting Through My Father's Books 287

Acknowledgements 291

Text Permissions 293

About the Author 295

PROLOGUE

Let me tell you a story, about a seventeen-year-old. No longer a child but not yet a man. An adolescent, with all that entails. His father had been away for the first two years of his life and their relationship had never been able to cross the gap.

His father kept his distance during most of his son's childhood, even though they lived in the same house. They rarely spoke about anything meaningful, never touched except by accident, and were too embarrassed to be left alone in a room together. The gap between them grew wider, both emotionally and physically, as the son grew older.

A lay preacher from a Nonconformist background, the father had conformed to almost everything his own parents demanded. He kept his nose to the grindstone, obeyed the letter of the law, and married his childhood sweetheart. He found it impossible to tolerate the way his teenage son flitted from one interest to another, from one girlfriend to the next, and seemed to have no plan in life except enjoying himself, no matter what the cost in drink and late-night cards. The more headstrong the son became, the more angrily the father reacted, in a vicious circle. The mother tried vainly to keep the peace between them, unsure about whose side she should take in any argument. The son's elder sister worked hard for anything she achieved and resented her brother's casual attitude to life. She and her father sought solace in each other's company.

An explosion was bound to happen. It came about, ironically enough, when the son squared up to a boorish neighbour who had criticised his father's lack of ambition.

'The trouble with your father is that he's wanted to do all sorts of things with his life but never had the courage to try them out. No wonder he can't stand the sight of you and the risks you take.'

Instead of welcoming his son's support, the father rebuked him for his rudeness. And the son was left with no way of expressing his anger. He carried it with him to school and thumped his fist through the library door. He was called to the headmaster's study.

'I think it's time for you and this school to go our separate ways.'

'Are you expelling me . . . sir?'

'If that's how you see it.'

It was a short conversation, but it had a lifetime's effect at home. The mother sat on her son's bed and cried into the screwed-up handkerchief that all women seemed to have tucked up their sleeve those days. This was the final straw. She could no longer hold back the feelings she had tried so hard to control. When the dam burst, they came out in a rush.

'Everything's falling apart, I don't know where to turn next. Your father seems to hate you for what you do; you seem to hate your father for what he doesn't do. One or other of you has to go.'

The son solved her problem by moving out of his parents' house. He became a navvy on the roads in winter and erected show-tents in summer; and he put enough distance between himself and the battles at home to think more seriously about himself.

Using the qualifications he already had, he talked his way into university and went there a year later to study history, weighing a stone for every year of his life. He discovered too late that history was what his father would like to have studied too, if he had been left to his own devices. But he went back home so rarely that there was no space to share this common ground, and their emotional separation was complete.

Unable to free himself from his past, the son soon lapsed back into a life spent opposing all that the world, and his father, might have wanted from him. He drifted from history to law to a succession of short-term jobs, and finally sank into his first, overt and deep depression. His father lived on with his regrets into a demented and bitter old age. To the end, the mother tried to spread a blanket over anything that might disturb the surface. The son and his sister replayed their relationship with the parents, until they too became distant and uncommunicative. And the past entrapped them all.

A bleak picture? Yes, but it might have been so different. What if they had received help, to repair their relationships before it was too late, and to prevent the problems that awaited them down the road – the sort of help that this book is all about?

I have painted that bleak picture for two reasons. Firstly, it is a story and this is a book full of stories – true stories, just like the one above. I have spent my life listening to people's stories, as a teacher, as a newspaper reporter, as a hospital doctor, and as a psychiatrist. And I came into medicine thinking that was about stories too.

What patients want is the opportunity to tell their story, to someone they trust, who will listen to them with patience and respect. Who will recognise that this may be the first time that they have found the courage to share it with anyone. Who knows that they will be frightened, angry, bewildered and upset. Someone who will hold them in the intimacy of their relationship, until they find the strength to relive their story to a happier ending.

Was that a forlorn belief? Not where I began. The profession chose doctors who had nous, who were skilled, who were hardworking, innovative and moral in the widest sense of the word. And it chose them, above all, because they could listen. But I fear all that is being lost in the scramble for places at medical school, for academic achievement, research qualifications, and shiny new technology.

Even in child and family psychiatry, where you would think that listening to stories is paramount, services are governed by the medical formalities of symptoms, diagnosis, treatment and outlook, and by the economic pressures of short-term contact and throughput of patients. Meanwhile the problems of living in a more competitive, unequal, lonely and stressful society are reflected in increasing family strife.

Children and their carers are languishing on ever-lengthening waiting lists or are not referred for help at all. If they finally get there, their behaviour will be turned into a diagnosis for treatment, or dismissed as a social problem for which the doctor behind the desk has nothing to offer. And their stories will never be heard.

Forgive me, for I am beginning to rant; and I am aware that I have not been entirely honest. The second reason for painting that picture is that it was about me. The story that I began with was my family's story, with one crucial ingredient missing. I did find help, with my own problems and my attitude to life, even if it was too difficult to change much for the rest of the family.

When I became depressed, I was in the last-chance saloon. I had gone back to university to study medicine and was in my final year, already married and with children of my own. A few more months and I might have been condemned to the same academic rat race as my colleagues and to repeating the same mistakes with my own family in turn. Perhaps that's why I became depressed; my mind's last attempt to put things right.

Whatever the cause, that depression and the help I received taught me lessons that have permeated every stage of my career. They have helped me understand the importance of our patients' stories, and how we might learn to listen to them with an open mind, from whatever quarter of life they come and whether they have a diagnosis or not. The growing pains in this book are the growing pains of my patients as they struggle with those stories; but they are my growing pains too, as I have struggled with what they have evoked in me.

I have railed against the medical model into which many children and families are artificially forced, and I have championed the ability to stick with the patient's story, no matter how confusing and disturbing it might be. But a book needs a structure or, like many of my patients, we won't know where we're going. I have used the stages of the therapeutic relationship for my structure – the beginning, the middle, and the end.

In the opening chapters, I have examined the three guiding principles that inform me as a therapist: self-awareness, the importance of the relationship, and patient empowerment. I learnt them with adults, as a medical student, an adult physician, and a psychiatrist in an adult mental health team, but they have been key to my work with children and their carers throughout.

In the closing chapters, I have tackled both the pain and the positive aspects of loss and separation. Leaving any sort of relationship, by death or divorce, leaving home, even the ending of therapy, can be fraught with regrets, but it can also be an opportunity for growth and a new and better way of life.

In between, I have tried to cover as many as possible of the issues that children and families have brought to me: the development of trust; the question of identity; how to communicate with little children; what adolescence is all about; the traps in which children may find themselves, in personality labels, family dynamics and culture; the handling of risk and its relationship to the law and to emergencies; peer group and social pressures; violence and stigma; and the varieties of approach.

Each chapter is centred around a story from the children, young people, families and carers that I have seen over the past forty years of my clinical life. Not all of them make comfortable reading. They may be sad or frightening or just perplexing. Others may even be humorous, if we can bear to see the funny side of life.

Some of them will be exactly what we are struggling with right now. Some will have disturbing echoes from the past. And some will make us thankful that we are not in the same boat. Most of them have led to a satisfactory conclusion. A few have a less than happy ending, but I don't think you would believe me if I pretended that they had.

★

I started this prologue with a story, so let me end with another. You will see that I dislike sitting behind the safety of a clinic desk. I believe in getting out into the community, where our children and carers live and work, to see at first hand the context in which their problems arise. But there are one or two clinics that I have valued, and one of these was at the top end of an old industrial valley, where the building was decaying as fast as the community around it.

The patients did their best to divide themselves into social strata. The better off came first, looking for a diagnosis for their children's behaviour that would exempt them from any responsibility for doing something about it. The single parents came next, pushing their children up the clinic stairs. Life had been tough on them, and they were tough on their children in turn. Finally came the professionals, who just happened to drop by when everyone else had gone – too embarrassed to make an appointment but needy all the same.

'Oh, there you are,' said one, as she poked her head round the door. 'I hoped you would still be doing the Thursday clinic.'

I looked at her, nonplussed.

'You don't remember me, do you? My name's Annabel. You saw us when our life was in a mess. I'm a counsellor myself now, you know.'

The details began to jumble in, like moths around her name.

'But you'll surely remember my son Jake.'

From behind her came a tall, gangling young man with tousled hair and an important-looking briefcase.

'He's home from college and he drove me up to see you. To see how it's all worked out.'

And of course I remembered him. I had seen him when he was seventeen, the age I was when my first story began, and his family had been in much the same mess. His father was a long-distance lorry driver and as remote from Jake as my father was with me. They struggled with a similar deteriorating relationship until none of them could stand it any longer. Like me, Jake took out his feelings at school and was suspended for his pains. And his mother had faced Jake and his father with the same agonising choice.

But they had help. They didn't wait for other people to refer them; a GP, a teacher or a social worker. They recognised their own problems and they came to me to resolve them.

I worked with the family for many months. Sometimes with all three of them together, sometimes with the parents to look at the future of their marriage, sometimes with Jake alone to explore what it felt like to be a teenager in such a hostile relationship. The parents decided to separate. Relieved of the pressure, Jake settled at home, went back to school, got good grades and went off to college.

Above all, the relationship between Jake and his father was healed. They lived apart but they were closer than they had ever been. The last time I saw them, they were giving each other a hug on the steps of the clinic.

Another story, about the power of therapy to change the lives of children and their families. And about the seeds of hope that we can plant in the most unlikely places.

CHAPTER 1

THE DEATH OF MR DOBBS
PHYSICIAN, HEAL THYSELF

When I rise my breakfast is solitary, the black dog waits to share it, from breakfast to dinner he continues barking, except that Doctor Brocklesby for a little keeps him at a distance . . .

Samuel Johnson in a letter to Mrs Thrale, 28 June 1783

One thing I've learnt the hard way: it takes more energy to run away from something than it does to face up to it. And I did a lot of running away.

I tried to put my childhood behind me, and all I did was to repeat my relationship with my father. First, to frustrate his ambitions for me by moving from one short-term job to another. Then, when I finally settled to medicine, to prove to him that I could be the best.

I had become obliged to many people for a second chance. I had responsibilities: to the college who agreed to take me back when others wouldn't; to the local authority who agreed to give me another grant; to my wife, her family and friends who supported me; to the two small children who depended on my succeeding. And to my own self-esteem. I couldn't afford to fail, in every sense of the word.

What I was really running away from, of course, was the fact that I had become depressed. I was just as vulnerable as anyone else, with my background perhaps even more so. And it took a dying patient to make me realise it, stop and seek help.

It was in the early hours of the morning, in my final year as a medical student, that things were about to change. A fellow student and I were ghosting through the surgical wards past rows of patients, rising and falling to the rhythms of their sleep like boats, tethered to poles with ropes of blood. We were trailing after Simon, the Senior Registrar – aloof, taciturn and straight-backed – who we had come to regard with a mixture of awe and fear. Who might at any moment demand to know the biochemistry of kidney failure or the distribution of the brachial plexus.

Simon's days worked on a different timescale to ours, but we were learning. Borne through the weekends on a tide of crises, eating in snatches, catnapping on trollies, able to carry out increasingly complicated procedures by rote when our brains were long since befuddled by fatigue. There would come a time when I would fall asleep at the operating table, when my two-year-old daughter would ask who I was, when I felt I just couldn't go on. But here we were, at two a.m., climbing the back stairs after Simon, to see one last patient for the night.

Mr Dobbs was in one of a string of side rooms reserved for seriously ill patients, hovering somewhere between life and death. We stopped outside his room while Simon whispered what he had learnt of his history. He was a proud man, a university lecturer, single, isolated and with no family or friends who had found time to visit him. Now Mr Dobbs was sitting upright in his bed, cradling a silver sick-bowl, his big moon face the colour of parchment. Alone, defenceless, and closer to death than life.

He had been brought in the previous day with a subarachnoid haemorrhage. A tiny, thin-walled, berry-like balloon in the wall of one of his arteries was oozing blood into the space between the membranes that surrounded his brain, raising the pressure in his skull and causing a splitting headache and profuse projectile vomiting – right in the middle of one of his tutorial classes.

In those days, before the neurosurgeons clipped off such aneurysms if they found them in time, and long before the radiology technicians were able to obliterate them from inside by passing a catheter through the femoral artery in the patient's groin and on up into their head, such bleeds were usually fatal. I had seen the pattern many times before. The initial insult, followed by a terrifying calm, and then the final bleed, irreversible coma and death. Mr Dobbs was in the eye of the storm and was doing his best not to cry.

Simon sat on his bed and asked him if he was frightened. Mr Dobbs nodded; he was beyond words. Then Simon, straight-laced Simon, the man we thought more suited to a brigade of guards than patient care, took him in his arms and rocked him to and fro like a baby, while Mr Dobbs sobbed into his shoulder.

Many a time we had walked the wards with Simon, ministering to the patients' physical needs; but I had never seen him do that before. By one simple gesture, he was allowing a drowning man to share his misery and receive comfort. Together they looked like the pietà I had seen in Italian churches, the Virgin Mary holding the dead Christ, alabaster-pale in their agony. Mr Dobbs was not yet dead but he soon would be, and Simon was holding him, physically and emotionally, at the very last.

Watching from the shadows at the foot of the bed, I felt devastated. Not at what Simon had done; it was magnificent. But at my own inability, I thought, to do the same. I had come from a family where no one touched each other or shared how they were feeling. I had become self-absorbed, stressed by my own problems and the work with which I was trying to blot them out. How could I ever hold a patient in my arms?

Later that morning, I was busy flushing through a patient's blocked drip, when a nurse from the side wards came up to me.

'The patient with the subarachnoid bleed wants to talk to Simon, but he's in theatre. Will you talk to him instead?'

I was terrified. I was in my final year as a medical student and this was not the first time I had seen someone so close to death;

death was part of the job. But there was always someone with me at the time. Nurses to share the drama of a medical crisis, senior doctors to share the news of a hopeless outlook. How could I find the words to talk to Mr Dobbs, let alone the sort of warmth that Simon had been able to show?

I busied myself some more with the drip, ordered a blood test or two, then made my way up the back stairs, unable to prevaricate any longer. But Mr Dobbs was already unconscious and died a few hours later, without being given the opportunity to share whatever he had wanted to say.

I sat with his body awhile, in the darkened room, nursing my sense of blame. I had become a doctor almost by accident. The university had only agreed to take me back if I passed three science exams beforehand, and I had failed the physics practical three times. I had been playing poker with friends the night before my final attempt. If I was in profit by three a.m., they would hose me down and I would try again. And thus began my medical career on the turn of the three of diamonds. Only later did they confess that they had fixed the game to make sure I won.

And now the prison walls were closing around me. In a few months' time I would pass the final exams and there would be no escape. Stuck forever in a career that I hadn't really wanted and at which I was no good – condemned to keep on running from the feelings I had been avoiding all my life.

I went to the Dean of the Medical School that afternoon and told him I would never be able to express the sort of compassion that Simon had shown to Mr Dobbs. I was giving up.

'I'm no good. I won't be any good as a doctor,' I said. 'I'm sorry for wasting so many people's time.'

The Dean, I know now, was a wise old man. He was a skilled clinician but his job, he believed, was a pastoral one. His students were his responsibility and he looked after their welfare as well as their academic progress. He had got to know us all.

'No, you're not giving up,' he replied. 'I've been watching you. You'll make a good doctor but you're depressed. And the worse you feel about yourself, the harder you work to prove you're wrong. You've been fighting against what you really feel for years. This was bound to happen. Mr Dobbs was just the final straw.'

I began to cry as he let down my defences, slowly, gently, bit by bit.

'So I shouldn't be a doctor after all. If I'm as shaky as you say.'

'We're all shaky, Michael. It's just that some of us show it more than others. But you'll have to learn to deal with it. I'll make an appointment for you to see a psychiatrist. When you've had whatever treatment you need, however long it takes, come back to me and we'll discuss your future again. With a clear mind.'

Given permission to face the feelings I'd been hiding, I plunged headlong into my first, deep depressive episode. I was convinced that the world would be a better place without me and that the only answer was to kill myself. Then I remembered the notice on the wall of the Outpatients Department, rang Samaritans, and was held just as surely as Simon had held Mr Dobbs. Until I was safely in the arms of the psychiatrist.

That depression took a year and a half out of my life and it has recurred many times since. As I get older, I have learnt to spot the earliest signs and to find ways of helping myself. Or, at least, to get help before it's too late. But that first episode was all but cataclysmic. It snapped whatever threads still bound me to my childhood; it strained my relationship with my wife; and it terrified the little children who had lost the father they once knew. After years of emotional, academic and financial investment, I was about to blow it all at the last minute.

There have been times when I've wondered if the Dean was right, in thinking that the self-doubts were part of my depression and that there was a good doctor underneath. But of course he *was* right, and I was lucky that he was so perceptive. Not only have I prospered despite my depression, but it has taught me many lessons, about myself, about my patients, and about how the lives of those patients and myself are intertwined.

To begin with, illnesses like depression are a product of both nature and nurture: of what I was born with in my genes, and of the rules and relationships I was surrounded by in my family upbringing. Undoubtedly, I was born with a biochemical vulnerability to depression, but it might never have surfaced if it wasn't for the events of my first twenty years – the relationship with my father, who might well have been depressed himself, my aimless drifting between one university spell and another, and a career chosen on a whim and fancy.

So what my psychiatrist gave me was a combination – tablets, which helped the biochemistry, and talk, which allowed me to explore the problems in my life. And with it came the reassurance that all this was not my fault, that I had the strength to withstand it however often it might recur, and that help would always be available. How have I applied all that to my own children and those I work with in turn?

I have handed on the vulnerability to at least two of my children. I can't change that, but I have made sure that our relationship is different. We can talk to each other openly now about how we feel, we can resolve our arguments without someone leaving home, and we can seek comfort, both emotional and physical, when we are in trouble. As a result, their depressive episodes are few, far between and short-lasting. And some of their struggles were part of the ordinary process of growing up and were not a part of their depression at all.

Similarly, some of the children I have worked with were clinically depressed and needed to be treated as such. But the pressures in their lives were just as important and required guidance, not a pill. Indeed, most of them were beset with problems that had nothing to do with illness – family breakdown, bullying, abuse and the like. Their lives were in a mess. They needed my help and they got it; not some invented diagnosis that would be more comfortable for everybody concerned, or a rejection because they had no psychiatric diagnosis that would fit their problems.

Secondly, the sooner we get help the better; but that is far too glib. It took me many years to recognise that we are all vulnerable to mental health problems, young or old, irrespective of what we are or where we live; and that I needed help as much as anyone else. I can hardly expect others to be more aware than I am. But if they aren't, they may go on defending against the feelings inside and holding their patients at arm's-length lest they remind them of themselves. Like me, they may fiddle with the drip until it is too late and the Mr Dobbses of this world would go uncomforted.

For children and young people, the difficulty of getting help may be even greater. Some adult carers are so alive to the possibility of things going wrong that they reach for a referral when the issues are a basic part of development, like the tantrums of the terrible twos or the skirmishes of adolescence. But most adults, in families, schools and the outside world, ignore children's problems until they too develop – into the full-blown breakdowns of adulthood, that destroy lives and cost many times as much in services and individual distress.

Even if their problems are recognised, the right sort of services have to be there to help them. I have spent many years in the third sector, as an officer of charities that work with children, young people and their families who have been dumped on the waiting lists of formal child and adolescent mental health services and despaired of ever getting seen. Or they have been seen over and over again without being truly heard by practitioners who are stuck behind the safety of diagnosis and the clinic desk. Working with them has taught me that we need to fit in with the child, their perception of their problems and the contexts in which they are expressed, and not try to cram them into our traditional ways of doing things.

And finally, did that encounter with Mr Dobbs change the course of my career? I finished my treatment and went back to discuss my life with the Dean, as he had promised. By now I was able to appreciate medicine in its own right, stripped of all the emotional baggage it had carried from my childhood. I repeated my final student year, qualified and spent a year or more as a physician and surgeon on the hospital wards. But its influence was far deeper than that.

The treatment I had received from my own psychiatrist convinced me that this was the sort of practice that I was looking for in the rest of my career. Simon had shown me an exceptional example of humanity amongst all the technology of modern medicine, and I am sure that there are still doctors in hospital and in the community who see beyond their patient's symptoms to the human being behind them, but in psychiatry it is the rule. Or it ought to be.

So when I had finished my stint as a physician and surgeon and was allowed to specialise in the branch of medicine to which I felt most suited, I decided to spend my next three years in a psychiatric training scheme. I tried very hard to remember that what we do best is to listen to the patient's story, to help them explore its meaning in their life, and help them to change it where they can. But it was difficult in adult psychiatry, with its increasing emphasis on academic achievement and research rather than the ability to talk directly with patients.

I had in my head the image of a therapist, able to see a patient's mental illness from every point of view, to offer treatment in its widest sense, and to extract from the bag of skills that I had learnt, the particular combination that the individual needed. But 'therapist' is a controversial title that contains within it a history of squabbling between medical and non-medical professions.

If a patient's mental illness can result from a combination of biochemical and psychological factors, doctors trained in psychiatry ought to have the widest view of their problems and offer therapy of every form. Pills and talk, as my own psychiatrist had done.

But many psychiatrists are wedded to a narrow, medical perception of illness and could never call themselves therapists in the widest sense of the word. Correspondingly, there are therapists who can see mental illness from many angles but who are not doctors and could never give the medical component of treatment if it was necessary. Child psychiatry seemed to offer the best of both worlds and I moved naturally into it when I was allowed to specialise even further.

And here I have remained. Have my own problems made me

better able to treat the problems of others? Perhaps, with one caveat. Just because I had difficulties in my own family and became depressed as a result, it doesn't mean that another child, another young person or another family has the same experience, and that I know exactly how they feel. I don't. The problems may be the same but everyone's expression of them is unique. We are all experts in our own story.

If we give them room to do so and have the patience to earn their trust, children will explore that story with a refreshing direct-ness of approach. For them the relationship is everything. With you as a person, not as a doctor with a stethoscope round his neck and certificates on the wall. Without the science to hide behind, it can be a painful experience. Feelings may be exposed on both sides of the relationship, for the patient and the therapist. But the rewards, for both of us, are huge.

CHAPTER 2

THE BENE'T STREET LADY
IT'S THE RELATIONSHIP THAT COUNTS

It is the province of knowledge to speak and it is the privilege of wisdom to listen.

Oliver Wendell Holmes, American physician,
poet and essayist, in *The Poet at the Breakfast Table*, 1872

I once asked a student what she had seen me do. We had spent the day tramping around the Welsh Valleys, seeing families in their homes, in draughty rooms on the top floors of Miners' Institutes, in social services training units, and in Portakabins in the school playground. We would have seen them on the street corner, if that's where they felt comfortable.

'Just listening, I suppose.'

I resisted the temptation to preach. It had taken me many years to learn the art of 'just listening' and it would take her years too. For listening is an active process. Listening with your ears, to what is being said within a family. Listening with your eyes, to what is going on between them. Listening with your heart, to the feelings they are transferring on to you as their therapist. And none of it is possible unless you have built up a trusting relationship within which all that can take place.

This principle has informed everything I have done with children and young people or within their family and carers. It is the relationship that counts, and the lesson began for me with an old lady I saw in the attic of a clinic in adult psychiatry, and who I would come to know as The Bene't Street Lady.

I heard her coming long before I saw her. Climbing slowly up each staircase, carrying something heavy. Stopping on the landings to get her breath. Until her head appeared above the final parapet, then her chest, and finally her whole body, heaved up the last step. Tweed coat buttoned up to the neck, her hat on slightly askew. Tesco bags of groceries in each hand.

The lower you were in the pecking order, the higher your outpatient room. I was a new psychiatric trainee, the lowest of the low. I swear that half my patients never made it to the attic – gave up or died before they reached the top – but I liked it there. It was sparsely furnished with a table, two chairs and an old sofa with the horsehair sprouting out. They were a present from one of the secretaries who was clearing out her mother's house and she had made her sons lug the whole lot up the stairs. A double wardrobe had defeated them and sat permanently empty on one of the landings. As if exhausted.

Mrs Garnett was her real name. She had been referred to our team by a GP who had diagnosed her as depressed. He had already started her, he said, on 'one of those new antidepressants'. He was concerned that she might be suicidal and left it up to us to decide whether she should be admitted to hospital, with or without the help of the Mental Health Act.

She saw me through the open door and put her bags down on the top landing. 'Eh, lad. Do you think I could rest myself on that settee?'

'Of course. Come on in. Would you like a cup of tea?'

One of the advantages of being in the attic was that it was so far down to the common room that it had been given its own kitchenette. Not much more than a gas ring, but enough to make a brew in the brown WI teapot and souvenir mugs I kept in the cupboard. In my years as a newspaper reporter in Sheffield, I had met many 'proper' ladies. Tea was very important to them; it was a whole language of introduction. And Mrs Garnett was surely from somewhere around the Sheffield outskirts. I could tell by the accent.

I could sense the distress underneath, but on the surface she was as straight, contained and matter-of-fact as any of the ladies I had met. I would have to earn her trust, respect her formality and keep hold of my own anxiety. Go for the problem and she would take off like a startled bird.

She arranged herself on the sofa, her bags at her feet and her hat still on. She clearly didn't intend staying long.

'Big shop,' I said, handing her the mug of tea. 'Big family?'

She was quiet for a moment. 'No. There's only me now . . . but I always do my shopping on Wednesdays . . . can't get out of the habit somehow.'

The silence went on but I could feel her willing me to take the next step. 'Anyway, what's a Sheffield woman doing in a place like this? You're a long way from home.'

It was enough. I've learnt over the years that people in tragedy are desperate to tell their story. What they need is a sympathetic ear from someone not afraid to bear the sorrow they have locked up in their box, and the right key to open it up.

Mr and Mrs Garnett, she told me, were Sheffield born, bred and retired. After a lot of discussion, they had decided to sell up and move to East Anglia to be near their only child, a daughter who was married to an American airman based in the heart of the Fens. But they were only just getting settled when their son-in-law was transferred to Germany and his wife went with him. Six months later, Mr Garnett died. Mrs Garnett was left alone, washed up on an alien shore, with no one she could really call a friend. She had gone to see her GP with backache and here she was.

We talked about her daughter, the American airman, and their inability to have children. And then, with more difficulty, about her own, dead husband. She wept a little as she showed me a photograph, extracted from her purse inside the tweed coat. Hot air from the radiators flooded up the stairs, but she kept her coat on. Grief is cold.

A much younger bespectacled man in a demob suit and open-necked shirt grinned at the camera over his ice cream. His free arm was draped around a slim woman with a 1940s hairdo and a mock-serious expression. It must have been them, snapped by a passer-by on a wall in Cleethorpes, on a weekend outing. She told me that he had operated a punching machine in the factory of one of Sheffield's 'little maisters' and that she had given up ideas of teaching to run the household. I'd no need of any more history. It was all there, in those spare details, a life both agonising and touching in its ordinariness.

After half an hour she got up to go. Suddenly. As if she'd remembered another appointment. She stopped at the door. 'Do you come here often?'

'I'm here every Wednesday morning.'

'That's when I do my shopping. Do you mind if I drop in? For a cuppa, you understand.'

When she was safely away, I went down to the secretaries and told them that Mrs Garnett would be back. Every Wednesday. At the same time. Book her in, but please don't challenge her, stop her or ask her for her appointments card. Just wave her up the stairs and let her get on with it. They did, and she turned up as she said she would, with her groceries, week after week. We talked some more about her family, about Sheffield and her friends there, but mostly we talked about her husband.

Slowly, he changed from Mr Garnett into Jack. We drank tea and she brought in some of his things, more photographs and the objects that he had given her which reminded her of him. A cruet set he'd bought her in Belgium and two pink glass clogs from Holland, which had survived intact when a shelf broke and sliced through her souvenirs. And then I remembered the jacket.

My father-in-law was a pipe smoker who used a particular brand of tobacco: Gold Flake and Cherry Rub. When he was away on business, his wife would take the jacket out of the wardrobe and sniff it. Mr Garnett had a pipe in one of the photographs and I asked Mrs Garnett if his clothes smelt of tobacco too.

Her face cracked open with love, sadness, and not a little embarrassment. She told me that when she was at her lowest, when she missed him most of all, she would take his jacket to bed with her and cradle his scent in place of his body. She brought the jacket in and we laughed as I tried to guess what tobacco he had used.

Gradually Mrs Garnett began to improve, to feel stronger and to talk more about the future than the past. I began to wonder how I would end the sessions when she had never known she was a patient in the first place. As usual, she beat me to it.

'I'm not sure how to say this,' she said. 'But I won't be seeing you any more.'

I held my breath; this was no time to interrupt.

'I've decided to go back to Sheffield. I didn't want to make the decision straight away, when Jack died. It would have seemed like running away. But I've made up my mind now. I've sold the house and I've rented a place near where we used to live. While I look around for a new flat. That's what Jack would have wanted. That's where our friends are. That's where I belong.'

She was leaving me, not me leaving her. And that's just how it should be.

We said our goodbyes and she turned at the door, one hand on the knob. 'Eh, lad. I'm right glad I never found that psychiatrist they sent me to see!'

At first, I was mortally offended, but the consultant I was working for put me right. When he had finished laughing.

'That lady has just paid you the highest compliment you're ever likely to get in this business. It's not what you are or how far up the ladder you might have climbed; it's who you are as a person that matters. The relationship you have with your patient. A safe space, open and honest, in which the patient feels they can tell you their most painful secrets.'

I have thanked Mrs Garnett and that consultant many times over, as I have tried to create that space for the children and families in

my care. The principle is true, of course, but there are adjustments
to be made.

Children have not usually come to me as autonomous beings,
on their own account. I would love it if they had done, knocking
on my door because they recognised their need for help and where
to get it. Most of them have been referred by adults – parents,
teachers and other doctors – who have felt that the children were
the problem rather than anything to do with themselves. And the
children are angry, sad, frightened, and made to feel guilty. Many
will be determined not to say anything, if they agree to come at
all; others expect it to be like a confessional box, with a penance
handed out at the end.

So the relationship is a staged one. It must begin with engagement, to earn the child's trust; it must give ample space to explore
their feelings, once the trust is established; and it must take its time
to say goodbye at the end, lest it compound the problems they
came with in the first place. So much like Mrs Garnett, but with
children that process may be even more difficult. I may have to
work hard with the adults involved before I can get their 'permission' to create that space, and they may want instant results.

'I want you to help my daughter,' said a female surgeon from a
neighbouring health authority, who didn't want to be seen on her
own patch. She had fought hard to reach the top of her profession
and her tone was forthright and explicit; she would not put up
with anything like delay.

'Believe it or not, she's fourteen now but she still acts like a little
child. See if you can get her to grow up faster. And by the way, I
can bring her every Tuesday afternoon for the next six weeks. She's
got exams after that.'

Behind those brief sentences lay a host of issues, but they would
have to be approached with care. I knew on the grapevine that the
surgeon was divorced, that there had been an acrimonious struggle
for possession of the children, and that Tasha, the fourteen-year-old,
was the only one living with her mother. Perhaps Tasha too might
wonder if she would lose her mother's love and be shipped off to

join her brother and sister. And perhaps her mother's brusque exterior hid her own worries, that Tasha might desert her in favour of the father.

My own anxieties were enormous too. I couldn't hope to achieve much in the timetable that was laid down, and yet it would be foolish not to comply. What might a senior colleague of my employers do if I didn't follow her instructions? Particularly to someone with a reputation for not following the rules and who many in the health authority might feel glad to see the back of. And the father, himself a local dignitary, might descend on me at any moment like the wrath of God. I might easily become part of the parental battle, just as the children had become in the courts.

Part of the engagement process is to hold on to everyone's anxieties, including your own, while the relationship is established. Mrs Garnett was an adult and had some say in the issue, though I could have overridden her wishes and admitted her if I thought the GP's anxieties were justified. But Tasha was tossed around on a sea of adult wishes and had no choice but to go along with them. My task was to help her find her own strengths, to explore her own identity, and to express herself, despite whatever role the adults might want her to play in their lives.

'Why don't we do what your mother wants to start with?' Tasha shrugged her shoulders as her mother walked out of my clinic room door and left us to it. 'Then we'll see where we get to. Who knows, you might get to like it here.'

I'm not a fan of seeing children in clinics; it smacks too much of the medical model for my liking. But Tasha needed an envelope of security within which to explore her feelings. My room was as warm and safe as a womb. She could grow at her own pace there and allow out her feelings when she felt ready. She could say whatever she liked and leave it with me at the end of the session, and I would not betray her to her mother. And she could use the toys I had around if words were too difficult or too dangerous for the job.

'Every time you come here, that's the first animal you choose.'

Tasha was cuddling a glove puppet kangaroo, as usual. 'Is there anything in her pouch?' Tasha put her hand in the kangaroo's pouch and shook her head.

'I'm pretty sure there used to be a baby in that pouch. Why don't you have a search around the other puppets and see if you can find it?'

Tasha searched and found it. A baby kangaroo, on the shelf where I had hidden it beforehand. And both of us knew it must be a girl.

'What was she doing there, I wonder?'

'She was hiding.'

'What was she hiding from?'

'People. Angry people. Shouting and making a noise.'

'Has the mother missed her?'

'She's been looking for her. But she's not very bright.'

'Who's not very bright?'

'The mother. Her baby was there all the time. Right under her nose.'

'Do you think you should put her back. In her mother's pouch?'

'For a bit. Until she doesn't fit.'

'Why wouldn't she fit?'

'Because she'll grow up and get bigger. Then she'll have a pouch of her own.'

The space was made, we had a relationship and her mother was content to respect it – once it began to have an effect on Tasha's behaviour at home. Over the weeks of work with Tasha, I worried about the mother's own needs, but I would have to get her daughter's permission to see her now. Exactly the opposite of where we'd started from.

'You remember you told me that the kangaroo mother wasn't very bright?' Tasha looked surprised. The kangaroo was sitting by itself on the shelf, her baby long since gone off again to play with the other animals.

'Do you think someone should check on how she's feeling too?'

'You could.'

And I did. Tasha's mother was bright enough intellectually, but she was as emotionally fragile as her daughter had been, and the divorce had left her scarred and defensive. I gave her some room to talk about her own feelings, independently, while Tasha was at school. We talked about her own childhood, which had been driven by professional parents who demanded academic excellence and left little space for her own wishes. And we talked about the trauma that she had gone through with her own children in turn.

'Tasha loves you. She loves her father too, despite what he's done. But it's you she wants to live with. She feels safe with you.'

'Safe?'

'So safe, she can explore other things in life now. You don't need to try and keep her as a little child, tied to your apron strings. Despite what you said about making her grow up faster when we first met. Leave her be, and she'll grow up in her own good time.'

I saw Tasha again a few years later, when she was an older teenager in all sorts of appropriate bother with her friends, but nothing that her mother needed to worry about. She came to see me at her own request, to talk through her feelings about her father's relationship with a new woman and how she might help her mother to adjust to it too.

She knew where she could get the space to think about it and the relationship to hold her, emotionally, while she did so. And the power in her life was in her own hands now.

CHAPTER 3

WAYNE, CHILDREN AND POWER
WHOSE BODY IS IT ANYWAY?

*Our body is a machine for living. It is organised for that, it is its nature.
Let life go on in it unhindered and let it defend itself, it will do more than
if you paralyse it by encumbering it with remedies.*
                                    Leo Tolstoy: *War and Peace*, Bk 10, Ch. 29, 1865–9

Nothing has been more important in the history of modern medicine than the rise of patient power. No longer do we assume that doctors know best and that they are entitled to do what they will, irrespective of the patient's wishes. Patients should be partners in their treatment, taking on board the doctor's advice, but making their own decisions about it wherever possible. Many people would shout me down for using the word 'patient' itself as both demeaning and old-fashioned.

But this is not always as clear-cut as it sounds, and nowhere is it more complicated than in the world of children and their carers. Having completed all my junior posts in adult medicine, surgery and psychiatry, I came down to South Wales as a senior trainee in child and adolescent psychiatry. It was a strange title for someone with five years of experience since qualification, but I was entering a whole new sub-specialty, and however hard I tried to get rid of them, I still had the remnants of an adult's philosophy hanging around me.

I developed a particular interest in the effects of chronic disorders on children and their families and spent much of my time working alongside paediatricians. And I was staggered straight away by the enormity of the decisions made by young patients about their illness – cancers, kidney failure, and the cystic fibrosis that destroyed their lungs. Wayne was one of the first.

One of the problems with hospitals is that they rarely have anywhere specific for adolescents to go or doctors skilled in treating them. So they sit on paediatric wards, surrounded by little children and feeling embarrassed, or on adult wards, along with dying old patients and feeling terrified. Neither is the sort of place that would encourage a debate about patient power. Wayne was fifteen and had been admitted to the paediatric ward.

His kidney function had failed after a streptococcal infection when he was a young child and he had been in treatment ever since. At first, he needed dialysis three times a week, sitting in a side room, hooked up to a machine that took his blood from his body, cleansed it and put it back. Simple if you put it that way, but simple it was not. Either physically or emotionally.

Wayne tried hard to strike a balance between his dependence on the technology and his own, separate identity as a boy. He described the machine as a friend and had a name for it: Charlie. But sometimes the fear broke through.

'That's me he's been fiddling with,' he said to me as I sat by his bedside.

His dialysis machine had gone wrong, flashed a red light and let out a piercing alarm that brought the technician running in his white coat. He spent an hour tinkering inside it with a set of screwdrivers, then walked away without so much as a word to Wayne on the end of its tubes.

'You mean the machine?' I said.

'No. I mean me. The machine is part of me now.' He was crying.

Over the years, like many children with long-term problems, Wayne became a much-loved part of the medical 'family'. In fact, he was more of a permanent fixture than the staff. I met lots of different doctors and nurses, as they finished their placements and moved on, but Wayne was usually there when I visited the ward on my way home. His own home was much less stable and I began to realise why he preferred it in hospital. Despite the alarms.

His parents' marriage was never a good one, and they used Wayne's illness as a battleground. Eventually, they divorced. His father left with another woman and his mother had a healthy new baby by another man. Though they were physically apart, they were still emotionally entangled and solicited Wayne's support against each other when they visited him on the ward or on the few days a week he spent at home. Wayne began to treat the staff as the good parents that he felt he'd never had.

He spent years on the transplant list, but eventually a match became available. It was rejected by his body, despite immuno-suppressive drugs which he hated but took regularly as he was bidden. He had a second transplant but that was rejected too and he went back to dialysis three times a week on the ward. He was tiny for his age, weak, pale and socially isolated from his peer group. The only friends he had were the children on the ward with illnesses like his own.

I don't think any of us had seen it coming, or if we did we tried to ignore it. One day, when Wayne came into the ward after a fraught weekend with his mother, her boyfriend and his half-brother, he told the staff that he wanted no further treatment. At first, the staff treated it as a temporary and natural reaction to what had happened at home; as a way of showing them how miserable it made him and a way of paying them back; it couldn't be anything to do with the treatment.

But it was soon clear that he was adamant. The treatment was the problem. No more dialysis; no search for another kidney to transplant. He was rejecting any further treatment as surely as his body had rejected the transplants. It was enough. They reached for a psychiatrist to help them out.

'Is he in his right mind, Mike?'

It was an understandable question from staff who had made many decisions to let a severely ill child die, but had never been faced with a child who was making the decision for himself. I talked with him long and hard. If I'm honest, I was as shocked by his decision as anyone else and would have loved to find a way out without him losing face; but there was none. He didn't want it.

Wayne was certainly in his right mind. He had thought through the consequences of having no more treatment to their logical conclusion; he would die. A gentle death, he argued, was preferable to years of painful treatment with no guarantee of anything getting better. And he did so rationally, with no trace of any mental illness that might have clouded his judgement.

The adults were split, just as I was split between my wish to save him from his decision and my respect for his right to make it. The staff closest to him were horrified and wanted something done about it; those less involved found reasons not to act. To treat Wayne against his will would be legally dubious and practically unfeasible in a condition that required his cooperation. The parents, as ever, argued with each other and threatened to go to the press.

'Whose body is it anyway, doc?' he said to me, with his tongue only lightly in his cheek.

He knew how difficult it might be for adults like me to put their principles of empowerment into practice in a situation like this. He was well aware of the agony his decision was causing his warring parents at home and the staff with whom he had shared a loving relationship on the ward. And he wanted somehow to help us all come to terms with the result.

In the end, Wayne died. The ward team looked after him with care and he looked after us. With my help, the parents were brought closer together and the feelings of the hospital staff were healed. It was, perhaps, his most spiritual of achievements.

I've started with Wayne's story, because there can be no greater challenge to our views about the empowerment of children and young people than a fifteen-year-old who chooses to die. But in truth, the pros and cons are just as complicated in other situations.

The United Nations Convention on the Rights of the Child is

the definitive statement on the right of a child to have a say in every decision being made about their life. The vast majority of countries around the world are signed up to the Convention, many of them have funded full-time posts of Children's Commissioner to watch over its implementation, and one or two have even enshrined the terms of the Convention in law. Ministers must take the views of children into account when they are framing any policy that impinges on their lives. The sensitive approach the staff eventually showed to Wayne would have been unthinkable a few decades ago.

But that Convention is not a compendium of all-or-nothing principles. It contains pairs of principles, opposite but equally valid. So the child's right to a say is balanced by their right to protection – the duty of adults to look after the child's welfare wherever they are incapable of doing so themselves. And thereby lies the question: when are children able to make a decision and when must adults step in and make it for them?

Any parent, of a two-year-old or a teenager, will have experienced that conundrum. How do we encourage our children to explore their surroundings, physically, emotionally and socially, within a framework of security? Unless we let them find things out for themselves, they will never have a stable idea of who they are and what they stand for. They will never learn how to cope with risk. And they will never hone the skills of communication, compromise and cooperation with others.

If we are too repressive, we risk tying them to our coat-tails for life. If we are too laid-back, our children may have to act out in ever more dangerous ways in an attempt to find the boundaries to acceptable behaviour. Most parents will solve the dilemma with only the occasional skirmish, but it is easy to fall off the tightrope on either side. And so it is in therapy.

In all the stories that follow, it will be clear that I have tried in every way to provide the space for children to explore their problems within the safety of our therapeutic relationships. They can try out new ways of thinking and acting with me that they couldn't begin to address at home, in school or the community; then they can carry them into the outside world with confidence. The end result is empowerment.

But I am a pragmatist. Children do not live in a vacuum and it may be necessary to work with the adults first. It would be easy to be a purist and lose the patient; to insist on working with the child only for the parents to take them out of therapy, angry that their own wishes have not been listened to and frightened that the therapist might become a pseudo-parent in their place.

Besides, the problem may well lie in the family relationships, in the parents' marriage or in the neediness of one of the parents alone. The job would then be to work with the adults, relieve the child of the adults' problems and free the child to strike out independently: empowerment again.

Age and intellect are further factors, but neither of them is a reliable guide to the child's ability to understand what is going on and to make a decision in their own best interests. We know that young children who have been allowed to ask questions about painful situations like death and divorce, to think about them and to ask further questions, are more able to deal with them emotionally than older children who have been sheltered from the experience. And we often make false assumptions about disabled children because of our own inability to communicate with them satisfactorily.

'How do you know what Daisy wants?'

I asked the question of another paediatric team who were explaining their decision not to pursue an operation on an eight-year-old girl with a learning disability and a serious illness. This operation might prolong her life, but it would be complicated and would entail a lot of post-operative management without the certainty of success.

'We don't. It would be too difficult to explain and she would never understand.'

'Do you have anyone on the team who can communicate with a girl like Daisy, or anyone you can bring in to help?'

'No. But it wouldn't make any difference. Daisy is far too handi-capped to cope with what would be required of her. And her quality of life would be awful.'

In fact, it was the team who were struggling. It was too difficult to talk with someone like Daisy, too difficult to explain the oper-ation, and too difficult to cope with all the post-operative care that they would have to give her. It was their quality of life that would be endangered, but perhaps that would be too cruel an accusation. I'm sure they had feelings that were just as raw as the staff who treated Wayne. And it was easier to hide behind her disability instead. In the event, they brought in a specialist from the learning disabil-ities team. Daisy decided not to go through with the operation after all, but at least she had been consulted.

Three final caveats to this issue of empowerment. Firstly, my wish to help children make their own decisions does not mean I have to approve of everything they say and do. For me, the principle of 'unconditional regard', so beloved of some therapists, seems to impose an impossible demand on my tolerance. More than that, it misses an opportunity for the patient to learn something about life. Many of the children I have seen from neglectful and broken fam-ilies will never have learnt that their mother can get exasperated with what they do but still care for them just the same. Love survives anger. They can learn that in therapy instead.

Secondly, the law may have something to say about the power of the child or young person to decide what is in their own inter-ests. Sometimes this will protect their power to make the decision, to opt into treatment, for example, where the parents or other adult carers disapprove and may risk the child dying instead. Though it is not always as understanding the other way round, where a young person like Wayne wants to opt out of treatment against the adults' wishes.

The law may even protect the decisions of a child when the adults have become confused by how bizarre they look and they have split the family down the middle. Recently, it upheld the right of a four-teen-year-old girl with an inoperable cancer to be cryopreserved after her death – frozen in the hope that she could be resurrected at a future date. The issue, it was quite rightly pointed out, was not the ethics of cryonics itself, but the right of the child to make the decision.

Crucially, in making its decision, the law will only intervene in pursuit of the child's best interests. But it is adult lawyers who decide what that is, and they are no more infallible than paediatricians or child psychiatrists.

And finally, I have written all this as if the therapist is making a decision about how much power the child should be given and how to help him wield it successfully. But some children may simply not want the power in the first place. Whether we like it or not, they may actually prefer to be passive recipients of treatment doled out to them by doctors who know best. While others may have grasped the power already, and acted upon it without discussion.

'I think we should try tailing off your medication now,' I said, rather pompously, to a young patient who was recovering from a psychotic episode. 'What do you think about that?'

'I'm glad,' she replied with a grin on her face. 'Because I stopped taking the tablets ages ago. I didn't think I needed them any more. But I didn't like to hurt your feelings.'

CHAPTER 4

BERNIE
INTIMACY AND TRUST

We give the doctor access to our bodies. Apart from the doctor, we only grant such access voluntarily to lovers – and many are frightened to do even this. Yet the doctor is a comparative stranger.

John Berger and Jean Mohr: *A Fortunate Man*, 1967

Trust and intimacy lie at the heart of successful therapy. Whether the patient is a child, an adolescent, an adult or a family, they are being asked to trust themselves to an intimacy of relationship that they may never have experienced in their lives before. And within it to share a story that they may have tried to keep secret, from themselves and from others, for years.

Trust grows with intimacy and intimacy relies on trust: over the course of therapy they reinforce each other in a virtuous circle, but their establishment is fraught with difficulties in every situation. Where the patient is a teenager and the essence of their problem is one of intimacy and trust, what happens in therapy may repair or repeat what happens in outside life. Where the issue is one of sexuality, that is a challenge for both patient and therapist alike.

Bernie was such a teenager. She was seventeen when I first met her and her age was significant. She was in the very throes of adolescence, struggling to work out her own identity in relation to the adults and peer group around her. Who she was and what she stood for, how she might come to terms with her own feelings, communicate them to others, and make compromises with those of a different persuasion. And like most teenagers, Bernie shifted backwards and forwards between different sets of feelings and behaviours over short periods of time. It would have driven her mother up the wall at the best of times; when it came to sexuality it drove her to despair.

Her mother had taken Bernie to see the GP because of her spots. For a teenager, acne is embarrassing enough; but the attitudes of adults are even worse. When her mother started talking about her worries about her daughter's sexuality, in front of her, Bernie curled up in a ball and refused to speak. The GP was at a loss and referred her on to me like a relay baton, relieved to hand her over to someone else but concerned that she might drop through the gap between us; and she nearly did.

Not surprisingly, Bernie found good reasons not to come to my appointment, but her mother came alone. She was a cut-glass sort of person, as precise in her speech as she was in her manner, and dressed immaculately. She was so desperate to tell me the story that she began before we were through the door and into the privacy of my room.

'I'm so sorry Bernie hasn't come, doctor. I tried everything to get her into the car but she wouldn't budge. It's just so typical. She needs help, I know she does, but she just won't accept it . . .'

She paused for breath and I held up my hand to slow her down.

'First things first, Mrs Waters. I know how worried you are, but Bernie is seventeen and she has every right to come or not as she pleases. I'll have to work out a way of seeing her, if it sounds as if I should.'

Bernie's mother delved into her handbag and brought out a tattered exercise book with Bernie's name in swirling colours on the front.

'That's Bernie's diary. I found it lying on her bedside table when I was clearing up her room. Read it and you'll see what I mean.'

It felt as if we were close to the heart of the matter straight away.

What I did next could make or break my relationship with Bernie, even though I hadn't yet seen her. I made her mother a cup of coffee while I thought about what to say.

'I'm sure you've every reason to be worried, Mrs Waters. You're Bernie's mother and it's your job to look out for her, after all. You wouldn't be sitting here if you weren't a good parent.' She relaxed a little as she cradled her coffee.

'You can tell me a bit about it if you want, but unless it's something personal to you I will tell Bernie what we've talked about. I can't keep secrets from her. It's her life and she has a right to know why we're worried about her.'

Mrs Waters sipped at her coffee, rocked a little in her chair, and then began to cry.

'I thought perhaps it was my fault. Bernie's father was a violent man. He treated me like a slave. And then, when I got older, he went off with a younger woman. I don't know where he is now and I don't want to. Bernie doesn't either.'

'So you're worried about how that might have affected your daughter? What her father did to you, what she might have seen?'

'Yes . . . but there's more.' The words were hard to get out now; she seemed as stuck as Bernie had been in the GP's surgery.

'There's more?'

Once released, the words came tumbling out. She would have nothing to do with men, she said, after her husband had left. They hurt you and desert you. Best never to give yourself to them again. And now she had passed on her feelings to her daughter. She knew she had, because Bernie was a lesbian.

'How do you know?'

'Because she dresses in boys' clothes and she calls herself Bernie even though she's Bernice. She's never had a boyfriend like all the other girls at school. And then there's this.' She pushed the diary across the table with a look of disgust. 'Assignations,' she said before I could stop her. 'With older women.'

We'd reached the end of our session and I needed to lift her to a level where she could get home with her dignity intact. I gave her another cup of coffee and told her that I would write to Bernie directly and invite her to come and see me. I would keep the diary safely and give it back to Bernie when she came, but I wouldn't read it. That was for Bernie to share, if she wanted to.

A week later Bernie turned up alone, as I hoped she would. The letter had worked up to a point, but she was understandably defensive. On the surface, she was the very opposite of her mother. She was sunk into a battered leather jacket, ripped jeans and close-cropped hair, dyed bright red. It was the only bright thing about her. She curled up in her chair, just as far from me as she could get, and turned her face away. It wasn't difficult to guess from her demeanour just how miserable she had become.

Bernie's diary sat on the desk between us like a challenge. I pushed it towards her unopened.

'Your mother brought it but I won't read it, unless you want me to. It's yours. And it's private.'

Diaries are a source of great friction in adolescence. They can be a comfort, a way of trying on worst fears and feelings without any real wish to act them out. Sometimes they are found by intrusive parents who ferret around in their teenager's possessions without permission. But they can also be a cry for help, deliberately left lying around for a parent to find when the feelings are too frightening to express directly. I wasn't yet sure which Bernie's diary was, and she wasn't going to help me out.

'Fuck off!' And then, with a bit more thought, 'Suit yourself.'

I told Bernie that her mother had been to see me and that she was worried about her. Did she have need to be?

'Why should she? It's my life, not hers.'

'That doesn't stop her worrying. When I was your age my parents worried about everything. One minute they treated me like a child, and worried about what I didn't do. The next minute they treated me like an adult and worried about what I did. Is that the same with you?'

'That's your problem.' She hunched her shoulder ostentatiously towards me.

'And is it your problem too?'

'About what?'

'Well, there's your father for a start.'

'What about him?' She had turned a little in her chair, enough for me to see her face.

'Your mother told me what he was like. She worries that you might hate him, for doing what he did to her. And she worries that you might hate her, for putting up with it for so long.'

'He's a scumbag. I hope he dies somewhere, of something horrible. She should have left him long ago.'

'That's pretty strong.'

'He's a man. Bloody men, they're all the same!'

'But I'm a man.'

'No, you're not. You're a doctor.' Bernie smiled despite herself and I laughed.

'Do you think your mother might have stuck with him for your sake?'

The question seemed to hit her hard and we spent the next few sessions talking about what it had been like, trapped between them, stuffing the pillow over her ears so that she couldn't hear the rows and the beatings. She talked and she cried; she was beginning to trust the intimacy of the relationship. It was time to dig a little further.

'You said you hate all men. Is that why you dress like you do?'

'What do you mean?'

'Jeans, jacket, short hair. It makes you look like a man.'

'I like it this way. My mother wants me to dress like a little girl. A frilly dress and everything, like she does. Haven't you noticed?'

'I have. And you've gone the opposite way. Does that mean that your mother has jumped to conclusions in other ways too?'

Bernie looked at me with a sneer on her lips. 'You mean my mother thinks I'm a lesbian? Just because I dress like a man?'

'Yes.'

'Well, I am. And I suppose you're just as disapproving as my mother. You'd like me to be a nice little girl too. To have boyfriends, who could push me around and beat me up. Just like my father did to her.'

Working out one's sexuality is a normal part of adolescence, but it worries parents intensely. Many young people have been dragged to see me because they have continued to be unsure about it. Their parents wanted me to turn them into confirmed heterosexuals, but that is no part of my job. All of the young people were unhappy when I saw them; they wouldn't have come if they weren't. It was my job to find out why they were unhappy. Because they were afraid of their heterosexuality, or because they were homosexual and pilloried for it. Bernie had begun to cry again.

'It isn't any of my business what you are. But I do care that you're unhappy. That is my business.'

We spent another few sessions discussing how Bernie felt about her sexuality. About her determination to make herself as unattractive as she could in her mother's eyes and about her flirtation with meeting older women, which she hadn't yet carried through. It would have been easy to set all this in the context of her feelings about her father. This would have been enough to explain the precariousness of her sexual identity. But it wasn't; there were hints of something more. And I thought I knew what it might be.

When I had first ushered Bernie into my room, I had placed my hand on her shoulder. It was a spontaneous gesture that was quite unthinking and meant nothing more than an attempt to defuse the tension. But I felt her freeze under the touch. It might have been her natural reaction to a power figure with an austere title. Patients do not expect to be touched by a therapist, unless it's something formal like a handshake.

It might have been her feeling about all men. It might have been her feeling about one in particular, who had been violent to her mother, and about the mixed messages of hate and desire that I guess her mother had given her. It might have been the adolescent's normal confusion about sexuality made even more complicated by her family past. Or it might have been something much deeper still.

The hand on her shoulder was entirely innocent on my part,

but it was a reminder that we need to put ourselves in our patient's shoes and be aware of what our behaviour might mean to them. It is not our intention that matters, but how it is perceived by the patient on the receiving end. As it was, it was the key to Bernie's unhappiness.

After two months of sessions, I thought that Bernie would have enough trust in our relationship for me to be more direct. To repay the honesty of approach that she had begun to show towards me with some honesty of my own, albeit less blunt.

'Bernie, when you came to see me for the first time, I put my hand on your shoulder.' I saw her flinch with the memory. 'You froze. As if it reminded you of something awful.' She hung her head and turned away from me. I waited for a while. We both knew what I would ask next.

'Has anyone done something like that before? Touched you, I mean. Inappropriately. Without your permission.'

Even with her head turned, I could see that Bernie was crying. But she had a new-found bravery now and was determined to carry on. I let her take her time; the normal limits of a session meant nothing in circumstances like these.

'He did it . . . my uncle . . . my mother's brother . . . when I was little.'

'What did he do?'

'He fondled me . . . my breasts . . . he said it was what all men did . . . and women liked it . . . or put up with it.'

'And did you tell anyone? About what had happened?'

'I couldn't . . . He was my mother's big brother . . . she looked up to him . . . and besides, he told me that she would never love me any more . . . if I blabbed.'

'And you've never told anyone since? Not even your mother?'

It was a while before she could answer.

'I couldn't . . . He died . . . I couldn't spoil his memory.'

Bernie had been left alone with the pain of the abuse and no redress. All physical contact with men was a potential re-enactment of her shock, her anger and her guilt about her role in what he did. Had she led him on? Was that really what all men did? Did all women have to put up with it? Was it her fault that she'd never told anyone? Trust in the opposite sex was impossible; any form of intimacy taboo.

If Bernie's uncle had still been alive, I would have had to consider the legal implications of child protection – of Bernie and any other children or young people with whom he might still be in contact. We would be discussing the limits of confidentiality, the therapist's legal obligation to disclose, and how to support her through the investigation and prosecution that might result.

But one thing remained the same. At some level, adolescents are aware of what their disclosure might entail. If they trust their therapist enough, they will use him to tell the appropriate people things they have never dared tell them directly. In this case, it was her mother, and the results were more dramatic than either Bernie or I could have guessed.

I checked with Bernie that she wanted me to be a message bearer and she agreed. We made an appointment for all three of us together, and Bernie asked me to talk on her behalf. Her mother burst into tears.

'The shock of hearing it has made you cry. What your brother did. And the effect it has had on Bernie.'

The agony on her face was almost unbearable and I could see Bernie squirming in her seat.

'Yes. But that's not all.' We waited until she had recovered enough to continue. 'He did it to me too. And I couldn't tell anyone either.' She turned to Bernie, pleading. 'Forgive me. I thought you loved him. I didn't want to spoil it all.'

I left them together for a while. They were hugging each other in a way they had never done before, awkwardly at first and then more relaxed as they cried on each other's shoulder. They needed privacy.

I saw them together for a few more sessions. Bernie was still unsure about her sexual orientation but she was able to talk about it more openly with her mother, and her mother worried less about its implications. Bernie took back her diary as if she was reclaiming her life. And I was confident that they would continue to work out their life together. They had no further need of a therapist in between.

I started this chapter by saying that trust and intimacy present a challenge to the therapist as well as the patient, especially when the issue is one of sexuality. And so it is. At the very least, it will be obvious that my sessions with both Bernie and her mother, separately and together, felt like treading on eggshells. They were so fragile.

It would have been difficult to get through it, even at this pace and with this caution, without making a mistake. Like putting a hand, unbidden, on Bernie's shoulder. The trick was how to be honest about the mistake and use it to take things forwards. Just like parents, we can only be good enough. It is good for the patient to see that we have feet of clay too. Perfection is a bad model.

But that is only half the story. I don't think that anyone with rigid scruples about sexuality should ever be a therapist with teenagers. Like parents again, we need to allow them to find their own sexual identity, while making sure that they don't come to any harm in the process. The last thing they need is some repressive direction from adults who purport to know better.

It is not for me to tell my patients what is best for them – though how I might react if I was dealing with my own teenagers' sexual problems at the same time as those of my patients, I'm not sure. And I do worry about them making irretrievable decisions that they might later regret.

Which brings me, finally, to the most difficult problem of all. A patient of any age can have a crush on their therapist. They may harbour sexual fantasies about their therapist that tune in to the fantasies the therapist may have about them. Their behaviour may be flirtatious at least, and it would be tempting for some therapists to respond in kind. Every year there are a few who cross the line into overtly sexual relationships and are rightly disciplined.

Such behaviour is a betrayal of the trust that allows us to lay our hands on the patient's life, just as intimately as the surgeon in his examination room. Trust in the doctor, that he will not seek more than the patient is willing to give; trust in the patient, that she is not offering more than the doctor is willing to take.

It is understandable but unacceptable. The answer, I think, is not to deny that those feelings exist – that would miss an opportunity – but to use the feelings that the patient transfers on to the therapist and engenders in the therapist in turn, to work out what they might reflect in the patient's life outside. And to learn more about the patient in the process.

Difficult stuff, and I wouldn't dream of tackling it without supervision. Not because I'm not skilled enough or don't have the experience to cope with it, but because it's sometimes impossible to keep an objective eye in the top corner of the room to tell you what's coming from the patient, what's coming from you, and where lies the cliff-face down which you both might fall. The 'objective eye' is like the guardian of intimacy within which you both may explore the world, without fear of further abuse.

CHAPTER 5

BRYN AND SIAN

IDENTITY AND THE DANGER OF LABELS

The first person he met was Rabbit.
'Hello, Rabbit,' he said, 'is that you?'
'Let's pretend it isn't,' said Rabbit,
'and see what happens . . .'

A. A. Milne: *Winnie-the-Pooh*, 1926

I began my adult psychiatric training when old-style institutionalism was still entrenched. Long-stay patients were imprisoned by their inability to survive in the outside world; acute patients, with their problems of life, were pinned down with a diagnosis and kept quiet with a pill. All in a symbiotic relationship with staff who had handed on their jobs from one generation to another and had grown to resemble the patients, like dog owners and their pets.

I left when a new-style institutionalism was fast taking over. Young men with strange behaviour, many more Afro-Caribbeans than their numbers would warrant, and paranoid Polish women left isolated by the deaths of their husbands, all plucked out of the community, labelled and put on depot injections once a month, with the threat of admission hanging over their heads if they didn't comply. Community Treatment Orders imposed just in case, tying them to the hospital as firmly as before.

Old-style or new-style. In each case the identity of the individual was subsumed into a category shared by many thousands of others. Easy to caricature, perhaps, but no wonder I came into child and adolescent psychiatry with a sigh of relief.

Identity formation is surely the very stuff of development. Or so I thought. Children and young people climbing upwards from stage to stage, securing a foothold on every new acquisition – cognitive, physical, emotional, social, sexual and spiritual. Stopping, for a while, to sort out relationships with adults and peer group at each stage. Emerging at last with a firm idea of who they are and how they get on with others who are different in their own, unique way. Well-being by any other name.

It was exactly what I had been looking for in all that journey, through history, the law, journalism, teaching, adult medicine and psychiatry. Working with the individual and all the rawness that might entail. But one of the first families on my caseload had a far more prosaic view of life.

Bryn was the eight-year-old's name. It means 'hill' in Welsh and he was in a whole heap of trouble. He had been referred to me by his GP, after his parents had gone to see him in desperation. In school, Bryn's behaviour had exhausted the patience of a string of teachers. He was an intelligent lad who asked awkward questions at the worst possible moment and roamed around the open-plan classrooms as if he owned the place.

'There must be something wrong with your son,' said his form teacher at a parents' evening. She quoted from a list of complaints from members of staff. 'They keep telling me he's old enough to know better.'

'But you don't think so?' Bryn's mother had begun to bridle at the criticism, even though she shared the school's exasperation.

'I'm not sure he can help it. Have you ever heard of ADHD?'

'Hyperactivity, you mean?' They had all read the newspapers, been on the internet, talked to neighbours in the same sort of situation. 'What do you suppose we should do about it?'

'Ritalin is what he needs. Your doctor could put him on it. Or a psychiatrist. We tried to get the educational psychologist to refer him but all he wanted to do was teach us how to handle his behaviour in the classroom. As if we hadn't had training in that sort of thing!'

The whole family came to see me: Bryn, his mother and father, and his younger sister, Rhosyn. Her name means 'rose' in Welsh and it was almost as if the parents had anticipated the difference in their children's personalities. While Bryn took the room to pieces, Rhosyn sat quietly smiling, as sweet and demure as a flower.

'Our son has ADHD,' declared his mother, as soon as they were in the room.

'No, I haven't,' shouted Bryn from the doorway.

'He's restless, can't sit still, can't concentrate on anything for more than a few minutes, interrupts and plays the fool.'

'She thinks I'm a loony,' said Bryn, opening and closing the door, much to the amusement of the children waiting their turn on the other side.

'You see what I mean?'

The father had been sitting close to Rhosyn, alternately scowling at what Bryn was doing and nodding at what his wife was saying about it. When he could stand it no longer, he jumped up from his chair, grabbed his son by the collar and plonked him down next to me.

'Just shut up and listen to the man!'

He knocked the remains of his coffee over the floor. Rhosyn picked up the mug and placed it neatly on the table. 'Thank you, Rhosyn. See, Bryn. Why can't you be more like your sister . . .'

The air was crackling with tension now and the mother launched into a lecture on Ritalin – or methylphenidate, to give it its generic name – the American drug of choice for recalcitrant children, which was rapidly flooding the child psychiatry clinics of the UK too. I gave an explanation of ADHD as I understood it, and the need to assess a child's behaviour in every context before any trial of medication was considered.

'You'll find he's just the same everywhere,' said the mother defensively. As if she had told me something obvious and hadn't been believed. But at least I had permission to take a look around Bryn's life.

I began with the educational psychologist. He was a kindly man who gave me the impression that he spent his life suffering fools gladly and had been ground down by it all. He wasn't long off retirement.

'Ah, yes. Bryn. You must make up your own mind, of course. But for what it's worth, I don't think he's got ADHD or anything else. What he's got is a family under pressure. And he bears the brunt of it.'

He told me that Bryn's parents were both professional people, struggling to keep up with the demands of their jobs and the responsibility of bringing up a family. And a huge mortgage to boot. He had tried to see them in school, but they worked all hours under the sun and he'd had to go to their house at the weekend. I was lucky to have got them all together in the clinic.

'They must be desperate. Or you've got more clout than me.'

Over the course of an hour or more at home, he said, Bryn had behaved exactly as he had for me, the parents had told him off, and he had deteriorated even further. In a vicious circle. The parents were tired out by their jobs and by their son's behaviour. What little energy they had left after shouting at him they reserved for Rhosyn, who was doing far better at school than her brother and for whom they had nothing but praise.

'Why don't you go and see Bryn in his scout group? I'll say no more.'

It meant an evening at work, but it was worth it. Bryn's behaviour in the scout group was so impeccable that they were amazed that someone like me should be involved at all. He followed all the leader's instructions, cooperated with his peers in the most complicated tasks, and above all he glowed with pride when they told him how well he had done. I could barely resist cheering when his patrol built a bridge across a stream faster than any of the others – largely as a result of his initiative. He showed me exactly how it was done.

Back at our next appointment, it would have been easy to give way to the parents' perception and confirm the diagnosis with a trial of medication. But I was determined, instead, to explain to them why he did not have ADHD and begin the difficult process of looking at the family dynamics that had got him the label. I was not looking forward to how they might react; but I was saved by the bell.

In the interim, they had read somewhere that such disorders could be caused by an allergic response to certain foods and drinks, so they had embarked on a complicated regime that Bryn was prepared to go along with because it hadn't yet involved beef burgers and cola. They also told me, in passing, that the grandparents had become so worried about how tired they had become that they had clubbed together to send them to Majorca as a wedding anniversary present. It would be the first holiday they had enjoyed together for years.

I saw them when they got back. Both parents were tumbling over themselves to tell me how well it had gone. Free of the worries of work, their own relationship had relaxed. Bryn and his sister were closer than they had ever been, and all four of them had done exciting things together.

'And you know what?' said the mother. 'It was all down to the milk.'

'Milk?'

'Yes. The milk was off so we couldn't drink it. And Bryn's behaviour changed straight away!'

It was clear to me what had happened. Because they were all relaxed and enjoying their holiday, the parents had been much more positive towards their son, and Bryn had responded in kind. They had reversed the vicious circle they had been locked in at home. The milk was quite coincidental, but it gave them all a way out without losing face. Unconsciously, of course.

Sometimes it's better not to ram explanations down a family's throat but to thank your lucky Spanish stars and move on. But here was a lad whose identity had been submerged by the parents' need for a diversion from their own problems, and who was free now from the diagnosis they had threatened to heap upon him. At the expense of milk. A small price to pay.

But this was just the start of a growing trend. Only a few years later, a former trainee of mine, now a consultant in his own right, came up to me at a conference.

'You've no idea how things have changed.'

'I could hazard a guess.'

'Seventy-five per cent of the kids I see have either got ADHD or are on the autistic spectrum.'

'Surely not. Isn't it just the way you choose to diagnose their problems?'

He's a good consultant, skilled, knowledgeable and experienced. So why have such diagnoses swamped his clinics and those of almost everyone else? Why are most parents and therapists so keen on a medical diagnosis for the children's problems? Why is it only possible to get help from some services if the child has a bona fide diagnosis? And why are so few of us left fighting the trend?

Much of the answer lies in an unspoken 'contract' between parents and doctor at the centre of the relationship. Child psychiatrists have a need to be seen as 'proper doctors', treating illnesses that are defined by research and the randomised controlled trial. It increases the esteem in which they are held by their medical colleagues, may encourage trainees into what is still a shortage specialty, and puts mental health on to a par with any other aspect of medicine.

For the parents, the idea of illness carries with it the whole medical model of symptoms, diagnosis, treatment and prognosis, which is not only comforting but is as fascinating as any other disease. It validates their worries and their request to see the doctor. It reduces the stigma of their child's behaviour amongst family, friends and teachers and is something that can be talked about openly in public. No longer do the parents have to be embarrassed, defend themselves against attack or hide away the problem in secret. And they can enlist the help of others. They might even get some sympathy.

'Oh, that's what she's got! I see now. What can we do to help?'

'You know, I think our kid had something similar when he was her age. If only we had got treatment for him too.'

'I saw something about that on the telly. They're putting money into it now, you know. About time.'

More than this, if it's an illness and we know the right treatment, no one is to blame. The parents have no need to delve into the mess of their own relationship and the impact it might have had on the development of their child. The doctor can only do what he has been trained to do. If the treatment doesn't work, it's not his fault. It must be something to do with the child. Treatment failure is treatment resistance, just like antibiotics. No one to blame, except of course the child again.

And this central contract is compounded by surrounding demands. Health authority managers want figures – their whole life is nourished on a diet of figures. Figures for types of diagnoses, figures for treatment outcomes, figures for the throughput of patients. Figures that treat children as medical units, which get what we've got to offer, not individuals in their own right. And money will be doled out to them by politicians who need hard evidence of the prevalence of diagnoses in the community and of the money they will have to spend further down the line if they don't spend it now.

The public define themselves in relationship to stereotypes. I know who I am, because I know who you are. And my child is not like your child, because your child is hyperactive or autistic or depressed. Public attitudes towards these stereotypes are founded on Schadenfreude, and the media build them up into concrete categories of childhood disorder that are difficult to shake. Heaven spare us if children are fluid in their development and can experiment with their identity like Rabbit, and our own children are just as vulnerable to their problems as anyone else.

So far, so clear. But we are getting close to something that is more insidious still: the fear of the chaos that might lie just beneath the surface of all our lives. Child psychiatrists are trying to define their remit in the face of overwhelming demands. They will squash children into diagnoses wherever they can; if they can't make them fit, they will be rejected as social and family difficulties that are not their problem.

The parents are looking for order, to know where they should be going and what must be done to get there. If diagnosis cannot give them the answer to their child's behaviour, they may fall back on harsh discipline at best, or rejection. It is the unknown that frightens us most and we'd rather not have anything to do with it.

Does all that matter? Or is it just the foible of someone like me, who hates being classified as a depressive, or as a particular type of psychiatrist who has one form of therapy to offer rather than a skill-bag of approaches to meet the individual patient's needs? Don't get me wrong; I am not opposed to diagnosis per se. I do have depression, after all, and the diagnosis was a relief for someone who had never met mental illness before and had no idea of what was happening to him.

And I am convinced that there is indeed something called ADHD, which may have a genetic basis and which we have underdiagnosed in the past. That some children's symptoms pervade every aspect of their lives and will wreck their futures. I have treated some of them myself, with methylphenidate, in addition to advice, and they have responded – to the relief of parents and child, who are freed to get on with their ordinary relationships. Without guilt or blame.

But I do despair of the way diagnosis has swept the board. Children's problems have been bundled into categories for treatment, and their broader identities have been swept under the medical carpet in the process. Sometimes I might cope with a bit of pragmatism and a tongue in my cheek, like Bryn and his milk. The end result was a good one and it wasn't worth the battle to make a point. But sometimes the result is much more serious.

Sian had been diagnosed as depressed. The label was understandable but it was misguided; and ironically it nearly caused her death.

She was fourteen when I saw her. I was a trustee of a national helpline and was contacted as an emergency by an old telephone counsellor who had little experience of children and young people. Luckily, Sian lived not far from me and I was able to see her straight away, in an anonymous cafe of her choice on a Saturday afternoon. She was far from the sullen teenager that I might have expected, and poured out her story over a cappuccino.

Sian was the youngest of three children. She adored her siblings, she said, but had no idea of how she might live up to their achievements.

'My brother, he's rugby mad, see. He plays for the school in the week and the local team at weekends. He's playing for them now. My dad's gone to watch. He'll probably play for Wales one day. We're all very proud of him.'

'And your sister?'

'She's the academic one and she loves animals. She wants to be a vet when she grows up. The house is full of animals. Cats, dogs. She had white mice and things when she was little. Now my dad's built her a cage for chickens. And Mum is trying to persuade him to buy her a pony.'

'And you?'

Sian dipped her spoon in the coffee and stirred it around, as if she couldn't decide whether to drink it or not.

'I've got to go to the loo.'

I checked with the waitress when she'd gone, to make sure there wasn't a back way out. Then I waited. She came back with red eyes. She had obviously been crying, but it was best not to point it out. I let her take her time and ordered another coffee. The old one had gone cold.

'You were talking about yourself.'

'Was I? There's nothing to say.'

'Perhaps you were trying not to talk about yourself. I learnt a lot about your brother and sister; not much about you.'

In truth, it was difficult to put things into words but she tried. She had never been sure about her role in life and what she wanted to do with it. Two years ago, when she was twelve and struggling with the move up to big school, her only friend had been killed in a road traffic accident. Her parents had taken her to the GP because of her unhappiness and he had diagnosed her as depressed and put her on antidepressant tablets. Unable to share the grief she felt inside, the diagnosis and its treatment had come to define her life, every bit as much as her sporty brother and animal-loving sister were defined by their enthusiasms.

'And now? What happened to make you phone for help?'

'A new GP stopped my prescription. He said my depression was better. Maybe it wasn't.'

'Or there was something else.'

We slowly unpicked the layers of her life. The so-called depression on the surface, her life-long insecurities underneath, the grief she still harboured for the death of her friend, and now another trigger factor. Three months ago her maternal grandmother had died at the end of a long illness. She had been the only member of the family who had treated Sian as her own person. Sian spent a lot of time with her when she was well and at her bedside when she was ill. Her mother had dismissed her death as 'for the best' but Sian was devastated.

'I've got no one now. Perhaps I ought to follow her. To be with her again.'

'To kill yourself, you mean?'

It was like naming the unnameable and her grief broke. Thankfully there were few customers and the waitress left us alone. I drove her back home and talked to Sian's mother, with her permission. We saw each other regularly for many weeks afterwards and explored the feelings she had about her identity. I talked with the parents, who had been blinded to the problem by her diagnosis. And with her siblings too. They loved their sister as much as she loved them.

A happy outcome? I'm sure a manager could label it as a depression well treated and cleared up, but it wasn't. It was much vaguer, deeper and more important than that. An identity given room to live and breathe for itself. And the label had nearly killed it.

CHAPTER 6

GAVIN

FINDING A COMMON LANGUAGE WITH
YOUNG CHILDREN

Out of the mouths of very babes and sucklings so hast thou ordained strength . . .

Psalm 8:2

If I was challenged to say what brought parents and their children to see me most often, it would be a breakdown in their communication. Parents who are frustrated by their inability to get through to their children; children who are frustrated at their inability to get their parents to listen and to fully understand.

I was thinking about frustration when I was sitting in a hot and stuffy lecture room in middle Europe, trying to work out what the psychologist was saying from the lectern. I've got mixed feelings about conferences. Some are vehicles for one sort of academic to peddle PowerPoint presentations that you could just as easily get from a book. Some are opportunities for another sort of academic to disappear into the obscure depths of their own philosophy. And just a few are worth it for an insight that rears up and hits you between the eyes when you least expect it. This was the latter.

The psychologist put up a diagram of a circle divided by a cross into four quadrants. A Johari Window! It was buried somewhere in my training, but as far as I remembered it had been invented by a couple of Americans to explain human relationships and the 'games' we play with each other, then elaborated upon by psychiatrists. It was intended for adults, but sitting there in a paediatric conference, it began to make sense of the problems we have in communicating with children.

The top left quadrant is the Blind Spot: the area of a child's life where adults may know more about her than she does herself and must decide when and what to tell her, if anything at all. The top right quadrant is the Open Arena: where the child and adults around her share their knowledge in equal partnership. The bottom right quadrant is the Hidden Facade: the area of life where the child knows more than the adults, and must decide what and how to disclose. The bottom left quadrant is the Unknown, where the child and adults are similarly ignorant but may find out what's going on together.

It would be tempting to discuss the problems of communication in relation to both young children and adolescents at the same time; they pose some of the same issues. But they are quite different stages of development, with different needs, requiring different approaches. We should begin instead by travelling clockwise around that circle with young children and their parents – and one patient in particular who has had the most profound effect on the way I work.

It was a spin-off from working alongside paediatricians in different parts of the country, that I was occasionally asked to see children from their area if the local service was not able to help. One of these was Gavin. He was five years old and he had neurofibromatosis. Patches of granular tissue were growing in various places in his body. They were benign and would not spread like cancer, but they were locally destructive all the same.

The disorder is surprisingly common and most of its sufferers have few problems. But it can cause major disabilities in some children and there have been heart-rending stories about them in the media. Gavin had a patch behind one of his eyes, so that it filled half his face and stuck out, the eyelid stretched tight over it and the eye blind. Another was deforming the bones in his lower leg, so that he was wheelchair bound and couldn't walk.

Gavin had been fostered when his single-parent young mother could not cope with his needs. His foster-father had given up his job to look after him and his foster-mother was working long hours to cover the loss of his salary. His older, foster siblings helped where they could, but they had left home and had lives of their own to pursue.

In other words, Gavin's disabilities were imprisoning his foster-parents as much as himself. He was in the kitchen when I went to see them all. Hidden from my sight as he had been from the rest of the world. He was said to be depressed. 'We daren't let anyone see him,' said his mother. 'Even the family are shocked at the sight of him. It's best that no one knows.'

'Until we can get something done,' his father added. 'But no one seems to know when that will be. No wonder he's depressed.'

Gavin was surprised when I went into the kitchen to see him, and so was I. Quite frankly, he was as horrendous to look at as his parents had described. I could understand that other adults might recoil too, though my experience of children is that they're more curious than frightened in this sort of situation. I tried to keep my adult feelings to myself and normalise things by asking the sort of questions about his deformities that the children might ask. But Gavin wouldn't speak to me at all and I didn't expect him to. We agreed that I would come and see him regularly, or rather we agreed for him.

I brought big sheets of paper to our next session and spread them out on the kitchen table.

Gavin's foster-father made us a drink and left us alone; his foster-mother was out working as usual. I suggested we play the squiggle game with thick, brightly coloured pens. Gavin said nothing but he picked up one of the pens when I invited him to and drew me a squiggle. I made his squiggle into a picture, then I drew him a squiggle and encouraged him to make a picture out of that.

At first, I tried to make the game as simple and unchallenging as possible. I could shepherd him to more sensitive areas later when we had got used to each other, through the story our pictures began to tell. But I needn't have been so careful.

Every time I drew Gavin a squiggle, he turned it into a huge monster, weeping technicolor tears from its single eye. There could be no doubt about Gavin's image of himself and he seemed very willing to share it, once he had found someone who might understand. I wondered how I could possibly address such unhappiness when the reality of how he looked was not far short of the pictures he was drawing; but he led me to it. Strange floating figures began to appear in his pictures, carrying knives and spears and poking the monsters in their eyes.

'Do you think these might be doctors, come to operate on the monsters?' Gavin nodded. He had heard the surgeons talk to his parents about operations.

'That must be very frightening.' He nodded again.

'But it might be a good thing too. If it made things better.' Gavin had begun to cry from his one eye. It made him look even more like his pictures.

'Would you like me to talk to your parents and the doctors? About the operations, and what you want to happen? If that's the way you feel?' This time his answer came in a word. The first he had said to me. Barely audible, but I could just make it out.

'Yes.'

Gavin's parents were distraught when I told them what he wanted, appalled by how he saw himself and how he had hidden away his feelings, just as they had hidden him. And because they were faced with the reality of the operations, despite what they had said initially about getting things done. What they had wanted was a miracle. We talked it over in a session by themselves and then I helped them to ask their son directly.

'Don't you think you ought to wait, with your eye?'

'No. It makes me look horrible.'

'And your leg. Shall we ask them to try again?'

'It wouldn't work.'

We discussed it together, again and again, until they were reconciled: Gavin to what he had said he wanted but which still frightened him in prospect; and his parents to what he had decided.

The surgeons in the eye hospital told me they had decided to wait until Gavin was older and more adjusted to losing his eye, but they had little idea of when that might be. The orthopaedic surgeons had already tried to save his leg three times, bypassing the granulomatous tissue with an artificial blood supply, but it had failed each time and they were running out of options.

Both sets of surgeons were relieved to hear that I had checked it out carefully with Gavin and that he wanted them to operate. There would be no better time for them to do so, and they should go ahead and remove his right eye and left lower leg. The parents had agreed.

Gavin approached the operations with a mixture of excitement and fear, both good and bad doctors chasing the one-eyed monsters across his squiggle game. But the game was now an introduction to words, as he talked more fully about his feelings and his wishes to be a 'normal' child. After the operations, his face was not so disfigured, he was given a prosthesis for his leg and he left the wheelchair behind. He became more sociable as his self-image improved and his parents relaxed, feeding into each other in a mutually positive way.

When I last saw him, he no longer wanted to play the squiggle game at all. He preferred to talk about friends and football, normal childhood things, while he beat me at noughts and crosses and other competitive games. He had lost two bits of his body, but he had become more emotionally whole. In due course, Gavin went off to a special school and I waved him goodbye.

It was ten years before I was contacted about Gavin again. He was spending most of his day now in a normal secondary school, but was still on the books of the special school over the wall. It was difficult to know why. Ostensibly it was something to do with follow-up and the need to check on his physical progress. In reality, I thought, it was more their unwillingness to let go.

The staff at the special school were confused. Gavin was refusing to be part of their team for the Special Olympics, where he could have been a star and won gold medals in the swimming events. They decided he must be depressed again and reached for 'that psychiatrist' who had got on so well with him before. I said that I would not treat him as a referral but was happy to bump into him when I just happened to visit his school.

Gavin was playing football when I arrived. He was amazingly mobile on his false leg and the others weren't giving him any quarter. A small group of peers were watching them, including his girlfriend, and we chatted as they walked to the changing room. He told me about the exams that were coming up and that he had been so interested in other activities that he wasn't going to do very well. He exchanged knowing glances with his girlfriend as he did so. Eventually, I slipped in the question I had come to ask.

'If you're so good at football, how come you don't want to go to the Olympics and win medals?'

Gavin stopped and looked at me quizzically.

'Mike, I'd rather be last in a normal race than first in one for those disabled people.' His political correctness left something to be desired, but I knew now that his rehabilitation was complete. It was the special school staff who needed my help, to adjust to it.

So back to that Johari Window, how it applied to Gavin and the lessons we may draw for all parents struggling to communicate with young children.

The journey around it begins in the top left-hand quadrant, the Blind Spot; an unfortunate title for someone like Gavin. This is where the adults think that they know more than the child, and tailor what they say in the child's best interest. In an awful situation like Gavin's, it was natural for his parents to protect him by keeping his looks out of public view and his feelings out of theirs. Together with the surgeons, they made huge decisions about his life without consulting him on his wishes for his own body. In so doing, of course, they were protecting themselves from the pain of it all; but their intentions were honourable enough.

The idea that adults know what's best for children was once the philosophy of all paediatric wards and it still is in some. And it lives on in most families who are in the midst of crises like death and divorce. Best to keep the children in a happy ignorance. In fact, there are two big problems with that. Children are never wholly ignorant of what's going on around them, let alone within them. The clues are there for all to see. And they will fill in the rest out of their imagination, which may well be worse than the truth.

Children develop normally by being involved in family life, being told what is happening, asking questions, trying to figure it out and asking more questions, in a circular fashion that may annoy the adults but is essential to their children's understanding. We know that children who have been allowed to go through that process are more mature than older children who have been excluded from it.

Better still, their voice is listened to and their views are taken into account when decisions are being made that will affect their life, like Gavin and his operations.

Which takes us to the top right-hand quadrant, the Open Arena. The child and adults struggle to share what they know and feel, together. There are problems here where words are not enough to describe what the child is going through. The misery is too great to express and the consequence of speaking too terrifying to contemplate. How could Gavin say what it felt like to look as he did, how could he say that he wanted to be operated on, knowing the effect it would have on the parents he loved?

Listening to the views of young children is an active process and it takes time. It requires attention to every way they have of expressing their feelings: listening to what they say, if they speak at all; watching how they behave, in the family and in the outside world; noting how they make you feel, when you are with them. Using every means of communicating that is to hand: toys, books, TV programmes and electronic games. Everything can be shared and everything can carry a message, if the adults are prepared to sit down with their children and an open mind.

Communicating with young children does not depend on their

intellectual ability. I have had some of the most insightful and ethical conversations with children who have Down's Syndrome.

'Basically, Mike, what they're trying to do is rid the world of people like me,' said a girl of nine, who was talking about new techniques to pick up the syndrome in the womb and give the parents the chance of an abortion. 'They don't want us around. We're a nuisance.'

Conversely, I've been as frustrated as parents and teachers, trying to hold a conversation with a highly intelligent young lad with Asperger's Syndrome who was developmentally unable to put himself in anyone's shoes but his own, could not draw inferences from what was unsaid between the lines, and needed everything spelt out clearly, in words of one syllable.

The most useful clinic I have ever had was in the midst of a crowded hospital wing. There was a pit in the middle of the room, full of toys and books for the children, while the parents sat around the edge waiting their family's turn. Dental clinic, paediatric clinic, hearing clinic, baby clinic and me. I would stand at my door and watch the children at play with each other. Children of many nationalities, with many different disabilities and many different illnesses, all finding a happy way of communicating together. Except for the children on the autistic spectrum, who were left out and alone. It was a message for all the adults, including me. Which disorders can get in the way of communication, what few barriers there are to most other children, and if the children can do it, why can't we?

The answer to that lies in the third quadrant at the lower right: the Hidden Facade. Here the child knows more than the adults and must decide what to tell them, if at all. Sometimes this is positive, a private part of the child's life that is their world, that they may share with their friends but which adults intrude upon at their peril. Many are the parents who have complained to me about being excluded from that world.

'He just won't talk to me about school,' said the mother of a six-year-old. 'I sit down with him over tea and ask him what's happened in his day, like a good mother should. But he just shrugs his shoulders, wolfs his tea down and wants to get out and about.'

He could, of course, have been hiding something awful at school. Bullying by one of his peers, being picked upon by a teacher, struggling with the work. But children do not usually keep their upset in watertight little compartments and his general demeanour was fine. It was the mother's sense of being shut out of a new and exciting part of her son's life that was the problem. A good mother, who had spent a lot of her time with her son in his childhood and must now learn to share it with others. She was right to ask questions, it showed that she was interested, but not to pry.

But other children are not so fortunate. They know more about their life than the adults around them because they are holding on to secrets. Secrets that are terrifying, shameful, anger-provoking or just plain miserable. Secrets that they dare not share, because the consequences would be catastrophic. Someone might be upset at least, like Gavin's parents; someone could be found out and punished; someone might die.

Bernie was a teenager whose life was still dominated by the need to keep secret the sexual abuse she had suffered as a child and there have been many more that I have seen and could have described in her place. Chun was still a young child, six years old, and had a different secret. But she had one thing in common with Bernie: she was giving off clues that there was something wrong in her life. If anyone was prepared to work them out.

Chun was an elective mute. That is to say that she chose not to speak in some situations, but did a little in others. Her teachers hadn't heard more than a whisper from her in the two years she had been in their school. She sometimes looked sad and distracted and sometimes tired and pale, as if she wasn't getting enough sleep. Her work was as good as they might have expected from a child with middle-of-the-road ability, and she had friends. The friends seemed to protect her in the playground and spoke for her in class. And everyone had adjusted to her silence.

The story came to me round-about. I shared a friend with one of Chun's teachers and the friend was more worried than the teacher. She persuaded the school to refer her but that was the easy part of the process; they had no real permission to talk to me about Chun and I certainly had no permission to see her.

Chun was of mixed race. Her mother was Welsh and her father Chinese and they helped run one of the restaurants in town. The teachers had been able to talk briefly to Chun's mother when she came to collect her, but she said that Chun spoke normally at home. She was always accompanied by the father's mother, who they were convinced had been sent as a minder to make sure she didn't say too much either.

I visited the school unofficially and saw for myself just how difficult it was for teachers to stop the other children intervening; no wonder they had given up. I also watched Chun in the playground and saw her talk a little to other children. Her vocal apparatus was clearly intact. I asked one of Chun's friends if she'd ever been to her house or had her for a sleepover. She had not, and neither had any of her other friends. Chun was isolated everywhere except school.

It seemed to me that the possible dangers to Chun outweighed the protocol, and I went down to see the parents in person, on an afternoon when the restaurant was closed. To my surprise, they agreed to see me. I was even more surprised when they agreed to let me talk directly with Chun, on the grounds that I was a doctor and there were medical worries about why she didn't talk in school. I could see her on their territory, in her bedroom, when they would both be around in the background.

I knew from her teachers that Chun could speak English so language was not a problem, if only she chose to use it. But she was as silent in our first few sessions as she was in class and all she wanted to do was play games on her tablet.

'You're very good at that, Chun.'

She smiled and leapt unscathed to a higher level of the game, manipulating the tablet with both hands at increasing speed.

'I don't think I could do that. I couldn't use both hands at the same time.'

She smiled again.

'Do you think you could teach me how to do it?'

Whatever Chun was frightened to talk about, it was obviously something that she felt powerless to change. But she was a powerful games player and she welcomed the chance to exert her power over me too. It was a good lesson. Sometimes it is best to admit our own fallibility as adults, to ask children to help us out and put them in charge. The very opposite of a parent's normal perception of their role.

Within a few sessions, Chun was instructing me verbally. I improved a little but she got angry when I made mistakes and hit me, just the once but it shocked her as much as it hurt me. Many of the games she chose to show me were violent, with fights and deaths amongst the characters. She flinched and poised in mid-flow when raised voices came up the stairs from below. And on one evening, when she had been off school for the day, both Chun and her mother wore dark glasses and high-necked sweaters and were sad and subdued.

'Chun, it seems to me that you are frightened of something.'

She stopped playing and hung her head.

'Something that's going on in this house.'

No reply.

'And you're scared what might happen if you tell me.'

She dropped the game on the floor and buried her head in her hands.

'Is somebody here being violent to somebody else? Your father, perhaps, hitting you and your mother? When he gets angry?'

Chun nodded between her tears.

I told Chun that it was right for her to tell me, that the law said that I must tell other people too, but that I wouldn't let anything happen to her and her mother as a result. I took them to the house of one of Chun's friends and rang the child protection team. But when they went to the house, the father and his mother had cleared out their things and left. As if they had a premonition of what was about to happen. They have never returned.

Despite my reassurances, Chun was as sad at what she had done as her mother was relieved. I worked with them for several more sessions together, until the freedom of not having to keep things secret overcame her sense of guilt. And her life in school was released.

Like Gavin, Chun had been round much of that Johari Window. Ways had been found for them to voice their deepest pain, their voice had been listened to and believed, it had been acted upon and the results were life-changing for them and the adults around them. Extreme cases they might seem, but there were lessons for every parent along the way.

One final thought. The lower left quadrant of the Window is the Unknown, where neither adults nor children know what is happening now or what might happen in the future. I have spent a lot of time persuading paediatricians that it is not a sign of weakness to admit their ignorance. They should not invent certainties to fill the gap. If the child finds out, however would they believe them again? More than that, for doctors to tell children that they don't exactly know what's wrong with them but together they might try and find out, enlists the children in a partnership and increases their sense of self-importance. The prospect is less alarming for the children than for their doctors.

And that is true of families too. Children cope well with change if they are given a clear role in the direction of travel, despite the uncertainties. Exploring the Unknown, children and parents together, can be one of the joys of family life.

CHAPTER 7

LIAM

THE NATURE OF ADOLESCENCE

So the first step out of childhood is made all at once, without looking before or behind, without caution, and nothing held in reserve.

Ursula K. Le Guin: *The Farthest Shore*, third book in the Earthsea
Cycle, 1972

Over the years, I have asked many adults the same question: if you could go back to one period of your life, which would it be? Not one of them has ever chosen adolescence and most have thrown up their hands in horror when I have said it was my favourite.

There is something about the unpredictability of adolescents, their moodiness and their switchback ride from one apparent drama to another that still terrifies those adults. Something that they must have been through in their own lives but have buried as deep as possible in their memory. This goes for my colleagues as well as their clients; therapists who prefer the certainties of little children, where they can be more instructional, like old-style doctors with disease. Perhaps that's why I have had so many adolescents on my caseload. Their unpredictable lifestyle and the directness of their approach are a challenge, but they are exactly what I value most. And Liam was a prime example.

It was late Thursday afternoon in a far-flung clinic, where mothers

brought their children to see me and the fathers were at work, if
they were lucky, or were already in the pub or had long since left
the family. Most adolescents were in school or playing truant and
I had to go out and find them if they were referred. But in this
case all three of them came up the stairs, both parents and Liam.
It was a measure of the distress on all sides of the fence.

Liam was fifteen, lean and wraith-like, with long ginger hair.
Neither of his parents had ginger hair and it set me wondering
immediately about his parentage. He sat angrily in the corner of
the clinic room, playing with the building blocks in a box of toys,
making as much noise as he could with them and throwing them,
in his mind, at the three of us in turn. He gripped them so hard
that I thought he might actually decide to do it.

'Look at him,' said his mother, without looking at him at all.
Liam scowled. An imaginary brick hit her on the back of the head.

'See, he doesn't listen to anything we say,' said his father. Liam
had heard every word his father said. An imaginary brick hit him
too.

'We can't do anything with him,' they said in unison. 'Now it's
your turn.' A whole broadside of imaginary bricks exploded around
them as they spoke.

I asked Liam if he would come and join us, which he did, reluctantly. He sat a few yards from his parents at the other end of my
desk. Whatever the gap between them, it was too dangerous to close
here, even in the safety of the session, and I suggested that I saw
them separately. The parents agreed; Liam shrugged his shoulders
and went off, slightly less angrily, to play on his phone in the waiting
room.

'You said it was my turn.' The parents looked even more uneasy
without Liam in the corner. 'What is it you can't do anything with?'

What they gave me was the adults' view of a typical adolescent.
It reminded me of a workshop I had run for counsellors, when I
had asked them to shout out their similar stereotypes.

'He's lazy,' said Liam's mother. 'He'd lie in bed all morning if
you'd let him. And getting him off to school is a nightmare.'

'Yes,' agreed his father. 'But when it comes to going to bed, he doesn't seem to want to sleep at all. He's awake at all hours, watching the television in his bedroom or playing on his computer. And heaven knows what he's doing on his phone all day.'

'Then there's the risks he takes.' His mother was warming to the task. 'I don't mind the drink so much. I quite like a drink or two myself, on a Friday night. And he's a lad, so he's got to learn about hangovers.' She took a sideways glance at her husband. 'But the drugs . . . I'm sure he's on something. They all are.'

'I wouldn't be surprised,' added the father. 'He's so moody. He's in his own little world most of the time, just doing what he wants. Then he flies off the handle whenever you try to correct him. The slightest thing.'

'He lost his mobile the other day and I found it for him,' agreed the mother. 'It was where it always is, under the mess on his bedside table. It wouldn't be a problem if he kept his bedroom tidy. But he stormed out of the house when I suggested it.'

Nothing that they told me sounded like 'the slightest thing'. They were skirmishing about almost everything now, whatever sparked it off. And it might easily develop into a full-scale war.

'Have you tried telling Liam what you're thinking?'

The father looked exasperated and the mother spoke for them. 'Oh, yes. We've tried. We asked him why he behaves like he does but he just said he didn't know.'

'Then we got angry about it.' The father had found his voice again. 'And all of a sudden he was quite nice again. And we were left with our anger in mid-air, with nowhere to put it.'

'So we had a row, with each other.' They both hung their heads, as if they were unable to look at each other. I finished off the words which were dangling, unspoken, between them.

'Perhaps it feels as if Liam is doing it deliberately, to get in between you?'

It was the opening I had been searching for and they poured through it. Liam's natural father had left three years earlier and his mother had met her current partner soon afterwards. It would have been difficult for Liam to adjust to at any time, but coming at the start of his adolescence it was a nightmare. For all of them.

'I know it must be difficult for him, his father walking out like that. But his behaviour is impossible.'

'So she gets frustrated and looks to me to do something about it. I get angry with him and she gets in the way. Like I'm his father but I'm not allowed to be his father. If you see what I mean.'

'That's a lot you're trying to deal with. And a lot for me to take in just now.' It was important to validate their distress. If it had been easy to sort out, they wouldn't be sitting in front of me.

'I'm aware of Liam out there, wondering what's going on. I'm going to give him a chance to see me by himself next time. To have his say. And if you'll give me a minute, I'll go and explain that to him.'

There are some people who think of adolescence as a modern phenomenon, made possible by western educational systems that prolong a period of self-absorbed introspection, on the one hand, and fostered by the media that prey on the teenager's desire to be like everyone else, on the other. In truth, it has been there ever since Plato moaned about young people's behaviour on the streets of Ancient Greece, though it may not have been named as such until recently. Adolescents are not just overgrown children or immature adults, but something in their own right; and a confusing mixture of biological and psychodynamic factors at that.

In many ways, they give parents another shot at the 'terrible twos'. Armed with a constitutional urge to explore the world and the legs to do so, the two-year-old will strike out on his own, knowing that the parent will still be there when he comes back to check. If he falls over, his parent will dust him off and send him out again with pride. But adults know there are dangers out there too. Roads and dogs and strangers. So the reasonable parent will set limits, the toddler will have a tantrum when he runs up against them, is cuddled and the process starts again.

And so it is with adolescence. Able to think now in the abstract, the adolescent will use their relationships in school and the community to work out who they are in the widest sense, what they stand for, how they can communicate their wishes to those around them, how they can relate to those with different wishes, and how compromises have to be made. The components of psychological well-being that politicians and policy makers talk so much about without a clear idea of what it is.

But there are problems in the way here too. Unless they are given a free enough rein to explore these relationships, to make mistakes and learn from them, the adolescent will not be able to cope with risks as an adult; their development depends on experiment. But parents know that there are limits to safe experiment and will impose boundaries to their adolescent's behaviour. Some parents may be repressive and impose them too tightly; some may be too laid-back and impose them too loosely. Most parents will get it about right and whatever the adolescent may say about it on the surface, they will test out the limits by their behaviour and be comforted when they find them.

What's more, we know now that some of this is programmed, not only psychologically but in brain chemistry too. The adolescent's brain is moving from the primitive tasks of survival to more sophisticated tasks of social relationships. Some connections are being pruned, some speeded up. But the process is in a fluid state. Most aspects are immature and many are quite different from what we might find in adulthood. So it turns out that the adolescent's apparent laziness, their self-centredness, their risk-taking and their emotional fragility, are laid down in brain structure and their behaviour reinforces the biology in turn, in a virtuous circle.

Parents who have managed to steer a path through all of this will recognise it as the normal process of adolescent turmoil, from which everyone will eventually emerge, a little scarred but intact. The key thing is that they can talk about what is happening, how they feel about it, and how they can work out a satisfactory compromise. Rows and resolution; rupture and repair. Though it is asking a lot of parents to remember when they are battling over the cornflakes that the daughter who is obsessed with her mobile and ignoring the need to get ready for school probably can't help it.

In other words, what Liam's parents were faced with were the tasks facing all parents of an adolescent son or daughter. And I would not have quibbled with their wish for help with that. It is part of my job to help families cope with the normal stages of development, the terrible twos, adolescence, and everything in between. It's complicated stuff and few parents get any sort of training in how to do it in an age where extended families are stretched to breaking point. But there was something more in this family, which made their frustrations very difficult indeed.

As I expected, Liam welcomed a private space to explore his feelings with a neutral person like myself, in a way that he couldn't at home. The tensions there were just too great.

'You've got very ginger hair, Liam. I couldn't help noticing it when you first came to the clinic, with the sun on it. It was almost as if your head was on fire.' He smiled at the description. 'Did your father have ginger hair too? Your natural father, that is.'

'Yes. Ginger and long, like mine. He wore it tied back in a ponytail. I think he was trying to look younger than he was. My mother didn't approve.'

'Was that what split them up?'

'No. It was the girlfriend. But I suppose his hair might have had something to do with it. She was much younger than him and he was trying to impress her.'

'Did he tell you that?'

'We weren't talking by that stage.'

'Do you still see him?'

'Now and again. Not regularly. He's got another girlfriend now. He tells me to grow up, but maybe he should too.'

We talked about his feelings towards his father. About the role model he had given him as a child – exciting and a bit edgy – but how he had let him down now he was older. Almost as if his father was trying to be an adolescent himself, stealing his son's thunder and no longer someone to look up to. He needed his father to be different, wiser and more mature.

'And now you've got another father. Is he different? Is he a role model?'

'Couldn't be more different. He tries his best, I know, to show me what's what. Then I get angry and he gets angry. And my mother comes in between.'

'They think you do it on purpose. Because you still love your natural father and you want to split them up.'

'I do still love him, I suppose, in spite of everything. But that doesn't mean I want to live with him. I'd be happy where I am, if we could sort it out.'

He was silent for a while.

'I can't help it sometimes. What makes them so angry.'

'I know. It's called being an adolescent. If that doesn't sound too patronising.'

Gradually, the three of them were brought together. At first they used their respective space to explore their own viewpoints, then they began to think about the viewpoints of the others in the family. Then it became safe enough to do that in the same room. And finally they found ways of getting around the upset of the past and the disagreements still to come. Almost as if the therapy took them through an adolescence of their relationships. Difficult enough in this family, but sometimes things are compounded by more hidden dynamics.

Take Craig, for example, referred to me at sixteen because his work had deteriorated rapidly in the upper school after what had seemed a promising path to university and beyond. At home he had become increasingly isolated from his peer group and alone in his misery. His parents were completely unable to explain what was happening. They were beside themselves with worry.

In therapy, Craig seemed to have got stuck somewhere in his development and to be retreating from any of his former successes, but it was difficult to say why. He played idly with a set of Russian dolls as we spoke, and I took the chance to probe a little deeper. I asked him how old he would have been if the dolls represented his life and we peeled off the outer layer. What was happening to him at that younger age? Slowly we went backwards, doll by doll, layer by layer, age by age, with Craig becoming more and more upset as we did so. Something terrible was sitting deep inside.

When we reached the centre, quite unknown to me, the smallest doll had been broken in two and fell apart in his hands as he took it out. Craig burst into tears. He told me that he had been born a twin but that his baby brother had been stillborn. His mother told him that he had been close to death in the womb too, but that he had survived by seizing what he could from her failing placenta, at the expense of his brother's life. His parents saw that as a triumph of resilience, but Craig had felt guilty about it ever since.

Now, on the brink of adolescent achievement, he felt he was being disloyal to his dead brother and should retreat into failure, so as not to surpass his memory. He had never been given the chance to grieve the loss of his twin brother, turned his feelings into behaviour instead, and became stuck with the consequences. Through the metaphor of the Russian dolls, he had found the language to understand what he was doing and to share it with his parents.

That story is an example of how adolescence can be undermined, but it illustrates other things too. I have deliberately used non-verbal ways of tackling feelings that are beyond words for some children and young people, and age is no barrier to doing so. The toy box is an invaluable aid, whether the therapist sets out to use it or is alive to the possibility, as with Craig. That is not some sort of magic, but an open mind and the skill to take advantage of the chance when it occurs.

Craig was able to use the metaphor within the safety of the session, but it would not be so with all adolescents. I have congratulated myself at using non-verbal methods, only to lose the patient. They have felt tricked into revealing their story, too much and too soon. And they have lost face. How they are seen is crucial to adolescents, though it may not appear so to their parents. Craig was able to maintain face, despite the revelation, and so were Liam and his parents. One of the tasks of therapy is how to let them all out of their corner without losing their dignity.

Adolescence can also be disrupted by constitutional factors, inflicted upon them, like illness, or conditions they were born with, like those on the autistic spectrum. The difficulties of children at the higher functioning end of the spectrum can often be accommodated in primary schools, with their smaller classes and closer liaison with home. Their academic achievements may outweigh their social problems. But it would be impossible to design a stage of development more challenging for them than adolescence; and big school can be a nightmare.

I was asked to see Mikey when he was fourteen. Like many young people with autistic spectrum disorder (ASD), Mikey had an all-consuming interest and would lecture anyone who asked about it for hours. In his case it was monkeys. Some children will steer clear of behaviour they don't understand, but some will make fun of it. Mikey's classmates called him 'The Monkey', they made monkey noises behind his back, mimed eating bananas and swung from imaginary trees. The fact that his nickname was quoted in his referral shows just how angry the adults around him had become.

Because of his ASD, Mikey found it difficult to put himself in other people's shoes, could see no one's point of view but his own, had little idea how to make compromises and cooperate with his peer group, and could not draw inferences from anything that was not spelt out in black and white. In other words, he was unable to satisfy the demands of adolescence. If he had been at the harder end of ASD, he might have survived in his own little bubble. At the softer end, Mikey knew he was living in someone else's world, whose rules he didn't understand, and it made him miserable.

It would have made him even more unhappy to try and train him to do things that were genetically beyond his capability, despite his academic intelligence. It was better to talk to the teachers, to increase their understanding of the disorder and make appropriate allowances, to rely on them to curb the worst excesses of the other pupils and to teach Mikey and his parents some alternative strategies to cope with life.

'Why did you hit her?' I asked him, when he had been thrown out of the swimming lessons because he had clobbered one of the girls.

'Because she hit me first.'

It was no use appealing to the morality of not striking back, especially with girls, because it would just have seemed unfair in Mikey's book.

'So what happened when you did it?'

'I got punished.'

'And what did that feel like?'

'Horrible.'

'So wouldn't it be better if you didn't do it next time? For your own sake, I mean.'

I put my arm round him and he began to cry. But he had learnt, not how to make things better for others, but how to make them better for himself. And it was a start.

There are many lessons in these stories, about how parents should handle their adolescent's behaviour, whether it is the normal behaviour of adolescent turmoil, behaviour made worse by family dynamics – open like Liam or hidden like Craig – or behaviour made even more difficult by constitutional factors, like Mikey. This is the job of the good-enough parent, not repressive and not laissez-faire, muddling through the problems as best they can. Not perfect but good enough.

And the same is true for the good-enough therapist. As with the parents, there are tightropes to walk, to fall off and to learn in the process. How can the therapist offer the wisdom of experience and objectivity without becoming a better parent than the ones the adolescent already has? Patients will not develop without taking risks with their lives, but how can the therapist offer the chance to experiment within an envelope of safety?

Both parents and adolescents may value the privacy of independent sessions, but how is the therapist to balance confidentiality with a greater need to share? How can a therapist maintain impartiality while disapproving of how the clients might behave? And if we get close enough to help, how can we deal with the feelings stirred up in our own lives, or events in our own lives that threaten to influence the therapy?

In the middle of my work on an adolescent unit, my own adolescent daughter ran away. It came on the back of an argument with me about boyfriends, something that many fathers will have experienced when they realise they are no longer the only man in their daughter's life. And during that time, I swear that every parent of every adolescent runaway in the country was referred for my help. Exaggeration, of course. It was one or two at most, but such was my confusion that it felt like many more.

I learnt three lessons: safety, dignity, and the connection between them.

However much the therapist within me might have sympathised with my daughter's search for independence, my first duty as a parent was to make sure she was safe. In fact, her elder brother found out where she was and assured us it was so. Beyond that, I would not pry. Confidentiality balanced with a need to know.

And how to preserve her adolescent dignity, and mine. We resolved the problem by passing a message to her through her brother. We would be going away for the weekend. If she was home when we got back, we would be delighted. And we would say nothing more about it until she was ready to talk.

She was home and we kept our promise. Everyone was out of their corner, safely and without loss of face. Just like Liam and his parents.

CHAPTER 8

CAMERON AND CHERYL
THE PROBLEM OF PERSONALITY

The most important kind of freedom is to be what you really are. You trade in your reality for a role. You trade in your sense for an act. You give up your ability to feel, and in exchange, put on a mask.

Jim Morrison, lead singer of The Doors 1943–71

The modern idea of personality is of a stable bundle of characteristics with which we face the world. Consistent over time, pervasive through every situation, provoking the sort of behaviour that marks us out from the rest. We have no choice; that is who we are. Personality will out, and there is nothing abnormal about that.

This perception is quite the opposite of the original concept. The word 'personality' was borrowed from the masks worn in the theatres of Ancient Greece. It was what the actors wanted the audience to see, not the actor himself. The real self was hidden behind the mask. Now, there are many of us, therapists as well as patients, who are prepared to play a part for a while, to fit in with the expectations of other people, to avoid harming their sensitivities, or to get what we want. And there is nothing abnormal in that either.

But this book is full of children and young people who do not have the luxury of being themselves at all. Sometimes they are forced into a role by families that have a need for them to behave in particular ways. Sometimes they are branded by the class to which their helpers in medicine, education and social welfare say they belong. Sometimes they are seen as the very stereotypes of the culture into which they are born: geography, nationality, race, religion and gender. And sometimes they become prisoners of personality and the labels of disorder that adults have heaped upon it.

There is no doubt that personality can be strained over time. If a child is weighed down by the burden of other people's views, those views may become the way they see themselves, the whole world and their place in it. The role has become their life and there is no room left to develop their individuality. The job of therapists like me is to help them shed that burden and become the person they really are; to fulfil Jim Morrison's wishes for themselves.

That is painful and difficult, once everyone's expectations are set. Better to start at the beginning, where parents and professionals confuse difference with pathology. Cameron's mother brought him to see me because she was worried about his behaviour and his GP had talked to her about something called 'oppositional defiant disorder'. This could describe the sort of defiance you might have expected from a toddler, and Cameron was two and a half.

She had three children by three different fathers. The eldest, a daughter, was five and at school.

'Sara is a lovely child. She hardly ever cried in her cot; you wouldn't have known she was there most times if it wasn't for the cooing noises she made. And her teachers tell me she's lovely in school too. Never answers back. Not very bright but . . . Cameron!'

She jumped up in mid-sentence to rescue Cameron. He was roaming happily around the room as she was speaking. Now he had found the open door, sidled halfway through it and looked over his shoulder to see if anyone would do anything about it.

'It's OK, there's nothing in the clinic to hurt him and there are plenty of nurses and other children around to play with him.'

'But he might fall over.'

'Then they'll pick him up and make sure he's all right.'

'But they'll be much too busy. Shouldn't I be doing that?'

'Yes, if that's what he wants. Tell him you can keep an eye on him through the door. He can come back and check on you whenever he wants. And you'll still be here if he gets upset and needs a cuddle.'

She sat down reluctantly and folded her hands over her pregnant belly. Her third child was not yet born but it soon would be.

'How long?'

'Another month.' She smiled and smoothed her dress over the bump. 'This one's lovely too. Aren't you?' She paused and smiled again. 'Oh, by the way, my daughter's white and this one will be too. Cameron's mixed race.'

She said it as if it confirmed how difficult it would be to handle someone like him. But the difficulty she was struggling with was a difference in personality, and was nothing to do with race.

'I noticed. Now tell me what you think is wrong with him.'

'It's the whole way he is. He's always been a handful, right from when he was in the womb.' She stopped and smiled at the bump again. 'Not like you. Cameron kicked me all night; I could hardly sleep a wink.'

'Maybe that was his way of getting your attention. This one doesn't have to; you talk to it all the time.'

She thought for a bit, her hands in her lap. 'Then he cried a lot. When he came out, I mean. He was a whingey baby.'

'And what did you do when he cried?'

'I picked him up. To see what was the matter.'

'Good. Communication again. Babies don't cry for nothing. They cry because they're hungry, or wet, or something hurts. A good mother like you will pick him up and put it right. It's the baby's first lesson in self-mastery. If I cry loudly enough, someone will come and help.'

'So I did it right?'

'Of course. My guess is, you picked him up just as soon as you could. Do it immediately every time and the baby will never learn to tolerate delay. He'll grow up expecting everyone to come running at his beck and call. Fail to respond and the baby will learn that his cry for help is useless; no one will help. Worse still, get angry. Crying is wrong and he'll be punished for it. We've all seen those awful pictures of babies weeping silently by themselves in the cot.'

She was quiet again for a while. 'But now he's everywhere. I only have to turn my back a second and . . . Cameron!' He had reappeared and clambered on to her lap.

'Give him a cuddle, I think he needs it. And let him have a feel of your bump. It's his baby too, you know.'

I let them cuddle for a while. 'So you're not a bad mother and Cameron isn't going to grow into a monster. He's just different. You've had one placid child and you may be having another. Cameron is active and curious and a handful at times, and he came as a shock. But that's the way he is.'

'So I should be happy that they're all different? In personality, I mean.'

'Exactly.'

Cameron's mother went away a little reassured. Cameron could be difficult and demanding but he did not have a disorder and she could be more confident in her mothering of him. And she could always come back for a top-up if she wished. One session was not going to change her world, but it was a start.

In contrast many people – professional mental health workers and political policy makers included – have a pessimistic attitude to real personality disorders that develop early and become entrenched, as if they are fixed and unchangeable and that's the end of the story. But they can be helped, even those who look most destructive to the sufferer and everyone around them. Like Cheryl.

Cheryl was admitted at a weekend to the local mental hospital; she was just nineteen, at the top end of my remit, but she stood out amongst the older patients in the adult ward. She had taken an overdose, though there were questions around what tablets she had swallowed and how many. A new psychiatric house officer had been pressurised into admitting her by the consultant in accident and emergency who knew this was the latest in a succession of overdoses, admissions and self-discharges over the previous two years.

In accident and emergency, no one had been able to agree whether her behaviour was deliberate and deserved to be punished, or unconscious and worthy of treatment. So they hedged their bets and stomach-pumped her, which was unpleasant, and referred her anyway. On the psychiatric ward, no one could decide whether she was psychotic and out of touch with reality, or neurotic and manipulating her environment. So they hedged their bets too, called her a personality disorder, then threw up their hands and added even more medication to the long list she was already on. I was asked to see her as an outpatient.

Cheryl's life was in a mess. She was an only child and had lived with her mother since her father had left when she was young. Now her mother had died and Cheryl remained alone in the family home. She had held down a regular job in a library since leaving school but had no close friends and just one or two, short-lived relationships with men. She had cut herself and attacked others when she was disturbed and had been carried off to police stations, hospitals and other places of safety.

No one seemed to have noticed that in the midst of all this mayhem, Cheryl's life was disturbed but stable in its pattern. It was those around her who were driven to distraction by the way she seemed to swing between calmer periods and bouts of violence or self-harm. Neighbours reported to me that Cheryl had been devoted to her mother and rarely went out, but that they had heard slanging matches coming from the house before her mother died. Work colleagues spent hours trying to get help for her until they lost hope and gave up. A man with whom she had an affair took out an injunction to stop her following him around. And now she was my responsibility – or that's how it felt.

Cheryl came to see me in the clinic, slim, smart, good-looking and bang on time. She complained immediately about the latest medication and was taken aback when I took her at her word.

'You're quite right. I don't think they should have added more to the list.'

'So why did they do it?'

'I guess it was a measure of their confusion. About the mixture of your symptoms.'

'You mean they didn't know what to do.'

'They hoped it might help.'

'Well it didn't. Now I suppose you're going to add some more.'

'No. I'm going to start taking them off. One by one. And we'll see how you get on each time.'

'How will you know?'

'Because I'll be seeing you here each week, same time, same place.'

'But you'll hand me on as fast as you can. As soon as anything happens. Just like everyone else.'

'No, I won't. I'm going to stick with you. Whatever you do.'

The promises seemed important and she tested them out with another overdose before I saw her again. So I went round the GP, the police station, the accident and emergency department and the adult psychiatrists, explained what I was doing, persuaded them to patch her up as appropriate each time they saw her and gave them a list of her outpatient appointments to see me. I would take the risk, not them.

If anyone could be said to have a personality disorder, it was Cheryl. She seemed to have a totally negative view of herself, the rest of the world and her relationship to it. Her behaviour was confusing but it was consistent in its self-loathing and mistrust of others. It was undermining her life in the long run and led her into repeated short-term crises.

The next step was to work out what sort of disorder it was, when and why things had gone wrong, and how I might help to put it right. Cheryl was outside anyone I had come across before, and it was no good reaching for the textbooks – nothing has emerged from the history of mental illness with such a mishmash of classical myths, derogatory stereotypes, psychoanalytical mumbo-jumbo, pseudo-scientific empire building and questionable psychological rating scales, as personality disorder.

Psychiatrists have argued about the most basic issues of type and treatment, and their confusion has been reflected in classifications of disorder that change every time a new one is produced. It's hardly surprising that in the midst of it all, a government, exasperated by high-profile incidents of violence, invented its own label, 'dangerous and severe personality disorder', and tucked away its sufferers in secure detention. Safely out of sight. None of which was a help with Cheryl and how to unlock her own problems.

Eventually, I found the key in a much-thumbed concept of child development: borderline personality. The writing was often turgid but the arguments made sense of Cheryl, how she behaved, how she made me feel, and above all what I should do about it. In a nutshell, the problem had developed between her and her mother in the first three years of her life and had coloured her attitude to those around her ever since.

The newborn baby is defenceless and needs its mother's protection as much as it did in the womb. It lives within the shelter of its mother's care, with little physical or emotional separation between the two. As it grows and acquires its various faculties, it separates out in every sense and becomes an individual in its own right, to the mixed pride and anxiety of its parents. Like Cameron, with a bit of comfort and reassurance for his mother that he was progressing normally.

But that separation process fails in the infancy of someone like Cheryl. The parent demands a slave to their own wishes and makes their disapproval clear whenever the infant tries to follow its own path. The young child never dares to explore its own identity and lives in constant fear of being rejected for doing so. It fills in that emotional black hole with a bewildering array of impulsive and self-destructive behaviour that confuses everyone who comes into contact with them, including psychiatrists.

Cheryl's mother was dead, so there was no hope of redressing their relationship directly. And so primitive was the legacy she had left in Cheryl's feelings, that I couldn't work openly on them; they were much too dangerous to put into words. But I did have those feelings by proxy and could give her a different model in the way I worked.

She feared that I might desert her at any moment, hence the importance of regular sessions in the face of anything she might throw at me. She lived in a world of angels and devils, the image of a good mother that she fought so hard to preserve, and the bad mother she really had been but was too precious to criticise. I resisted the temptation to be over-happy or over-angry at the way she saw me, and met her with as constant a level of care as I could manage, no matter how she made me feel inside. And I refused to accept the appalling image she had of herself, which she hid under her smart appearance and criticism of others.

To put it bluntly, the only way to address what had happened was to 'breastfeed' her again with the reliability of my sessions, and then to 'wean' her off with encouragement and congratulation for every hesitant step she might take. Whatever happened, she would never find herself being put back into hospital until she behaved herself, because this would simply repeat her mother's threats of rejection. The very conditional love where it all began.

Slowly, Cheryl learnt to trust this new way of doing things, to understand where her development had gone astray and how different she might be.

'So I could never be loved by my mother, if I became my own person?'

'I think that's so.'

'For what I am? Rather than what she wanted me to be?'

'Right.'

'And I just had to obey the pattern? Without understanding why?'

'Right again.'

'Until she died, and I treated everyone just like my mother?'

'Until you were sure that you couldn't be loved by anyone if you developed healthily.'

'And now?'

'What do you think?'

'It isn't true.'

The whole process took about three years, as it would have done naturally in a good-enough family life in which infants, children and young people are brought up with a normal mixture of love and exasperation. It would have been even better to do it with Cheryl and her mother together, to free the mother from her own needs, which had no doubt been imposed upon her by her own parents in turn. But her death made that impossible, and we had to work with what she had left behind.

It is difficult enough to work backwards with someone like Cheryl, once her personality disorder is established, but the principles are well founded. What about working forwards, to help those at risk before the disorder can develop?

To begin with, that relies on the ability of adults to spot the problem and reach for help before it is too late, as it was for Lauren. She was a teenage girl who had hovered on the edge of anxiety all her life and had occasionally been tipped over into a disabling panic by events at home, in school or in the community. Parental rows, teachers' criticisms, other girls whispering behind her back – she took it all to heart and treated it as her fault.

People made allowances for her wherever they could, 'because that's just the way she is'. They tiptoed around her and nursed her back into circulation without thinking what it must be like to have such a chronic lack of self-confidence and a punitive sense of guilt. She had an anxious personality, they thought, fixed and unchanging, and beyond the reach of help.

But school can be a very cruel place. Lauren had two weeks off with aches and pains that were almost certainly a reflection of emotional distress. She had been left out of a shopping trip by peers who felt that her anxiety would dampen their fun. And in her book that must mean that no one liked her or would ever want to hang out with her again, because she wasn't worth knowing.

Once again she was eased back into school but had a minor-sounding argument with another girl at lunchtime and went missing. She was found two days later after a full-scale search. She was lying in the bushes at the foot of a cliff in a nearby beauty spot.

It was impossible to tell whether Lauren had jumped to her death or been careless and lost her footing. But what is certain is that she had got as far as adolescence with a twisted view of herself and life, and now found herself totally unable to cope with the emotional ups and downs it was bound to entail. I was invited to help with the anguish of the parents, her teachers and the girls who had crossed her path; valuable, necessary, but too late.

I should say that it is quite normal for children to get anxious in difficult situations like family problems, moving up to secondary school or exams. In fact, I would worry if they weren't. And most of us are phobic about one thing or another: spiders, clowns, heights, flying and the like. The anxiety diminishes when the situation improves, we avoid the spiders or get some help to overcome our fear. Other children have a more free-floating anxiety, unconnected to anything, and which becomes their normal approach to life.

'She's our little worrier. Good job too. There are lots of things that could have gone wrong if she hadn't checked.'

To that extent, an anxious personality is as normal as Cameron and his active personality. It is not a disorder and can be put to good, constructive everyday use. It only becomes abnormal when it pervades every aspect of life and gets in the way of outlook, functions and relationships. Rigid and inevitable. Undermining the normal flexibility of childhood development.

Kelly was eight years old when her parents came to see me alone. They were worried that her anxieties would be made worse if she talked about it, especially to someone called a psychiatrist.

'She's worried all the time, doctor.' Her mother was as worried as her description of her daughter and dabbed at her eyes with a screwed-up handkerchief. 'She seems to wake up worried, worries all day and lies awake at night . . . or has bad dreams . . . awful dreams . . . monsters and things going wrong.'

Her husband put his arm around her but she shook it off. 'It's beginning to affect all of us, as you can see. Most nights my wife is awake, worrying if Kelly is awake. Or she goes to sleep with her, to calm her down when she has nightmares. We might as well be living apart.'

They gave me a long string of Kelly's symptoms. She was eating little, was irritable most of the time and frequently flew into uncontrollable outbursts. She was tense and fidgety, had unexplainable aches and pains and went to the loo several times an hour. She had a negative approach to everything and everyone, including herself. And she had had one or two full-blown panic attacks when faced with things that other children coped with quite well, the last one when they were getting on the bus for a school trip.

Kelly's anxiety had developed gradually over the years and had got steadily worse. It was not connected to any specific situation and was not part of another disorder like hyperactivity or the autistic spectrum. She was shy in all social situations, her schoolwork was deteriorating and she had few friends. She had reached the point where she was chained to the house and her mother's apron strings; and her mother was chained to her.

This level of anxiety was no longer a normal part of Kelly's personality, but had become an identifiable disorder. A disorder that was unlikely to get better with a bit of understanding on the adults' part. A disorder that might progress in adolescence into an illness that would disable her life, and which she might try and cope with by drinking, drug-taking or self-harm. The parents were quite right to be worried; but it could be helped. And it was.

Talking about this sort of anxiety does not make it worse; children need the opportunity to explore their feelings, but it has to be done sensitively and at a speed that they can manage. I visited her at home at first, where she felt safer, and only moved her to my clinic when I had earned her trust. My clinic room became her territory and her parents were freed to repair their own relationship at home. No mean feat when their life had circled for so long around their daughter's needs.

Over the course of many sessions, we examined Kelly's anxieties and what evidence she had or had not for her attitudes to herself and life. What I offered her was not a cure; she would always be an anxious person but her anxiety could be managed. We developed coping strategies for dealing with situations that she found impossible, which she faced in fantasy in the clinic first, then with my company outside, and finally alone. In other words, what we might now call cognitive behavioural therapy, though that is just another phrase for what young people like Kelly have always required.

On an individual level, Kelly's anxiety disorder could be understood, contained and treated. It is more difficult to work out why anxiety levels are said to be increasing amongst children and adolescents in general. It might be a real increase in the sort of feelings and behaviour that had interfered with Kelly's life. We might be learning to recognise it more often and bringing its sufferers into help, instead of making allowances for a girl like Lauren. And the stresses of modern life may have become more than vulnerable children should have to cope with.

While politicians have been searching for the keys to public happiness, we have had successive reports from the Joseph Rowntree Foundation, the World Health Organisation and others that the UK is now the least satisfactory country in which to be brought up in the developed world. Our children and young people are subject to a constant pressure for success: academic success, social success, career success. And the internet is the means by which they can check out how they're doing, morning, noon and night.

Achievement at all costs is the driving force in an increasingly competitive world; and children and young people are telling us what those costs may be in terms of their anxiety, depression and self-harm, as we shall see in later chapters. Individual therapists can help parents cope with the disorders of individual patients like Kelly, but the disorder of society is a global responsibility.

CHAPTER 9

GWEN AND RYAN
ANOREXIA AND FAMILY DYNAMICS

> . . . Freud is all nonsense; the secret of neurosis is to be found in the family
> battle of wills to see who can refuse longest to help with the dishes. The
> sink is the great symbol of the bloodiness of family life. All life is bad, but
> family life is worse.
>
> Julian Mitchell: *As Far As You Can Go*, Ch. 1, 1963

Children do not grow up in a vacuum. Most of them live in families of one sort or another and the nature of those families has shifted over time and culture. In my lifetime, for example, professional women have begun to have their babies later so as not to interrupt their career; and young girls have given birth in their teens as a way of securing some sort of status in an uncaring environment. It can have profound effects on adolescents with more elderly parents or parents not that much older than themselves.

There are single parents and two-parent families with a history of multiple marriages and numbers of step-children. There are same-sex marriages, foster parents and adoptive parents. Some families have many children, some have an only child, and some have none at all, by accident or design. There are families with several generations living in the same house, those living within extended networks of relatives, and those who have moved far away from their origins in search of work and a better life.

In other words, there is no such thing as the archetypal family. Each is normal in its own eyes and any therapist must know what sort of normality that is. But they are all held together in the same way: by the relationships between family members, by the roles that have been built upon those relationships and which members must perform, and by the ways of doing things that have been handed on from one generation to the next, until they have solidified into family rules.

Families can be kept together by negative feelings or fear of the unknown, just as surely as by loving care. 'It was only the fighting that kept us going,' said a mother when I asked her why she and her husband had stayed together so long. They had been giving each other hell for years. 'I think we both missed it when it was gone. The fighting, I mean. And I got depressed.'

Where this is so, it is often the children and their problems that divert the parents' attention and keep them together. It can take a great effort for those children to escape the stickiness of the family web, and sometimes they do it by behaving dangerously – consciously or unconsciously. Like Gwen and Ryan.

Both of them had anorexia nervosa, and in both of their families the eating disorder had become as important for the family structure as it was for themselves. They taught me everything about the systems in which we live and work. About the young person at the centre of the family, about the family at the centre of the wider system of health, education and community, about the way they may influence each other in concentric circles, spreading out and back again, like ripples in a pond. And about the therapist trying to change it all, without getting trapped too.

Gwendolyn was fifteen when she came to us from the paediatricians. Everyone called her Gwen for short, except for her maternal grandmother, after whom she was called and who insisted on her full name. She had an eating disorder, anorexia nervosa, which had developed insidiously over at least three years. It was serious, but it was built into the family dynamics and the parents fought hard to stop it disturbing their image in the community.

Gwen was the only child of a middle-class professional family. Her father was a solicitor and her mother an ex-teacher and local councillor. Her maternal aunt, her mother's younger sister, had come to lodge with them for a while after her own marriage had failed when her husband ran off with a prominent businesswoman, much to the glee of the local weekly newspaper. She too could have been an embarrassment, but she had lived on in an annexe to the house, with the family appearances smoothed over her like a pearl growing around the grit in an oyster.

The father had done much to modernise the firm that his own father had started, but it was having difficulty coping with the twenty-first century and clients were moving off to firms that were more comfortable dealing with custody and access disputes, sexual abuse, domestic violence and the like. All the grandparents had now died, except for the maternal grandmother, who lived in an expensive nursing home nearby, holding court at her bedside, or so it seemed. She demanded regular updates of the family affairs and made her disapproval clear.

Gwen had failed to get a scholarship to the girls' public school on their doorstep but had been admitted there in her early adolescence as a fee-paying pupil after her father 'pulled a few strings' (his words) at the golf club. Money had become much tighter than it might have seemed because of her fees on top of the amount they had to pay for the grandmother's accommodation, but appearances were important to both parents and they continued to give money to local church and community events though they could barely afford it.

Anorexia nervosa is a complicated eating disorder, in which its sufferers starve themselves down to precariously low weights; as opposed to those with bulimia, who binge on food then make themselves sick or use laxatives to stop themselves gaining weight. It's complicated, in that it can be the end result of many different factors – physical, psychological, and mutually reinforcing cycles between the two.

The latest research has suggested that there may be a biochemical vulnerability that could be genetically passed on, and Gwen's mother certainly had issues with food. She was a good cook but ate little herself and was noticeably thin. But you could say that the family traditions that Gwen inherited were just as important. Appearances were everything in this family and made her especially susceptible to the sort of peer pressure that she came under at school.

It is quite normal for adolescents to worry, not only about what they think about themselves but also what others think about them. Most adolescents get the balance more or less right, despite media scares about eating problems which, ironically, they may have helped to cause. We may even be seeing a backlash now against the cult of thinness, but female role models are still airbrushed into a perfect, slim-line elegance. And bear in mind that it was particularly important for Gwen to feel accepted amongst girls who might look down on her as a late school entrant who was only there because of her father's money.

Whatever the origins, Gwen had begun to eat less and exercise more in her first year. But both she and her family were unaware of the consequences or ignored them until she collapsed on a school cross-country run. She was taken to see the GP and admitted to the paediatric ward of the local hospital as an emergency, under a cloak of secrecy. As ever, the school were worried that bad things might spread if you talked about them, whether that was drugs or drinking or eating disorders. Wrong, but perhaps that was understandable.

I visited her in the hospital and persuaded the family and her doctors that she should be transferred to our adolescent mental health unit. It was made easier by the fact that they felt that it was inappropriate for a fifteen-year-old to be lying in a ward of little children, though her anorexia had so reduced her body to a child-like level that she fitted in physically quite well. She was hovering just above a dangerously low weight and could control its level to the last gramme. Control was going to be a key issue and it took us into another conundrum.

The paediatricians had got enough nutrients inside her to climb away from the very real prospect that Gwen might die, but the biochemistry of low weight had affected the image she had of her body size. So eating became even more of a problem, her weight was compromised even further, her body image was even more distorted, and so on, in a vicious circle. It was a perfect example of how physical and psychological factors can combine together to defend everyone against doing something about the root cause.

If we ignored the precariousness of Gwen's weight, we risked her slipping back into the hospital ward. But while we concentrated on her physical state, there was no room to talk about the emotional need for control that lay behind it. And there was plenty to talk about in this family.

There was little love lost between the parents and the need to think about problems like Gwen had just about kept the family together. In my opening sessions with them, there seemed to be no good role models for a teenager in the throes of growing up in general, and for her sexuality in particular.

Her mother kept her own feelings firmly buttoned up, while her more flamboyant aunt crossed and recrossed her legs in front of us, dressed in a faux fur coat and thigh-high white plastic boots. It was almost as if they were two halves of one female personality, that for some reason could not be put together. Her father circled around the two halves, subtly undermining one and flirting with the other. And in the face of their skewed relationships, Gwen's anorexia had taken her body back to the safety of a pre-pubertal state.

In essence, this family were prepared for Gwen to die rather than change. That would have been much too blunt for what was an unconscious process and blame would get us nowhere. But Gwen knew the score.

'Why don't you sort yourselves out and leave me alone,' she blurted out when she was beginning to find her self-confidence. 'I don't want to be stuck in the middle.' Like glue, I thought to myself.

'But we only want what's best for you, Gwen. We're doing everything we could possibly think of to get you better,' replied her mother.

'And what would you be doing if she wasn't ill?' I asked. The parents stared hard at the floor. Nobody spoke for a while. It didn't need putting into words, but the aunt had a go.

'Separating,' she said. 'But he might wheel me in instead.' It was an outrageous thing to say and perhaps deliberately so. She looked sideways at her brother-in-law, a half smile on her lips. 'But Granny wouldn't approve. And anyway you'd be broke after the divorce. You couldn't afford me.'

The feelings in this family were so dangerous, and Gwen was so implicated in maintaining the status quo, that it was no surprise that her eating disorder had become a last chance to exert some control over her own life. Putting weight on her was the easiest part of the bargain; it took many months to extricate her psychologically from the role she had been performing.

She had weekly individual sessions to explore her feelings about herself, what sort of person had been hidden under all those family expectations, and what she wanted to do with her life. She had daily group sessions to challenge and be challenged by the other adolescents on the unit, each with their own problems in development. And she took part initially in the family work.

There would have been an argument to keep the aunt in the family sessions too; she had been part of the problem after all. But she had no more business there than in the house; and certainly not in the middle of the parents' marriage. She left all three. Gwen concentrated on her own life, and I worked with the parents together.

At length they decided to separate, whatever the outcome of Gwen's disorder and its treatment. It freed their daughter to be the person she wanted to be and she experimented with her new-found identity in friendships on the unit and with her peer group when she went back to school. She lived with her mother after her father left, though she saw him regularly and he continued to pay the school bills.

I saw her for a while as an outpatient. It was not her fault that her parents had separated, but for a while there was part of her that felt it was. We worked her way through the guilt of it, with a reassurance from both parents that their own, independent lives were happier too. Eating never again became a pleasure for her, but it was no longer a battlefield on which to fight the family dynamics.

Change is difficult for families. Given that the relationships within them are intermeshed like a spider's web, there is no way of changing one thread, independent of the rest. If one person changes, all the rest must change too, and they may resist it in any way they can, unless the situation is so abusive that the child has to be rescued and the rest must look after itself. Or a young person has help to leave it all behind.

In Gwen's case, the ultimate change was what the family had been fearing most and what her illness had been protecting them against: the parental separation. No wonder it was so difficult for them to achieve. But change can be difficult even where things appear to be improving and the outcome, you would think, would be positive for everyone concerned.

Chronic, serious physical illnesses in children, for example, can have profound effects on family structure. If the child is hospitalised, it is usually the mother who stays on the ward while the father looks after the other children at home, with wider family support if he is lucky. Even in these days of greater parental flexibility, of open visiting times and staff sensitivities, it is easy for that split to widen.

The mother and her sick child become part of the ward routine, defined by the illness and its needs – tablets, injections and operations; groups of doctors and nurses who come and go on their shifts; and friendships with other sick children and their mothers on the ward. Meanwhile the father and the rest of the family must get on with their life outside. When the sickness improves and the child goes home, it may be difficult for everyone to get back to their former existence. The sick role has become the child's way of life and the family structure has been built around it.

Some families find the whole prospect of change so frightening that they decide not to risk it. I have seen families where the children are driving coach and horses through the gap between parents who have no tradition of talking privately about what to do and facing their child with a united front. I have helped the parents decide on a new regime and warned them that things may feel worse for a while as the child tests it out. And I have promised to help them weather the storm, only for them to decide not to tackle the behaviour. The pain of change would be greater than the pain of what they've got.

That is their privilege, providing that no one is being significantly harmed by what is going on, and needs rescue. If Gwen's family had refused to change, we might have reached that point. And it was certainly so with Ryan. The signs were there from the very start.

Ryan was one of those supposedly rare patients – a male with anorexia nervosa. The research base on these boys is poor and myths have accumulated around them. Not so many decades ago they were thought to be non-existent. Even now the textbook numbers are many times less than their female counterparts, though they are more equal at the bulimic end of the eating disorder spectrum.

In fact, anorexic boys are far less rare than we care to admit and their prevalence is increasing fast. This may be partly due to the media pressure they are coming under from slim-clothed male models, and partly because some of their activities designed to lose weight, like gym workouts and sports, are not included in the classic definitions. We simply don't recognise them soon enough; and since boys are able to lose weight faster than girls, the result can be even more tragic.

Ryan came to us from the paediatricians too; he was sixteen years old and looked about ten. Pale, thin, very small for his age, with floppy hair over a cherubic face. Unlike Gwen, he was from a poor family but their relationships were just as twisted, and entangling. Ryan's mother was a typical matriarch; her husband had been invalided out of his job as a steel worker and he was at home now, hanging on her every wish, but in truth she had always been the dominant one in the family and came from a long line of similar women.

Some of the traditions the women brought with them were bizarre. No one in the family was allowed to express angry, fearful or miserable feelings. When they threatened to surface, the culprit had to stand on their head in the corner of the living room and let the feelings drain out of their mouth. Feelings were a crime and the sentence a penance. I had never met such a concrete metaphor before, but it was no more extreme, perhaps, than a middle-class family like Gwen's, sleep-walking towards their daughter's death in order to keep up appearances.

All the children in Ryan's family had found perverse ways of fighting off the clutches of the system. The eldest son had gone to prison after a string of burglaries; a daughter had become a prostitute on the streets of Cardiff; and the second son had joined the Army then been charged with desertion. Which left Ryan, who his mother was determined would not leave like the others. He was the youngest, the last in line, and the clutches of the family wrapped tightest around him. Try as we might, we could not relieve him of his role by getting the rest of the family to change. His mother demanded that she take him out of the unit, and was beside herself when he decided to stay. At sixteen, he had a right to decide for himself and we supported him in his decision.

Ryan improved on the unit. It was too late for him to grow in height, but he grew emotionally and socially to the point where he could contemplate trying out new relationships in the outside world. He went off with staff and a party of adolescents on a weekend trip to the seaside, and there he met a girl of the same age (seventeen by now). The relationship deepened with letters, telephone calls and visits afterwards, and Ryan asked if we would help him break the news to his parents. There was still a part of him that needed his mother's approval.

'There's something I've got to tell you.' Ryan approached it with the air of a guilty confession rather than something to be proud of. Such was the court-like atmosphere in the room, he might as well have been in the dock.

'I've been to Bournemouth . . . and I met a girl.' His father gave him a sly leer; there was no doubting the view of women he had beneath his subservience to his wife.

'We want to get together, up here, when I'm well enough to leave the unit.'

Ryan's revelation sat in the middle of the group, as if it was challenging each one of us to react. It was good to hear of his independence, though I doubted that he would be able to take it any further for a while.

'That might be a year or so, Ryan.'

'That's OK. We can wait.'

His mother certainly could not. Knowing her, I was prepared for her to be devastated to learn that her son had a healthier relationship with another woman. But I was not prepared for the drama of what she did.

She dropped to her knees and crawled across the carpet to clutch her son round his ankles.

'If you go out with that girl again, I will die!'

I met Ryan again many years later. He was married now to the woman he had met at the seaside and was with her for an out-patient session with one of the adult psychiatrists. She had become depressed after the birth of their latest baby but was recovering fast. Ryan was still small and thin, but he was holding down a good job and had fond memories of his time on the unit.

'Life's OK, Mike. For me, that is, not my mother. She never got over it.'

He told me that his mother had died of cancer a few years before, lonely and bitter, though her husband had done his best to nurse her through it. Ryan was the only one of her children to attend the funeral. He said he still struggled with a sense of guilt, especially around the anniversary of his mother's death, but he refused to let it interfere with his new life.

'Don't worry,' he said, putting his arm around his wife. 'My daughter's just got herself a boyfriend. I don't much like him but she'll have to find out things for herself. I'm not going to make the same mistake as my mother.'

Gwen, Ryan and their anorexia nervosa showed just how powerful family dynamics can be. When families are going right, it is difficult to think of a better vehicle to carry children and young people through their development towards an identity of their own. When families are going wrong, they can trap them in a role of the family's choosing. But the situation is more complicated still.

The child is at the centre of the family's relationships and those relationships influence how the child thinks, feels and behaves. But the nuclear family is at the centre of the wider family of the helping system: health, education and the social services. Relationships in that wider system can reinforce or repair the relationships in the nuclear family and the child in turn.

If GPs, hospital doctors, teachers, social workers and psychiatrists are themselves at loggerheads, they may feed into the battles within the family, and the mixed feelings inside the child. Where they are working together in cooperation, they may bring the family together and heal the child at its centre. The helping system has a responsibility, not just to offer therapy, but a role model too.

But the ripples flow both ways. Just occasionally, a child may act maturely enough to bring the adults together around him. Like Wayne with his decision to turn down any further treatment for his kidney disease. When that happens, we should be truly amazed..

CHAPTER 10

NATHAN AND CHRISTINE
TALES OF PRIDE AND PREJUDICE

> *Timothy Winters comes to school*
> *With eyes as wide as a football-pool,*
> *Ears like bombs and teeth like splinters:*
> *A blitz of a boy is Timothy Winters.*
>
> Charles Causley, 1957

Two home visits in the same morning. They couldn't have been more different and they couldn't have been more the same.

The first was to a council house at the far end of one of the poorest estates in the country. Litter was strewn across the streets, last year's Christmas trees rotted in the gardens, and the local supermarket had its windows boarded up and its doorway narrowed against a quick get-away. Poor, but the family were glad to see me and welcomed any help I could give them.

The lad I'd come to see was slumped on the sofa, playing Zombie Shooting games on his smart phone. 'We didn't think you'd want to come out so far,' said his mother, snatching the phone out of his hand. 'But now you're here . . .'

The second was to a gated community in one of the wealthiest areas of the country. The streets were swept, the gardens immaculate and the deli down the road was full of expensive foreign food.

Wealthy, but the family were suspicious of my involvement, had barely agreed to the visit, and denied any need for help.

The young girl who had been referred was in her bedroom, safely out of sight. 'I'm not sure why you arranged to come,' said the father, looking at his watch. He motioned to his wife to keep quiet. 'Could you make it quick, please. We've all got to be at work . . .'

They sound like caricatures, but I only wish they were. They were real, and they set me thinking about something we're not supposed to talk about these days – class. The differences between the haves and have-nots that increase daily amongst my patients, the way they affect our attitude to help, and their attitude to the sort of help we have to offer in turn – it pervades every aspect of our work, whether we admit it or not, and it is every bit as entangling as the family dynamics in the last chapter.

And yet the situation is more complicated than it might first appear. I have spent a great deal of time trying to persuade governments that we should not equate family problems with run-down housing estates. I understand that most children on those estates are living in material poverty, that generations of adults on them have had no work and no prospects, and that the children are losing their faith in the ability of education to get them out of the mess.

But this misses two crucial facts. One of the joys of working on those estates is that every now and then you meet a family that has not simply survived, but has prospered emotionally amongst all the mayhem around them; while some of the most emotionally sterile families that I have worked with have been in comparatively rich, professional homes. Material poverty does not necessarily mean emotional poverty; material wealth does not guarantee emotional prosperity, as those two home visits proved. So different in their circumstances; so similar in their need for help; poles apart in their response.

Instead of poverty, we should talk about deprivation. Deprivation is to be found across the board, but class attitudes get in the way of help from traditional services. The children on those lower-class sink estates are every bit as entitled to our help as any other, but they do not fit easily into clinic-based psychiatric services, whose therapists are likely to dismiss them as social problems and drop them off their list at the slightest excuse. The children in middle-class professional homes are entitled to help too, but their parents are often prickly at best, threatening at worst, and services avoid them wherever possible or underestimate their need. The result may be the same: they don't get helped.

Nathan and Christine came from very different backgrounds, with the same, near-tragic ending. For one of them, psychiatric services felt it beneath them to be involved with the family. For the other, the family felt it beneath them to have psychiatric services involved. Both were stuffed full of pride and prejudice, on all sides.

I came late to Nathan's story, when he was already an older teenager, and I had to piece it together from many people's notes. And that is significant. Children like Nathan are passed on from one service to another like a relay baton without much being done. He first presented to the local paediatric team when he was just four years old, referred by a locum GP because of his failure to thrive. His failure; no suggestion that society might be failing him.

He was small for his age, pale and pasty, and had a host of phys-ical difficulties. He had a stammer, was clumsy and uncoordinated and was still wetting the bed at nights. He had a ripe choice of swear words without understanding any of them. On the hospital ward, Nathan hid in a corner or played aggressively until there was a fight and the nurses had to step in. Twice he was found pinching food from the trolley, and the only reason he didn't tell the dinner ladies to 'fuck off' was because he couldn't pronounce his 'f's.'

It would be very easy to blame Nathan's mother, but in truth she had as many problems as her son. She was a single parent, had herself been in care and had no support from a family who were scattered between prison, prefabs and heaven-knows-where. She had a string of broken relationships with unsuitable men and children by most of them. Nathan's own father was a heavy drinker and killed himself in a road smash when his son was just two. When she lost her temper with Nathan, which was often, she screamed at him.

'You're just like your fucking father. No good. You'll end up the same fucking way!' And Nathan believed her.

There were good grounds for taking action, but little seemed to have been done. None of his physical complaints were deemed worthy of treatment in their own right, and no one saw that, put together, they were shattering to his self-esteem. His mother could have been accused of neglect, but that itself was a neglected diagnosis. And in any case, they would have seemed little different from hundreds of other families on the local authority's books. He was discharged to follow-up in a GP practice where the locum doctors moved on every few months and were lost to follow-up themselves.

Nathan surfaced again, a day after his seventh birthday, as a referral to the child and adolescent mental health service (CAMHS). At home, his mother was struggling to cope with a physically handicapped infant and a new baby; she had no time to do anything about Nathan's destructive behaviour. Neighbours said he was often seen wandering around by himself at night and begging for food from passers-by. They had called the police because of shouting from the house, but they had no idea if this was ever followed up.

At school, Nathan interrupted everyone around him. He seemed to find it impossible to concentrate on lessons and played the fool to get attention. The other children egged him on or ignored him and he had no real friends. He was referred after going missing on a school trip and then being found in the clutches of a local shopkeeper. He claimed he was buying a present for his mother but he had no money and the shopkeeper said he was thieving.

The referral letter came from the educational psychologist who had seen Nathan only once, and that in the school classroom. He had told the teachers to try rewarding him for good behaviour instead of punishing him all the time. The teachers, who were angry with Nathan and just wanted to get rid of him, said there was no good behaviour to reward. They said he was hyperactive and needed 'a course of that medication'. The psychiatrist who assessed him thought there was good enough evidence for a diagnosis of ADHD and planned a trial of Ritalin; but that was the last he saw of them. Nathan's mother failed to turn up for two further clinic appointments and he was struck off the list.

At some point, Nathan was taken at last into the local authority's care. He was placed with foster parents who handed him back when he attacked other children in the house. He went next to a small group home, where he did better for a while and excited the attention of his mother; but she was unable to keep consistent enough contact to reform their relationship, to bring him home or to help him settle elsewhere.

He was suspended twice from secondary school and sent to special education – which was neither special nor educative. By fifteen, he was roaming the streets and being used by older gangs as a look-out. He was usually the one caught and had built up a list of minor charges. He used any money he could lay his hands on to buy drugs and alcohol, and slept in shop doorways. He was seen in accident and emergency with occasional overdoses but discharged himself each time and was not followed up.

I was told about Nathan when he was seventeen, but by that time he was caught up in the baton-passing battle and there was little I could do. Nathan was virtually homeless, was drinking heavily and in a poor physical state. He was picked up by the police and taken to see the GP for his hacking cough. He was given a course of antibiotics and referred again to CAMHS because he was depressed; but CAMHS said he was over sixteen, out of education and the responsibility of the adult services.

The adult mental health service thought that Nathan's drinking was the main problem and referred him to the addiction psychiatrists. The addiction team said they couldn't take him on because he was still drinking and showed no motivation to stop. While they were busy passing his referral around between them, Nathan took another, major overdose and very nearly died.

He was admitted to the adult ward on a section of the Mental Health Act and began a career in psychiatric care. More comfortable than the streets, perhaps, but it buried any real hope of change and made sure that he would repeat the problems with his own children, if he ever had any. As his parents had done before him.

Nathan's story makes grim reading. I could be accused of beefing it up if it wasn't so common in an age when more and more young people like Nathan are ending up on the streets after a lifetime shuffling between services. Services whose own resources are being cut and are wary of taking on anyone who doesn't quite fit their criteria. Criteria that become tighter the greater the fear of being deluged by referrals. And people like Nathan, whose referrals are rejected or who are not referred at all.

Christine's story is just as painful and increasingly common; we simply don't hear about it so often. She was born into a family that was already creaking at the edges. Her father left a well-paid executive post to set up a business of his own, in the middle of the financial recession. The business thrived at first but soon required his full-time attention to keep it afloat. He began drinking socially with clients, but it became the only way he could cope with the workload.

Her mother was a music teacher who had the threat of redundancy hanging over her during local authority cuts. She had frequent days off work with physical pains that were never satisfactorily explained and took to her bed for periods of time with depression. (Children are not the only people who convert emotional problems into bodily symptoms.) Another daughter, Christine's older sister, was herself a musician on a further training course that needed a lot of financial support. She seemed to be separating from the family, both physically and emotionally.

Christine was a late child who the parents described as 'a mistake'. She was born into the first flush of her father's success, at a time when her mother was out of bed, less depressed and functioning well. The pressures on Christine's shoulders were huge from the beginning.

'The only way to survive in the modern world is to be more successful than the next person,' said her father. 'Devil take the hindmost.' Just at the point when his own life showed how difficult that might be. Her mother agreed.

The key to success, they said, was academic, and at first Christine fulfilled their hopes. She was a high flier at primary school, head of her year in every test, with impeccable homework that was way beyond what she was expected to do. Some of the teachers were worried about her lack of social skills, however. They never caught her playing games when she should have been concentrating, none of the other children invited her for a sleepover and the world of Harry Potter seemed to have passed her by, but her academic work amazed them and compensated for it. Only one of them was brave enough to ask the educational psychologist what might be happening at home.

'There can't be anything wrong,' he said. 'Everyone knows them. Her mother's a teacher too. And I wouldn't want to get on the wrong side of her dad. He's a powerful man, a successful businessman and very jealous of their reputation. Rather you than me.'

But things were not as they seemed. The father's business was floundering and his drinking getting worse. The mother was now so listless that she had been put on half pay and then lost her job completely. They were having difficulty with the mortgage and the bank were threatening to foreclose on their debt. And there was a hidden agenda lurking in the background: if it carried on like this, they might have to sell up and move somewhere cheaper, if there was any equity left on their house.

Christine worked even harder at school and in the evenings. No friends were allowed to visit. TV was strictly limited and bookwork put above all play. At night she slept with her head under the pillow so that she couldn't hear the arguments between her parents – downstairs if her mother was out of bed, or upstairs if her mother was bed-ridden again. A neighbour had called round on some specious excuse, to see if things were all right, but was fobbed off with smiles and a pot of tea when she did.

It all began to crumble when Christine went to secondary school and her parents diverted their upsets into endless complaints. The form teacher became so wary of the father's temper that the head was forced to intervene. Christine bore the brunt of the school's reaction and was increasingly isolated. She seemed to be ostracised by her peer group and was taken to and from school in her father's car, or by taxi, even though her house was walking distance away. To the teachers' secret relief, Christine developed aches and pains like her mother and was sent home by the school nurse. She spent long periods off school and her work went downhill.

At home, the atmosphere was tense. Her father was drunk most days, her mother was deeply depressed, and Christine was trapped somewhere in between. Her father had lost interest in her academic achievements and demanded that she do her mother's work; her sister had stopped visiting altogether. The GP found no physical cause for her symptoms but referred her to the hospital to make sure, against her father's grumbled objections. The paediatricians were at a loss too and suggested a child psychiatrist. The father exploded and stormed out of the clinic, trailing his daughter behind him.

How do I know all this? Because Christine told me herself. At the age of fifteen, her physical symptoms became critical and she was admitted to the paediatric ward: weak, tired and without any of her former energy. Tests showed nothing specific. Her mother visited her regularly and the nurses felt she enjoyed being in the hospital more than at home. The father made brief, angry appearances, demanded to know the diagnosis, and berated the doctors when they failed to give him clear answers. And I became involved.

My base, of course, was in the child and adolescent mental health service. Some of my patients needed the safety of my clinic room, but the rest I would see wherever they were. And that included the hospital ward. I don't believe in psychosomatic illness, as if it is something separate. All physical illnesses have a psychological component, and all psychological illnesses can be expressed in physical symptoms, like Christine's. But parents and patients are often made frightened and angry by a psychiatric referral for what they are convinced is a purely physical illness. As if we are saying it doesn't exist, it's all in their head at best, or they're going mad at worst. But they might just put up with a psychiatrist being a familiar part of the ward routine – even the father of Christine.

She spent hours telling me what had happened to her over the years, and her mother joined us when she dared. I began to see them as joint victims, with similar symptoms and similar needs, but the father was just as much a victim in his own way. Life in the household had become intolerably pressurised, and all of them were looking for ways out. Christine with her physical collapse, her mother with her depression, and her father with his drinking, though he wouldn't have admitted it. The elder sister had escaped and failed to answer any of my attempts to contact her.

Gradually, we got Christine back on her feet. We had to restrain her or she would have tried to do everything too soon, to prove to herself and her parents that she was still their champion. I got her mother into adult help for her depression, to spare her daughter from having to look after her. And I assuaged her father's continued objections by reintroducing her to a more reasonable programme at school. Then I lost touch with them and have regretted it ever since.

It is difficult to know exactly what happened. Her teachers told me that Christine did well enough to get a place at university, which must have gladdened everyone's heart. But it was the first time she had been let out of the family and the first time she was being asked to function outside its pathology, to become her own person. She would have been totally unprepared for it, and that must have been very scary.

She saw the university GP with a recurrence of her aches and pains and he referred her to the university counselling service, hesitantly, because he had been warned by the father not to drag up the past. Christine agreed to see them and they contacted me, knowing that I had once been involved. Before I could talk to them, she was arrested on a charge of possessing cocaine, which she said she was holding for a friend. And she was admitted to intensive care a short while later after taking a major drug overdose.

Whether her overdose was deliberate or accidental, I doubt even Christine knew at the time. Most people are pretty ambivalent in the heat of the moment, careless of what might happen as they take the tablets or stand on the motorway bridge. But it took her into adult psychiatric care and undermined her hard-won independence.

So there we are: two equally horrendous stories, starting from widely different stations in life, but with the same ending. And leaving us with the same messages. To begin with, neither Nathan nor Christine could have had any sense of being wanted for their own sake.

Nathan was seen by his mother as the reincarnation of his father's faults, and he did his best to prove her assertion that he would end up the same way. Christine was her parents' great hope, the saviour of her father's failing ambitions and her mother's protector. She was never allowed the space to develop the social relationships within which she might have found her place in the world.

Both of them reflected this in their behaviour, and it was our job to work out what that behaviour might mean. Nathan's bad behaviour fulfilled all his mother's expectations at home. In school, he could only get attention by playing the fool and anything was better than nothing at all. Christine turned her emotional distress into physical sickness, which took her out of the pressure at school and carried her home, where she could get between her battling parents and prevent her mother being beaten up, emotionally if not physically too.

Armed with those insights, it was the role of the services to act. But I'm not surprised that they compounded the children's problems more than they helped. It is often said that such children are hard to reach, yet their history shows that they are seen by almost everybody. They just aren't properly heard. Instead, they were passed around like hot potatoes, no one being willing to hold on to them long enough to tackle their distress. Which must have convinced them that they were truly unwanted, that their situation was too difficult and worse, downright dangerous.

In both families, there was ample evidence of neglect. It is just as destructive in the long run as sexual and other physical abuse, but it has the reputation of being difficult to prove. In fact, all it requires is perverse parenting, thwarted child development, and a connection between the two. It was overwhelming in both cases, but Nathan was only removed belatedly and for Christine it was never even considered. They had to find their own, pathological ways of getting out of the situation.

Why? The answer, I think, lies where this chapter began: in a mixture of pride and prejudice. Social workers must have heard stories like Nathan's many times over, to the point where managers felt they would be less criticised for spending their time in sexual abuse teams, where they can make a more obvious difference. And many mental health teams would have considered Nathan's social problems to be outside their remit, unless they were disguised as a diagnosis like ADHD. Pride at doing something more incisive; prejudice against getting involved in something untreatable.

At least one teacher and one neighbour had spotted the warning signs of what was happening in Christine's home, but the prospect of doing something about it in a middle-class, eloquent family with an angry and potentially litigious father would have been very threatening. It was understandable that all the professionals chose to accept her symptoms at face value and not dig deeper. Pride of a family that thought it could consume its own smoke; prejudice of services that failed to consider that such a family might be on fire.

The word we are skirting around, again, is class. I have no doubt that there are some services that would handle Nathan and Christine with greater insight, but they have needed wholesale changes of attitude that can only be pushed through by local like-minds and central government backing. Not every service has the benefit of either.

And I have no illusions about my own role. I have been accused

myself of pride and prejudice many times, of class issues. I can only
be more aware of my own pathology and work on it as far as I
can. Like Nathan and Christine, and their helpers.

CHAPTER 11

ABDI, HASSAN AND HIJAB
CULTURAL DIFFERENCES

Before French culture, German culture, Italian culture, there is human culture.
Ernest Renan: *'Qu'est-ce qu'une nation?'* address, given 1882

Children are born of their culture, just as they are of their personalities, their families and their social class. Some of them work hard to escape its clutches; some are content to live within its expectations; some struggle anyway, to no avail, and are distressed by the fight. But what is culture, and what are the implications for trying to help?

Descriptions of culture tend to stress its consistency: a soup of knowledge and experience, values and beliefs, customs and practices, that distinguish the taste of one group of people from another and whose recipe is handed down through the generations. But culture is not so easily defined. It can vary, not just between racial groups, but within those groups themselves. And I include myself in that.

I am English, from the coalfields of the Derbyshire–Nottinghamshire border, where anger was expressed by 'going mardy' on each other. We retired in silence to opposite ends of the house and the last one to speak was the winner. I married into a Welsh family from the Gower, who chucked bricks at one another and made up again at the drop of a hat, if you'll forgive the mixed metaphor. Culture shock, but at least I knew what to expect. The differences are much less clear when it comes to mental illness.

My self-contained English relatives found it difficult to show any emotions, let alone madness. A mental hospital was akin to Alcatraz and a threat with which to frighten the children.

'If you don't behave, the men in white coats will come and take you off to the loony bin!'

And yet, despite that background, I have talked openly about my own depression on these pages, on radio and television, from the public platform, and to anyone who has the time to listen.

In contrast, I have spent most of my life practising psychiatry in that open Welsh society where people will tell you their life story at the bus stop and women wear their heart on their sleeve.

'We're all related anyhow. So we all know each other's business. No secrets here, love.'

But in contrast to that sense of community spirit, the men from the Valleys are so shy of getting help for their mental problems that the suicide rate is high and climbing.

All of which is a reminder. Therapists must be aware of the cultural difference between ourselves and the patients in front of us, must never make assumptions about them because they are from one sort of group or another, and must always try to work out what is coming from their life and what is coming from our own.

Ironically, this may be easier when we work abroad because the cultural differences are so obvious and nothing will last very long unless we embed it within the needs and skills of the local people. It is much more difficult at home, where we may not be sure whether we are dealing with something cultural, that needs cut-glass handling, or something universal, that needs the usual treatment no matter what culture it has cropped up in. The Somali boys were a case in point.

The Somalis have a proverb: 'A person who has not travelled does not have eyes.' A brave assertion, but it covers a very chequered history. They came to the UK first as seamen from the Horn of Africa, soon after the opening of the Suez Canal. They were allowed to settle temporarily in boarding houses on the dock fronts and send money back home. But the outbreak of civil war in Somalia in the 1980s had dire results, here as well as back in Africa.

They brought their families over to escape, but the journey was horrendous. Many of them came out in cattle trucks, through hostile communities in Eritrea and Djibouti. Some of the women were raped and gave birth in the trucks, and all of them had been reviled in one way or another. What they suffered en route compounded the trauma they had endured in their home country, and what they needed here was sympathetic handling. What they got was a social services hostel in alien territory, and a growing resentment from the local population.

A few months before he made it to Cardiff, Abdi had been defending the remains of his family with a Kalashnikov rifle; his father having been abducted and killed along with all the adult males in the village. We have become used to the stories of child soldiers but they are still shocking, and Abdi was just twelve.

In Cardiff he was placed in a secondary school, where he sat in the back row of a maths lesson with little English language and no preparation. He was bullied by the other boys in the playground who took their cue from their parents' attitude in the docks. And he did what he had been trained to do. He defended against violence with violence, pulled out a knife and tried to stab his assailants.

The authorities were convinced that Abdi had mental health problems; he had, but they were not the product of a mental illness. What he needed, like all the Somali children, was a period of careful debriefing from the events of the war and their journey out, and a preparation for their new life here.

'You can't do that,' said an official. 'It would make them different.'

'But they are different,' we replied. 'This is a cultural issue, not a diagnosis.'

Abdi's was a classic case of mental illness worries and misplaced political correctness, overcoming the emotional and practical realities of the Somali cultural needs. The problem with Hassan was the opposite, and this time I was the one who made the mistake.

I arrived at our in-patient adolescent unit one Monday morning to find the staff jumping up and down with anxious anticipation. Somali boys are very tall for their age and look older than their years. Hassan had been admitted to the adult psychiatric ward over the weekend under a section of the Mental Health Act, and been diagnosed by the on-call team as suffering from a psychotic breakdown. He was actually in his mid-teens and was due to be handed over to us for treatment at any moment.

Hassan escaped his nursing escort and began running around the grounds of the unit, muttering out loud in Somali and dropping to his knees to scoop mud and grass into his mouth. I had a dim memory of prayer rituals and the need to take in water or a substitute during the incantation. He was not psychotic, or so I thought. He had been terrified by the experiences he had been through and the forced admission must have been the final insult. He was praying for deliverance.

The nurses were sceptical but I resisted their wish to give him antipsychotic medication and called in the elders from the Somali community to come and advise me on what to do next. They watched Hassan for a few minutes, spoke to him in his mother tongue, then turned angrily towards me.

'Call yourself a psychiatrist?' one shouted. 'Don't you recognise an illness when you see one?'

'He's mad,' said another. 'Now get on and give him the medication he needs.'

'Just because he's from another country,' said the first, 'it doesn't mean he's not entitled to treatment like everyone else.'

We did what they ordered, Hassan's psychosis settled over several weeks on the unit and we were able to talk with him about the trauma that he had been through and which lay, raw and untouched, underneath. He was discharged to the Somali community on medication and close follow-up.

Two very different situations, but the same difficulty in working with foreign cultures in a UK setting. Sometimes, like Abdi, a young person's behaviour is the product of a different culture and its trauma; we must not confuse it with a diagnosis. Sometimes, like Hassan, it is the symptom of a universal mental illness; we must not confuse it with culture. But how easy it is to get it wrong, especially when we're trying to be politically correct.

At least there was no question in either case of the patient and his community refusing our help; they were only too glad for us to be involved. But that is far from the situation with the Muslim and Hindu girls I have seen with worrying frequency, after they have taken an overdose of tablets or harmed themselves in some other way. Like Hijab.

There was a world of difference in the background to her referral. The Somali boys were hotfoot from the war in their homeland and taking their first, traumatic steps in the UK. Hijab was born here. Her name means 'daughter of a scholar from Baghdad', which was near enough. Her father was from a town only twenty miles from the Iraqi capital, had been to the university there, and came over many years ago as a lecturer. He brought his wife, a son and two daughters with him. Hijab, the youngest, was born soon after they arrived.

Despite how long they'd been here, the rest of the family still thought of Iraq as their home. They were steeped in the Muslim tradition, visited relatives in their birthplace regularly, and might one day return for good. Britain was Hijab's home and she was caught between the western, more liberalised expectations of her friends in school, and the Muslim, traditional attitudes of her parents and siblings in the house.

The contrast must have been more than Hijab could bear, and she took an overdose of sleeping pills that she pinched from her mother's drawer. I would learn all this, gradually, over the months I worked with them; but the referral was stark and insensitive.

'Are you the psychiatrist on call? Right, we've got a sixteen-year-old Muslim girl in accident and emergency. She's taken an overdose. Can you come and see her before she's discharged?'

'Could you get her admitted, to the women's ward? I'll see her there.'

'But she doesn't need admitting. She obviously didn't mean to kill herself. Either that or she's not very bright.'

'Doesn't need it physically, perhaps. But she does if I'm going to be allowed to help. If a psychiatrist appears down there, the family will whip her away and I'll never see her again. Not till she takes another overdose. And this time she might make sure.'

The first job was to engage her enough to help, and to do that I would need to work within her cultural heritage. The mental health services are even more stigmatised in many sections of the Muslim society than they are in our own. Their whole concept is alien and they are viewed with incomprehension and mistrust. A history of contact with them could ruin a woman's marital chances, and a good marriage would be the height of ambition.

Better to see her in a more familiar setting, a physical ward, surrounded by women with a physical illness, where I could be a doctor in its widest sense and appeal to her father's natural respect for authority. He would be less likely to take her away from there.

Which brings us straight to the point. Hijab was sixteen, born in Britain and desperate to have the same chances as her friends. Should I not have respected her right to autonomy, to privacy, to see me wherever she wished and alone? That might have been difficult with any adolescent, and with Hijab it was impossible.

Her culture revolved around the family. It was dominated by the father's wishes and those of his own father before that – the very tradition from which Hijab was trying to break away. But unless I sought his permission in some way, I would lose her. And she would not openly challenge him. Sometimes we have to be less purist and a little more pragmatic to do anything at all. A tough lesson.

Next, how to establish the sort of therapeutic relationship within which we might begin to address her problems. Muslims have no tradition of patient and therapist working together in an equal partnership like that. Personal disclosure means weakness, disloyalty and shame. The Muslim medical students who have been placed with me and watched me work, have taught me much about how I should conduct myself with someone like Hijab.

'You can shake hands, Mike, but don't touch. Keep a respectful distance. And be careful how you look her in the eye.' Difficult again for someone like me, who has striven hard to escape from his own cool, distanced background. It could have been my family speaking.

What the family required was old-style medicine. They wanted the doctor to give them a clear explanation for the patient's symptoms, a diagnosis for what was wrong, an argument for the treatment of choice, and a step-by-step set of targets on the way to a cure. Wouldn't a lot of people like that sort of help for emotional problems, therapists as well as patients, and to whatever culture they belong? To that extent Hijab was no different, but her culture made it even more difficult for us to get away from the medical model.

I brought in the whole family and listened to the father and his son telling me how things were, or should be, while the women sat passively by. Including Hijab. But bit by bit, I earned enough trust to lift the lid on their relationships and find out what lay beneath. I learnt that one of the older daughters had fought against an arranged marriage, had been sent back to Iraq to learn the error of her ways, and had given in.

I learnt that the mother had risked her reputation by using her own education to get a job as a secretary in the university, without confiding in her husband, who was a lecturer in the same department. I learnt how they were worried that Hijab might throw over the family traditions and break away completely. Something that might sound familiar to any parents faced with a rebellious teenager leaving home.

And I learnt that I was not alone in trying to help. A younger daughter had been to consult with 'al-fataha', the female fortune teller, who had told her that there was an arranged marriage in the offing for her too. The father and his son were being instructed in the scriptures by 'moalj belkoran', the elders who knew best.

'Anyone who is a day older than you in age,' said Hijab's father, 'is a year older than you in understanding.' It was a proverb that settled on the shoulders of a sixteen-year-old like a dead weight.

But we began at last to seek out a compromise. Hijab was discharged. I worked with the family at home and in the sessions I was allowed to have with her alone in the school. The family agreed that they would not arrange a marriage for either Hijab or her sister, over the head of their own wishes. They would respect the careers they might carve out for themselves. And in return, they were comforted that the girls would remain more happily within the family and its religious beliefs.

Hijab was allowed to go shopping with her friends on a Saturday afternoon. She texted them, played computer games with them, and brought them over for a taste of Arabic cooking – much to the parents' pride. Together they discussed the political situation, and worked out strategies to deal with the worst of the racist attacks they had all received in the wake of ISIS and the wars in the Middle East: Hijab in school, her father and brother at work, and her mother in the supermarket.

A compromise, yes. Not wholesale multiculturalism, in which the family traditions are preserved intact at the expense of new-found expectations. Not wholesale assimilation, in which the traditions are deserted in favour of a new-found home. Not what the purist might wish for. But it was a compromise that Hijab and her family could live with; and so could I.

We never referred to the hijab that she wore around her head, though it was there as a metaphor throughout. And Hijab told me in our last session, with her tongue firmly in her cheek, that her name had another meaning too: 'a veil'. Her head had remained covered, as the family wanted, but her emotions had been uncovered, to work on openly. She no longer needed to express them by harming herself.

You could say that most of the work with someone like Hijab and her family was political in its widest sense, and some of it was certainly so. It is impossible to tackle cultural problems without any reference to the context of the time – whether that is the invasion of Iraq, the war in Syria, or the increasingly bitter debate at home around immigration. Hijab was consumed by her own cross-cultural battles, but she was aware of how they were a microcosm of what was going on around her.

'Wouldn't it be good,' she said, 'if we could get everyone admitted, for help.'

'It would have to be a big ward,' I replied, 'and a hell of a therapist.'

'And they'd have to want to be helped. Too big.'

'But your family changed. And your school is changing. It's a start.'

The task in working with different cultures is to relieve the suffering of the patient trapped within. Sometimes we can do that directly, as with the Somali boys, Hijab, and similar young people and their families. Sometimes the first responsibility falls to someone else, like the police and the law. But psychiatry cannot wash its hands of the situation.

We owe our support, for example, to girls who are still subject to genital mutilation; and to the women who speak out against it. We should fight for them verbally as courageously as they have done with their own bodies. The practice is abhorrent in countries where it is endemic; in the UK it is totally unacceptable. But it goes on here, in FGM parties, as a rite of passage.

And that, of course, raises the most difficult problem of all. In families like that of Hijab, we might try to modify their cultural attitudes, to help a young person fit in with her westernised expectations and relieve her distress, to the satisfaction of everyone involved. But at what point do we say that a cultural practice is beyond the pale, abusive, and needs rescue, not therapy? Is that just a quantitative spectrum, with something like FGM at one end of it, or is it qualitatively different?

Is there a culturally sensitive compromise to be reached there too, or should there be no compromise at all? With any such cultural practice and whatever the repercussions, for once, politicians, the law and therapists are in agreement. Compromise in this case would simply be immoral.

CHAPTER 12

BECKY

HANDLING RISK

Life is a gamble at terrible odds – if it was a bet, you wouldn't take it.
Tom Stoppard: *Rosencrantz and Guildenstern Are Dead*,
Act 3, 1967

Life is full of risk. The risk of hot ovens, busy roads, animals and abusers, that lie in wait for young children at home and in the outside world. The risk of bullying, of social isolation and academic disasters at school. The risk of alcohol, drugs and wrong relationships as they grow up.

There are many adults to defend them against those risks. Parents must decide when to rescue children from their own behaviour, and when to let them find things out for themselves. Teachers have pastoral duties way beyond their academic training. We argue about how much responsibility the social media firms should carry for keeping the internet clean and safe. And when it all gets too much, the Mental Health Act and the courts may step in and protect children and young people from themselves and others.

But taking risks, we know, is essential for healthy human development. Unless they are allowed to take risks in childhood, young people will find it difficult to cope with risk in adult life. They may never learn self-mastery of life's problems, or how to cooperate with their peers in solving them. Without their own experience of freedom, they may become adults who smother their own children with anxiety in turn, in an increasingly risk-averse society.

Risk cannot be eliminated, but it can be managed. And it can be helped if it all goes wrong, as long as we are given the licence to experiment, within appropriate boundaries. Children must learn how to take risks, and parents must take the risk of allowing them to, within their watching brief. Patients must take risks in order to improve, and therapists must take the risk of allowing them to, within the therapeutic relationship. And the helping system must take risks with its practitioners, within what is reasonable and effective, however perilous it might first appear.

That requires nerve, and sometimes it's the young people themselves who are the bravest. As it was with Becky. I was working on an adolescent in-patient unit at the time, with a mixed bunch of young people, some caught up in family entanglements, others whose bodies had been blighted by physical disease, and others still reeling from death, divorce and other disasters. The development of all of them had been derailed, and they needed some sort of shelter while they got it back on track.

They weren't particularly interested in what had brought them there; only how they were going to put it right. And they approached each other's problems with a healthy degree of risk while they were on the unit and in their lives outside afterwards. We decided to run an evening group for those who had just been discharged but needed more work, together with others referred from elsewhere. A co-therapist and I, with a dozen shaky adolescents, came together one evening each week, in an outpatient building empty except for the cleaners.

'You're all mad there,' said one of the cleaners when I went to apologise to her at the end of the group. 'You must do strange things to each other in that group. Best not to go anywhere near, I say.' Which showed how little sympathy we would have got if it all went wrong. And it nearly did.

If we'd known a bit more about Becky, we would never have taken her into the group in the first place. But we'd had the wool pulled over our eyes by a psychiatric colleague who knew we were anxious to start and feared that the sheep would begin to leave the fold while we were waiting to complete the numbers. He seized the chance to offload someone with whom he'd failed, repeatedly, by selling her to us in disguise. She was seventeen.

'Becky has a personality problem,' he said. What he meant was a personality disorder, but his language showed how judgemental he felt about her. 'She's ideal for group work. Right up your street, Mike.'

Now here she was, lying curled up on the carpet, in the middle of the other adolescents. She had arrived late and sat silently through the first half hour, her head bowed over her handbag, chewing at her cuticles until the blood ran down her fingers and dripped on to her feet. She seemed immune to either direct encouragement from the group, or interpretation of what her behaviour might mean. Then she sank slowly to the floor and curled up, foetus-wise, before us all.

When I bent to touch her, Becky ran out of the room and up the back stairs, clutching a broken milk bottle she'd taken from her handbag. I heard her slam the lavatory door with a noise so loud it could only mean come and get me.

For a moment we were all stunned. How we tackled this situation might be a turning point, for Becky, for the rest of the young people in the group, and for my co-therapist and me too.

'Well, there are two of you.'

The comment came from Ross, a tall, thin and pale-faced youth, who had been a patient on the unit and who we thought we might help further with the relationships in his family.

'One of you could stay with us while the other goes to see what's happened to Becky.'

It was a solution so simple that I convinced myself I had been waiting to see if the group would come up with it. I bounded up the stairs to the lavatory.

'Becky, are you in there? Unlock the door.' Silence. 'You can't hide away forever.'

The lock was fragile and it burst open when I put my shoulder to the door. Becky had cut her wrists with the milk bottle but the wounds were superficial. She let me clean them up without a word, bandage them with my handkerchief and lead her back to the group. She lay down on the floor in our midst, still silent but calmer now, my handkerchief turning pale pink with the water and her clotting blood.

'Has she ever done this before?' asked a young woman whose arms were rutted where she'd cut herself too, to relieve her own tension.

'Yes, quite often,' I replied. Her referrer had told me a little more when she was safely off his hands. Even though he was an adult psychiatrist and Becky was only seventeen, she had been admitted to his ward because of the anxiety that her behaviour evoked in everyone around her.

'And?'

'And she has usually been locked up under section and sedated when she does this. She's said she wants to die.'

There was a long pause while the group considered the new information. Outside, a man was mowing the grass and a car somewhere backfired. Becky twitched at the noise and half raised her head. She was in touch with everything going on around her.

'Well, it doesn't seem to have done much good.' Ross, the tall, thin youth again. 'Where did she come from?'

I told them that Becky had come from her home, ten miles away. By bus. 'So what shall we do with her, then?'

Another pause. Then Tina, an overweight eighteen-year-old with bulimia, who woke in the middle of each night and ate most of the contents of her parents' fridge until she was sick, answered without looking up.

'I suggest we put her back on the bus and tell her she can come to the group again next Thursday. Like the rest of us.'

We followed her advice, nervously but firmly, and took Becky to the bus stop together with one of the other group members who was going the same way. Becky went along passively with us and said only two words.

'Thank you.'

The driver was none too happy when he saw the bloodstained handkerchief, but he allowed her on to the bus and she presented her ticket and sat quietly as if nothing was untoward. I rang her home to tell them what we had done and went with my co-therapist to our supervisor. She listened to our story and told us that it was a risk we had been right to take. No other approach had made any difference.

In other words, our supervisor's matter-of-fact approach calmed our own anxieties, much as the group had calmed Becky. It was the group's bravery, not ours. This was the first time that anyone had carried the risk of Becky's behaviour, had proved to her that it would not overwhelm them, and had made her the stronger for it. She came to every group session thereafter, and made positive suggestions about herself, the others, and the relationships between them. Her life outside was turned around and she got a job she had always coveted as a saleswoman in a dress shop.

Becky's story was a perfect example of how essential risk-taking may be to healthy development, how it can go wrong, and how it is never too late to put it right. No one in her past had taken risks with her behaviour. Her parents had panicked and handed her over to the psychiatric services. Her consultant psychiatrist had panicked and tried to wrap her up in cotton wool. And Becky's reaction had become more and more extreme as she floundered around, looking for a balance between permission and protection. It had become a self-fulfilling prophecy: treat her as dangerous and she will become so.

Thankfully, most parents find a way of coping with the risks of adolescence and childhood, though there may be much heart-searching, many skirmishes, and the occasional pitched battle that brings a young person and their parents to someone like me for advice. Just like Liam. But some of them get it wrong, and their children may show it in the sort of behaviour that carries them into the paediatric ward. At which point I'm called in to help.

Two of them were admitted to the local ward within months of each other, and their families had fallen off on opposite sides of the tightrope of risk. The first because the parents were so diverted by their own problems that they had failed to put any boundaries whatsoever around their son's behaviour. The second because a history of disaster had made a parent so cautious that she could allow her daughter no risk at all.

Andrew was a boy of ten, who had come in repeatedly with fits and had been diagnosed by his GP as having epilepsy. Tests revealed nothing conclusive, Andrew seemed well on the ward, but fitted again just before discharge. There were no reliable witnesses and the paediatric consultant was sceptical. He asked me to visit the family home, where Andrew's mother was herself said to be ill.

I was met at their door by a wave of heat. The central heating was full on, despite it being the middle of a hot summer, and there was a fire in each grate. Andrew's mother lay on a daybed in the living room, swathed in blankets. She was huge, pale and cocooned, like a grub. She hadn't been upstairs for years, said her correspond-ingly small, wiry and attentive husband. He did everything for her. Everything. And no one did anything for their son. In fact, so absorbed were they with the mother's needs that they couldn't care less about his behaviour, once it had been diagnosed and he was safely away on the ward.

'Well we don't have to worry about our Andrew,' said the mother from her daybed. 'He's got epilepsy, you know. That's somebody else's problem now.'

Andrew's fits, real or not, seemed an entirely appropriate escape from home. His parents had been unable to provide the envelope of security that he craved, and the fits took him into the care of the doctors and nurses on the ward. He was able to behave as he wished there, knowing that he would be held within the bound-aries of its routine.

A case conference decided that it would be wrong to return Andrew to a home that was simultaneously so tightly organised around his mother's needs and so neglectful of his own. He was taken instead into a local authority foster placement and his parents put up little fight. His father, in fact, seemed quite relieved to have only one invalid to worry about. Andrew settled in the foster home, he visited the parents regularly at weekends, and his fits disappeared.

Alys was admitted as an eight-year-old, tired and dispirited but with no specific symptoms that the ward could identify. Within days, she spent more time out of bed, playing with the other children, but she got back in again as soon as her mother appeared. Bit by bit, Alys told her story to the nurses and I was called in to work out what to do. The story was a tragic one.

When Alys was a younger child, her mother had another baby. Her father was away a lot on business, which left his wife a prisoner in the house, looking after Alys and her baby sister and unable to drive. One morning, she left Alys in charge of her sister, sleeping in her cot, and nipped down to the shops at the bottom of the street. She was only gone a short time, but while she was away, Alys was diverted into a game with the neighbour's children. When her mother returned, the baby was dead.

It was a cot death, unexplainable and entirely unpreventable. It would have happened whether Alys or her mother were in the house and no one was to blame. But everyone blamed each other. The father blamed his wife for being a bad mother, and she blamed him for being away so much. They both blamed Alys and Alys blamed herself. The neighbours blamed them all.

The marriage did not survive what had happened and Alys and her mother were left, their lives locked together around the consequences. Her mother tried to slake her own guilt by removing all trace of risk from her daughter's life. It was because Alys had gone off to play that the baby had died, she thought. Play was dangerous and henceforward it would not be permitted. No friends were allowed in the house and Alys was barred from going to a sleepover elsewhere. Her toys were strictly educational and she played with them alone or supervised by her mother. Both of them were prisoners now.

'You look as if you could do with a good cup of coffee,' I said to the mother when I found her on the ward one morning.

The coffee in the ward kitchen was almost undrinkable and it was a perfect excuse to get her away by herself. My room was across on the other side of the hospital, nearby but far enough away to leave Alys playing with the other children and her mother to get some space of her own. Nothing would go wrong while she wasn't there. The cup of coffee became a regular pretext and I turned her visits, slowly and without threat, into a therapy for her sadness.

'You like playing with the puppets,' I said.

'Where did you get them?'

'I bought them all over the place. Here and on trips abroad.'

'And do the children play with them?'

'They were meant for the children, but it's the adults who seem to play with them most.'

She looked close to tears. She said nothing but cradled one of the puppets against her cheek. I let her be for a while.

'Forgive me, but I can't help noticing, it's always the leopard that you pick up. I wonder why that is. You could choose any of the others.'

She buried her head in its furry tummy. I waited while she got herself back together and wiped her eyes on the tissues I pushed across to her.

'The leopard?'

Her coffee was too hot and she spat it out, involuntarily, down her front. She was full of apologies and wanted to fetch towels to clean it up, but I waved her back into her chair.

'It's all right. The cleaners will cope. Right now there are more important things.'

Alys's mother sighed and picked up the puppet again. I could easily have slipped in an interpretation, but she needed to come to it herself.

'It's not a leopard. It's a cheetah.'

'Is that important? The name?'

'Yes . . . because I'm a cheater too.'

'In what way?'

It was some time before she could reply, then it came with a rush.

'Because I've cheated Alys. It wasn't her fault, what happened, but I needed something to blame . . . because I felt so guilty, I suppose . . . so I wouldn't let her play.'

'And the cheetah?'

'I'm cheating Alys. I've cheated her out of her childhood . . . and I'm cheating myself too.'

They were both brave in their own way. Alys and her symptoms, which brought the problem to our attention. Her mother and her revelation, which showed us what to do with it. And it was not too late. They began playing together on the ward and at home. Alys was given encouragement to make friendships and her mother began to make relationships outside the home too. It was full of risk for both of them, but it was a healthy risk.

Andrew and Alys were difficult to help, but demanded much less risk of myself than they did of themselves. Becky was a huge risk, as much for myself as for her own life. And some risks are so great, for everyone, that it's not worth taking. And they can come out of the blue.

I was asked to assess Jordan by a psychologist friend who had been seeing him in regular outpatient sessions. She felt they had been uncovering some traumatic issues from his past and she was worried about his state of mind. He was turning his day and night around and becoming suspicious and reclusive. It was a matter of time before they got to the abuse that she felt sure lurked somewhere in his childhood; but was he too fragile to face it?

Jordan was eighteen when I saw him. He was a pianist. He slept all day and played the piano into the small hours in city-centre bars. It could have been an occupational hazard, but it felt more sinister than that. I knew what she meant. He had said nothing civil to anyone for days, growled when they approached, and had walked out three times when asked to play 'Moon River'. He claimed that it contained hidden messages that he didn't want to obey. Most of the bar staff left him alone and breathed a sigh of relief when he was gone.

My friend had been unable to contact any friends and family who could fill in his history; even if he would have allowed them to. She was surprised that he agreed to see me and so was I. There was something important, he said, that only I could do for him. And he was prepared to come to the clinic to get my cooperation.

Jordan sat opposite me, playing around with a cup of coffee that I had made for him. He was untidily dressed, unshaven, and hadn't washed for some time; I could smell him from where I sat. He complained that he had to break his sleep to see me and seemed edgy and hostile. He jumped at every noise in the corridor outside and stared suspiciously at the door afterwards, as if we were about to be interrupted. I used the sun that was streaming through my window as an excuse to switch chairs so that I no longer sat between him and any possible line of escape.

It was a wise move; what followed was quick and decisive. While I was resettling myself, Jordan lifted the case he had brought with him on to his knees. He opened the zip. On top of the screwed-up clothes and bundles of sheets of scribbled paper, was a gun. He laid it on the floor beside his right foot.

'Get me a fucking taxi . . . on that phone. You're not leaving the room. I want to hear everything you say . . . no tricks . . . If you do it wrong, I'll blow your fucking head off . . .'

'Would that be wise – for you, I mean?'

'What difference would it make? They're all after me anyway . . . Do it . . . now!'

I might have been tempted to stick with it and hazard some interpretations. The gun and my name, for instance. Two shooters. But the risks were impossible. Ostensibly, I did what Jordan ordered and telephoned a taxi. In reality, I called the psychiatric team I had alerted earlier and used the words of alarm that we had agreed.

Jordan was on an acute psychiatric ward within the hour, under heavy sedation and the terms of the Mental Health Act. He had a florid, paranoid psychotic disorder that took many months to settle on medication and he has needed close monitoring from the adult community team since. When he was gone, I picked up the gun which had been kicked under his chair. It was unloaded, but somehow that made no difference. I wasn't to know that, after all.

It was reasonably easy for an experienced therapist to know when to take risks and when someone like Jordan needed a firmer intervention. Though Becky was the kind of test case that I wouldn't want to take on too often, and the threat of disciplinary action is making medicine more risk-averse by the year.

Parents must take risks with their adolescents' behaviour on an everyday level. Without the freedom to experiment, their offspring will not develop. The consequences of getting it wrong are rarely as crucial as with Jordan and Becky, but to parents worried about drugs and sex and social media, it must often seem so.

The vast majority of parents negotiate these problems successfully, with fingers crossed and the help of friends and family who have faced similar dilemmas and come out the other side. And in the last resort, most of them would feel that it is better to be safe than sorry. It would be both wrong and impractical to lay down rules for them all, but parents should never be afraid to call on help if they are unsure.

This book is full of examples where parents have asked for such help, when they have been uncertain what to do about their offspring's behaviour in prospect, or where they have made the wrong decisions, the behaviour has worsened and work is needed to put things right. The times when the situation is irredeemable are tragic, but few and far between.

CHAPTER 13

LIZZIE

A CHILD'S BEST INTERESTS

Kindness, the Family Division daily proved, was the essential human ingredient.

Ian McEwan: *The Children Act*, 2014

The one great principle of the English law is, to make business for itself.

Charles Dickens: *Bleak House*, Ch. 39, 1853

Children have rights; adults have obligations to make sure those rights are upheld. All in the child's best interests. A simple enough statement in theory, but life is never that straightforward in practice.

Sometimes children will tell me what they want to happen and the adults agree that it is in their children's best interests to let it be so. Everyone is happy. Sometimes the children's wishes are shrouded in the mists of anger, anxiety and fear. I have to infer their wishes from their behaviour, check out what I have learnt with them, and persuade the adults to whom it might come as a great surprise – as it often does when adults hear of children's wishes to be involved in the facts, emotions and rituals of bereavement.

Sometimes children want what no responsible adult can agree to, because we know better what is in their interest. Like protecting a toddler or a teenager whose behaviour has gone beyond the pale, no matter how upset they may be about it at the time. Sometimes the adults have a view that is more about their own interests than that of the children, the children react in their behaviour and they are sent to me for help. As in custody and access disputes after divorce. And sometimes the whole business is so confused, or the arguments are so finely balanced, that no one can be sure what to do and the law steps in to clear up the mess.

But even the law may find it difficult and distressing to decide what is in the child's best interests. Children who are being physically and sexually abused must be rescued, clearly enough. Now suppose that their parents are being neglectful, short of such abuse. Through no fault of their own, because they were poorly parented themselves, have had no parental training, and are struggling with their own overwhelming needs. Then social workers may be pilloried one minute for leaving the children where they are and working to improve the way their parents handle them, or pilloried the next for taking them away and not giving the parents a chance.

And the public will find it easy to criticise them from the safety of the breakfast table, with black and white opinions and no responsibility for making decisions in a fog of greyness in which it is almost impossible to make out the children's best interests. The press may fall back on stereotypes about the law, lawyers and the courts that are as prejudiced as their views on mental illness, and the children in the midst of it all are as confused as everyone else.

Lizzie's situation was about as complicated as it gets. She was fourteen when I met her, but her story began long before I was directly involved. She was brought up as the child of her maternal grandmother when, in fact, she was the illegitimate daughter of her sister. There are some who would call that pathological, but the family may see it as the best way out of the problem. The 'sister' is able to continue with her education, and the baby is cared for by the extended family. Until the whole pretence is blown by another child in the school playground, where everyone knows everyone else's business in a close-knit community.

But in Lizzie's case, things went wrong from the start. The

relationship between the maternal grandmother and her husband was already shaky when Lizzie was born. Lizzie's 'sister' had herself been placed for a while in the local authority's care because of her behaviour. She came out of care at seventeen to help look after Lizzie, who learnt of the true family structure from the social worker when they were building up her life-story book at the age of five. My sister is my mother: what a facer. She reacted with a mixture of anger, uncertainty and bewilderment and the relationship between the two of them deteriorated from then on.

Lizzie's mother called her 'one of them psychopaths', a fixed and unchangeable label that adults still fasten around the neck of children they don't like. The diagnosis may be frowned upon clinically now, but Lizzie certainly had the full house. She wet the bed into her early teens, was cruel to any children who rivalled her for attention, tortured cats in an idle sort of way, and played with matches whenever they were left in reach.

'I'm always having to stamp out fires,' said her mother. 'She says they're an accident, but she knows what she's doing all right.'

Her comment said less about what was wrong with Lizzie than the rock-solid, pathological partnership in which she and her mother were locked together. Her mother needed someone to blame to divert attention from her own problems, and Lizzie provided her with ample ammunition.

'What am I supposed to do with her?' asked her mother. 'She won't do anything I say.'

'Who would want to do anything you say?' replied her daughter. 'Look where it's got you.'

Earlier psychiatrists had fought shy of a child they felt they couldn't diagnose, and social workers were wary of a situation they felt they could not change. Just like Nathan. For me, the mother–child relationship had echoes of the borderline personality chain I had come across with Cheryl, except that this time the mother was still alive and the chain existed in fact, not just in the daughter's head.

I decided that I needed to tackle it by bringing Lizzie into the adolescent unit and working with her more safely there. If that was a test, it worked. The relationship between the two of them exploded, the mother ran off with a new partner, as her own mother had eventually done before, and Lizzie was taken into local authority care in her turn. She was given a brief foster placement and then a group home in the city.

Cycles of disorder repeat themselves. Lizzie's life had been more of a down-bringing than an up-bringing, in which she had ended up with little moral appreciation of what she did and her behaviour betrayed the emptiness inside. Every Friday night, she ran off from the group home, got as far away as she could, then gave herself up to the local police station. It was an attempt to find out who cared enough to chase her. And it happened so regularly that we formed a special rota of people who knew her well, understood, and were prepared to drive out and bring her back.

The staff needed a further test and they got it. Lizzie began sleeping around and became pregnant at sixteen, as her mother had done at about the same age before. She was told that the local authority would probably take her baby into their care at birth, with a view to adoption. Lizzie would not be allowed more than an initial and fleeting contact. And that would be it. The baby would be gone forever.

Miserable, angry and without a mature outlet for her feelings, Lizzie told the staff that she was going to set a fire under her bed. She did so, a small one that was easily put out, just like the ones at home. But fire was something that the group home were not prepared to handle, however much warning they were given. Lizzie was transferred, there and then, to a secure placement over the border. Whether she knew it or not, you could say that this was the containment she had been after and which her home had never been able to provide. But it was precarious.

Lizzie gave birth in the secure placement, the local authority applied successfully for an interim care order and the baby went to foster parents. She was given supervised contact, grudgingly and more difficult to arrange than it should have been. Reinforced in her anger, Lizzie escaped from the secure placement and protested in the only way she knew how. She set fire to a pile of rubbish in the yard of a deserted house that was boarded up in a row due for demolition.

Unfortunately for her, a homeless man had been sleeping in the house overnight. He was woken up by the smoke and injured himself climbing out of the window. Once again the fire was easily dealt with but Lizzie was arrested under the Criminal Damage Act and charged with arson. She was arraigned to appear before the Youth Court, and I was asked to prepare a psychiatric report.

I spent as much time on it as I dared, bearing in mind the urgency of the baby's situation and that we would have to take Lizzie through two different legal processes: the criminal case in the Youth Court and the custody dispute in the Family Court. The arguments were complicated, and I offered as always to appear in both courts to participate in them. So what did Lizzie's predicament illustrate about the law and its attitude to children?

The immediate issue was one of responsibility. The cases that hit the headlines are usually those where the court is assessing the responsibility of adults for the abuse of children: parents for abusing single children; groups of men for passing around young girls from bed to bed, as if they were parcels to be unwrapped and used at will. Directly, with the adults there in the dock and punished for what they have done. But the adults in Lizzie's case were at one remove. The issue was whether she should be held responsible for the behaviour they had caused.

As a result of her childhood, Lizzie had been left with the shakiest idea of whether anyone cared for her, she had no sense of security other than the restrictions imposed on her, and she had no acceptable ways of showing her emotions when she was at her most vulnerable. Her running away and her fire-setting were evidence of all of it. She just about knew the difference between right and wrong and the way she set her fires meant that she knew the possible consequences of what she did. But she was not in control of the feelings behind her actions and could hardly be said to have moral responsibility for them.

There was no easy excuse for Lizzie's actions and the law was entitled to express its anger for what she had done. But they were understandable in terms of what she had been through and the law had a chance to behave in a more forgiving way than any of the adults she had met so far. Just as I have tried to persuade parents in the clinic who have been outraged by their child's behaviour, and myself when my tolerance has been stretched to the limit.

Take, for example, the young parents who brought a ten-year-old lad to see me. He was surly at the best of times and openly destructive at worst. His parents could barely cope with his anger and the final straw came when he ripped up his older brother's homework. The brother was twelve, a high achiever academically, and as pleasant to live with as his younger brother was difficult. They had punished the ten-year-old by keeping him in indefinitely, which meant that one of them had to stay in too. I asked him to help the nurses make us coffee while the adults talked.

'But he ripped up his brother's homework,' said his father. 'He shouldn't be allowed to get away with it. Shouldn't you be doing something about it?'

'I'm not suggesting he should be allowed to get away with anything,' I replied. 'I would be angry too. But why do you think he did it?'

With their anger validated, the parents were a little more understanding.

'Because he's jealous,' said his mother. 'Jealous of his brother, I suppose.'

'That's right. His brother is much brighter and the homework proved it. I bet it was perfect.' They exchanged knowing glances.

'Now let's find an appropriate punishment for ripping it up – one that doesn't punish you as much as him – but work on what he's good at.'

'What do you mean?' said the father.

'Something that he's better at than his brother. Something that you can give him lots of attention for.'

'But isn't he just an attention seeker already?'

'Of course. But there's nothing wrong with attention seeking. We should be asking why he has to go to such lengths to get it. This way he learns what's acceptable and what isn't. That people will praise him for doing good things and get angry for bad things. He may get punished, but he will still be cared for and given another chance.'

Love survives anger; the most important lesson a child can learn from its parents. I could just spot the father's hand, reaching out to his wife, as the message sank home and their son arrived with tea. Not what we'd asked for, but it got him his first reward.

It was a simple lesson, perhaps, though it meant a great deal to the parents, the brothers and their future relationship. The decision facing the court was a great deal harder, considering what damage Lizzie had done, in a country that has a lower age of criminal responsibility and punishes more of its young people by imprisonment than most of the nations in the western world.

I asked them to give her a firm but non-custodial community order, a supportive social placement to live in, and lots of youth justice supervision while she learnt how to do things differently and got rewards for doing so. A virtuous circle, to reverse the vicious circle of her childhood. The Youth Court agreed. It was an outstanding example of how the law can understand a child's actions in the light of what has gone before, can set clear boundaries round its behaviour, but can trust that things can be done better in the future. If it crosses its judicial fingers, takes a risk, and sets an example.

What the Youth Court decided, I would argue, was clearly in Lizzie's best interests. But in the Family Court it was more complicated. I felt that it was too soon to know whether Lizzie was capable of being a good-enough mother to her baby or whether the local authority should be allowed to carry on with their plans for adoption. So far, the circumstances for Lizzie had been so intolerable that adoption had become a self-fulfilling prophecy. What she needed was a much longer period of regular contact with her baby, free of pressure, backed up by good-quality training in child rearing – the sort that her mother had never been able to give her, and that her mother had never had herself.

But here there were two children to consider: the baby and

Lizzie, barely more than a child herself. Whose best interests should take precedence, or was it possible to satisfy both the baby's best interests and Lizzie's best interests at the same time?

Looking back on it now, I can see that my argument could easily have gone the other way. Was it really for the best if they were not separated? Wouldn't it have been just as abusive to have left the baby with a mother so damaged, and to have saddled the mother with an emotional and physical responsibility to look after her?

Thankfully, it was not my job as an expert witness to make the final decision. That's why we have courts to do it for us where the evidence we give them is so finely balanced. Again, the court agreed with my request for Lizzie and her baby to stay together, but it was a close-run thing. Another example of the law's ability to listen to the arguments on each side, to steer its way through conflicting ideas of best interest, and to come to a sensitive and sensible decision, whatever the risks involved.

So far, so good. But the skills of the court will come to nothing if the adults who are responsible for putting their instructions into practice refuse to do so. And I can think of no clearer example than divorce and the disputes that ensue around custody of the children and around their access to the estranged partner. It is sometimes said that if parents could settle those issues amicably, they would never have got divorced in the first place. But they are usually so angry with each other that they use them as a continued battle-field. And the children are caught in a cross-fire of mixed loyalties and misery.

A recently divorced mother brought her two children to see me: a daughter of seven and a son of five, who were behaving badly at home and in school. So much so, that the school had called her in to complain, and the other parents were refusing to have them over for parties. All three of them were becoming isolated and ostracised by the community. The mother was alternating between punishing her two children and joining with them in a sort of bunker mentality: us against the world.

The court's job had been to give custody to whichever would

make the best day-to-day parent and in this case it was the mother. As it usually is. The father had made their choice easier with his own behaviour, drinking heavily and sleeping with other women, but there have been many cases where it is the other way round and the father has custody instead.

The court had backed this up with a stipulation that the children should see their father every other weekend and that he honour the arrangement by keeping to it regularly and behaving responsibly while they were with him. In fact, it was their mother who stood in the way. She found a succession of excuses for the children not to see him – they had a cold, they had too much homework to do, they would be away visiting her family, it wasn't right that his girlfriend would be there too. And above all, they didn't want to see him. Look how much worse they were when his weekend approached.

I saw the children together at the second appointment. The seven-year-old girl was defensive of her mother and tried to shut her little brother up whenever he threatened to become disloyal. He began by drawing a stick family quietly enough as we talked, but obliterated it so violently with black crayon that he ripped the paper.

'Was that your family you were drawing?'

'It could have been any family,' his sister intervened.

'It was our family,' said her little brother, firmly.

'You seem to be very angry with your family.'

'He's angry with everybody,' his sister intervened again. 'We all are.'

'I think your mother feels you're angry with your father most of all. For leaving you. For still trying to see you. For messing your life up.'

'It's not his fault. It's her who stops us going to see him . . .'

'Shut up!' His sister was beside herself now, unable to stop him saying what he wanted to. 'She can't help it.'

She tried to hit him before I could get between them, but it missed and I held them while they cried together. It was clear that he was speaking for both of them.

They were able to tell me how much they missed their father and how much they still loved him, despite everything. They were happy to live with their mother and they wanted to see their father regularly, as the court had decreed. They had lost their parents' marriage but not the parents themselves. The present mess was worse than when their parents rowed and fought each other before they got divorced.

I saw the mother alone next time. She was already embattled and it wouldn't help to heap blame on her head; but the children had asked me to tell her how they felt. And I needed her to hear it.

'It doesn't sound as though the children have seen their father. For some time.'

'No. I had to put a stop to it.'

'But the court said they should have regular contact with him.'

'The court was wrong. The children don't want to see him.'

'How do you know that?'

'Because they got so upset. Every time it got close to seeing him.'

'Perhaps that's because you made it clear that you didn't want them to see him. And they got all mixed up inside.'

I told her what her children had said and she began crying too. Just as they had done. She had confused her own wishes with what the children wanted for themselves and was using them as evidence in the fight. Right now it was the children who were being hurt. But she would be hurt in the future, when they were old enough to do what they had always wanted but had been prevented from doing, and blamed her for it.

She tried once more.

'But he was a terrible father and he still is. What makes him any better now that we're not living together?'

'You'll just have to trust that he will be. Not always, of course. Any more than you are always a good mother. But they still love him, with all his faults.'

In this case, the mother gave way to the children's wishes. Their settled behaviour proved that the court was right about their best interests, and they all settled more happily in the community. As it happens, the children's best interests were her best interests too, in the longer run.

The children had been able to confide their wishes within the safety of my clinic room. And the courts are keen to listen to the voice of children too, in a neutral environment, free of the parents' influence. They have done much to help them, indirectly through video links or by direct attendance at a wig-less, gown-less, jargon-free court hearing. And their instinct about the children's best interests is usually right. But we are all capable of being surprised.

Which takes me back to Lizzie. It was several years before I saw her again and could find out if what we did had served both her and her baby well. But it was worth the wait. I was asked to assess a child with kidney problems in my local district general hospital and walked into the paediatric ward to find her. I thought I heard my name called from a side room as I passed by, but I had spotted my kidney patient at the far end of the ward and made a bee line to talk to her. An hour later, I passed the side room again and this time the voice was louder.

'Doctor Shooter. Mike. You don't recognise me, do you?'

I peered into the darkened room. An obviously handicapped child lay sleeping in the bed, her mother beside her, tired but attentive. It was Lizzie. She was her baby's full-time carer now, of the baby for whom the courts and I had stuck our necks out in pursuit of what we felt were the best interests. The child had developed serious physical problems. Her mother needed to watch over her carefully along with the paediatric team. And it had been the making of both of them.

At last, Lizzie had found the affectionate relationship she craved; she was secure in the knowledge that she was both wanted and needed; and she had found through the medical system a channel for communicating her feelings when they threatened to get out of control. I wondered if this might be yet another link in the mother–daughter chain of borderline personalities, but the child was unavoidably dependent. She was unlikely to survive into adulthood and would need her mother's full-time care in the years ahead. Lizzie would be devastated when her child died, but the lessons she had learnt by caring for her would help her through the loss.

Lizzie had been to all the court hearings and we chatted about her memories of how it went. I was surprised to hear that she had been as torn as everybody else about whether she could look after her baby. She was certainly more unsure than she had admitted to me at the time, or I had guessed. Was I the one who had persuaded her, by the force of my argument from the witness box?

'Sorry, Mike. No. It was the old court officer who was looking after me. He persuaded me to have a go.' She took a damp cloth to wipe her young child's face. 'Still, it turned out all right in the end. Didn't it?'

CHAPTER 14

WILL

RECOGNISING AN EMERGENCY

I keep picturing all these little kids playing some game in this big field of rye and all . . . I mean if they're running and they don't look where they're going I have to come out from somewhere and catch them. That's all I'd do all day. I'd just be the catcher in the rye.

J.D. Salinger: *The Catcher in the Rye*, Ch. 22, 1951

It was just an average Monday; an average day on call. Or so it started.

The young girl who had come into accident and emergency the previous night with an overdose was still too ill to be seen. I didn't yet know much about her and she would keep for later. The adolescent unit was safely in charge of the senior staff, and the clinics were cleared for home visits. So I set off up a main road out of the city, to see a six-year-old the teachers were worried about. Not much, they said, but if I had the time . . .

He was standing in the corner of the playground, perched high up on the mountainside, engrossed in some complicated game with sticks and gravel that only he understood. None of the other children involved him in their games. If they strayed too near his, he threw the gravel at them, squatted down into his overcoat and burst into tears. At first sight, he was one of the most genuinely autistic children that I had ever seen.

'How long has he been like that?'

'Oh, years. Ever since I've been here.'

'Didn't you think of contacting me earlier?'

'Well, he's not been much trouble. We make allowances for him. And his brother's very protective. At least, he was. Until he went up to big school.'

I was planning what to do, when my mobile went off.

'Where are you?' It was the sister from the paediatric ward.

'Halfway up a mountain in the middle of nowhere. Where are you?'

'Don't get clever with me, Mike. We need you. I know you're on call.'

'I'll be there this afternoon. I've left a hole for emergencies.'

'No good. We need you here. NOW!'

I have come to appreciate that when a usually laid-back ward sister asks you to jump, you'd better do it. But someone had run into the back of a lorry on the approach to the city and I sat in the queue, pondering on that autistic boy, on what might be happening on the paediatric ward, and on the nature of emergencies.

The ideal therapeutic relationship is a rounded curve that allows for a slow build-up of trust, the space to examine what is happening in the child's life, and an equally gentle tail-off towards separation. There is a shape to the relationship, a beginning, a middle and an end; but that takes time and we don't always have it. If it's an emergency, we have to act.

Many children and young people let us know that they are disordered, in danger or distressed. They tell us that they are in serious trouble, by their behaviour as much as by what they say. But we don't always pick up the cues. Psychiatrists and social workers failed to see that Nathan and Christine needed rescue from their abusive families, though teachers and neighbours as good as told them so. And the situation was compounded until they nearly died.

At other times, the adults may not see it as their role to act on the situation, or are afraid to do so. A young girl on the adolescent unit reveals to a night nurse for the first time that she has been sexually abused. A child with a serious physical illness asks a night nurse if he is dying. And both are fobbed off with promises of a consultant in the morning. The window that opened in their life is shut again and may never reopen.

Some adults may be blind to the urgency because they think they can cope. How bizarre did that little lad's behaviour have to become, up there in the windswept playground, in class or back at home, before his teachers and parents felt they had to do something about him? The life of autistic children is full of crises, and we can usually head them off before they become a full-blown emergency. If we are called in early enough. But sometimes the problems are masked, by an elder brother watching his back or adults making allowances when they ought to know better.

Most often, the emergency is due to the needs of the child or young person at its centre; the test is in how we deal with it. I had no doubt that Jordan was in a psychotic crisis and that he needed to be admitted to a psychiatric hospital under a section of the Mental Health Act, straight away. Becky was also in a mental crisis, but she didn't need admission. Far from it. Admission would have been the easy way out and her consultant had taken it, over and over again. Two emergencies, one in the middle of a busy outpatient clinic, the other in a summer evening group. And two very different approaches, tailored to their needs.

But sometimes, the children and young people are caught in the middle of a situation that is not wholly of their making. A situation that is distressing enough for them, but has brought the adults around them to the end of their tether. An emergency that is born primarily out of the needs of the adults, but one which will only get worse for the children if we don't intervene, and quickly. So it was with Will and his tube.

William, 'Will', was a thirteen-year-old lad who I had seen occasionally, wandering around the paediatric ward with a naso-gastric tube held in place with sticky tape. He had cystic fibrosis and needed feeding through the tube sometimes, up his nose and down through his throat to his stomach, to get calories into him and gain weight. When I reached the ward, he was sitting in a corner, the old tube at his feet and a new one thrown across the floor, still in its packet. Will had been crying, the nurses were angry, and the other children had made themselves scarce. The atmosphere was explosive.

'What's wrong?'

It was a rhetorical question, because I could see that they'd reached some sort of impasse when it came to changing the tube. But it set the scene for the ward sister to vent her frustration.

'He won't have his tube down. He says he won't ever have it down again. But he needs it. How many times have we brought him back from the brink? And this is how he repays us.' She paused for breath. Will said nothing but scowled and sat tighter in his corner.

I resisted the temptation to get into an argument about naso-gastric tubes, picked Will up and carried him with me into the empty storeroom next door. I started talking about family and football (he was wearing an Arsenal shirt) and finally we got around to naso-gastric tubes. As luck would have it, the largest sized tube lay on the desk by my elbow.

'My God! I'm glad I don't need to have that thing up my nose. I'm not surprised you told the nurses to stuff it. Or did you say something worse?'

A brief smile crossed Will's face and was switched off again, in case I noticed.

'That's for big boys, stupid. Mine's much smaller.' Like most young people with cystic fibrosis, Will was a shadow of his real age.

'All the same . . .'

Will had begun to cry again. I put an arm around him. An innocent gesture, with a young lad who needed comfort, but I am aware of how difficult physical contact has become for many professionals, especially with children of the opposite sex and in highly charged situations. The rule, as ever, is to work out what the gesture will mean to the child, not what the professional intends. And in this case it was pure solace.

We talked about cystic fibrosis. How horrible it was to be ill and need treatment all the time. How he wished he could be like other boys, play football and mess around, without worrying about everything from bangs to bacteria. And how frightened he was that he might die.

When he was calmer, I opened a drawer and fished out a smaller tube that looked about his size.

'Is this the one?' Will nodded. 'I bet there's someone who's really good at putting these down.'

'Doctor Akbar.'

'Shall we go and find him?'

An hour or so later, I wrote up what I'd done in his notes. I suggested that Will could do with some longer-term help, and waved him goodbye as he helped the nurses with the drug trolley, his new naso-gastric tube firmly in place. The consultant rang me that evening to say thanks and to ask if she could take up my offer. And thus began a ten-year involvement with Will and the cystic fibrosis team. They were some of the happiest and saddest times of my life, and they taught me many lessons, about emergencies and how to handle them.

When we are called to help, we must never accept the child's behaviour at face value. We must try instead to work out what it means, and to contain everyone's anxieties while we are doing so. Including our own. In Will's case, it was about illness, its effect on the behaviour of the patient, its course and how children and adults can get out of phase in their grief.

Some childhood illnesses, like cancer, come out of the blue and both child and parents are plunged into grief at the same time. The issue is whether the adults are able to share the shock, the fear, the anger and the misery together with their children, or whether they become separate and secretive out of a misguided wish to protect them. Some, like cystic fibrosis and many kidney disorders, begin in early infancy. Parents may do their grieving when it is diagnosed, but the child grows up knowing nothing else. The illness, its treatment and the ward team become his world.

It's much later, when the adults are well over the shock and are expecting their child to take responsibility for tablets and tubes and injections, that the child may begin to realise for the first time just what the illness might mean for his future. It's now that he may begin to grieve, out of phase with the adults around him – parents, and staff who have looked after him for years and for whom he has become their child too. It happens classically in early adolescence; about Will's age. And the weapon most readily to the child's hand, with which to express their conflicting emotions, is the treatment.

There are no prizes for guessing where Will fitted in to all that and the meaning of his sudden rejection of the naso-gastric tube after years of meekly accepting it. The task was to let him know that I understood what he was going through, without ramming it down his gullet with the tube. I needed to shift his protest to a different arena, where he might more safely show his feelings about the illness without refusing to cooperate with its treatment.

Easy for me to say, but the parents and staff would have to go along with it. And that would be no mean feat when they had waded through their own crushed hopes and come out the other side. When they had for so long helped the child and were expecting him now to help himself. When they were becoming more optimistic about the child's future and wished him to be so too. Small wonder that they were surprised and reproachful when Will hurled the tube across the floor; and small wonder that the ward sister should call on a child psychiatrist to sort out the emergency.

A proper assessment of the situation will tell us what to do and how quickly to do it. When to act swiftly and when to slow it down; and usually it's both. With Will, I needed to defuse the immediate situation by taking him out of it to a private space. Where I could listen to his story more slowly, without the nurses breathing down our necks, and prepare the way for a deeper and more lengthy therapy later. That was relatively easy on the ward, with its rabbit warren of little rooms where we could hide without

being disturbed, knowing that the doctors and nurses were somewhere round the edge.

It was much more difficult, called as an emergency in the middle
of the night, to a stranger's house. Alone, in a situation fraught with
dangers, and with the threat of repercussions if it all went wrong.
And such was the case with Danny and his family.

Danny lived in the middle of an estate on the outskirts of his
home town. A locum GP rang the switchboard and demanded that
a child psychiatrist go out immediately. At midnight. A young boy
was threatening to hang himself and the parents were desperate.
The GP had no idea how old the boy was or how the situation
had developed. I doubt he had even been to the house and I could
have suggested, politely perhaps, that he do his job properly, find
out more exactly what was happening and report back. But it
wouldn't have done much good.

I know that not every crisis should be treated as an emergency.
If it were, we would spend our days and nights like Holden Caulfield,
the anti-hero of J.D. Salinger's book, trying to catch every child
who falls over in the rye. We might even make things worse, by
reacting too quickly and setting a precedent. Cry and I'll come
running.

But by sticking to procedure, I would have made the GP angry
at best. He would probably have refused and I would have had to
go out anyway, with a formal complaint to face when it was all
over. At worst, I would miss the chance to strike while the iron
was hot. In other words, to assess the situation for myself while
feelings were at their most exposed and raw. And I had to remind
myself that however sanguine I might be about the situation, for
the family and even that GP too it would be full of swirling
emotions.

In the middle of the night, after several hours of mounting
tension, everybody would be on edge. The threat of hanging would
be enough to push them all over it. We have all read stories about
children who have killed themselves. It's buried deep in our psyche,
the nightmare for every parent and for those who are supposed to

prevent it happening. In such circumstances, they should never be hesitant about calling for help, and we should never be hesitant about giving it. No matter whether I feel it is a real emergency or not, it is for them.

A man answered the door. He was angry and confused about what to do. Danny himself was standing on the landing, one end of a pyjama cord wrapped round his neck and the other tied to the railings. His mother was crouched on the hallway floor, pleading with her son not to jump and trying not to cry. The pyjama cord would have snapped if Danny had jumped, even if he had been able to climb over the railings. In fact, they had been like this for so long and it was so late that he was falling asleep where he stood.

They were all stuck and what they needed was something to defuse the tension.

'Is that really the time?' I said, looking at the hall clock. 'Sorry, I know you must all be on your last legs, but I've been at it since this morning too, and I'm desperate for a cup of tea.'

Danny's eyes were closing fast.

'Would Danny like a snack before he goes to bed?'

His mother disappeared into the kitchen and the man I took to be his father ushered me into the living room. Danny came in soon afterwards, followed by his mother with the tea-tray.

That may all sound banal, but banal was what they needed. An excuse to come out of their corners without losing face, and I was the excuse. That is not to underestimate their distress and, yes, my actions would probably have been very different if Danny had been standing on a motorway bridge. But the skill would have been the same. How to lower the temperature without everyone's fears being realised.

Danny was eight and he sat between the adults on the sofa, doing his best to stay awake. They told me that Danny was his mother's only child, that his natural father had left and they were divorced. He was remarried and had a new family. She had tried to keep him involved, but he wasn't interested and now he had moved away. It put an end to any hopes Danny might have had of staying in touch with his father; and it came just at the point when she had met the man who Danny had now slumped against, fast asleep.

The relationship between Danny and her boyfriend had been so fraught that they had decided not to get married until it improved; but it didn't. There were lots of arguments. The boyfriend tried to be firm but the mother intervened, Danny said he couldn't tell him what to do because he wasn't his real dad, and the boyfriend retired to a frustrated sort of limbo: a would-be parent with no parental power.

Tonight's problem had begun when Danny had wanted to watch a TV programme. The boyfriend had told him it was not suitable. There was an argument, the mother relented, her boyfriend exploded and Danny took to the landing and threatened to jump unless he got what he wanted. They were playing out what had been happening for months. And Danny was ruling the roost.

They put Danny to bed with instructions to keep an ear open for him. He might wake and feel terrified at what he had done tonight, let alone the power he was wielding in this family. If he did wake, the boyfriend was to go and cosset him back to sleep. And we made a date for me to come back and see them again. It was clear that they all wanted to change things, but they didn't know how to do it without tearing each other apart. They would need a referee. I would have liked to thank Danny for bringing them all to therapy, but at eight years old he wouldn't have understood. And it didn't matter.

'By the way,' I said as I was leaving. 'None of my business, but I think you should start planning the marriage. Make sure Danny has an important role.'

Both Will and Danny had been at the centre of the whirlpool. It was the adults who had called for help, but it was the children's behaviour that had pressed the emergency button. Both of them needed immediate action, but both needed a slower follow-up to work on the issues that had got them to that point. And it was the person who first saw them that should stay involved.

Thinking back to that ideal therapeutic curve and the time it usually takes to establish enough trust to work with them, it seems ironic that children and adults will latch on so tightly to therapists they meet in a crisis. You cannot hand them on with a sigh of relief, once the emergency is over. If more work is required, you're in it for the long haul, or they will feel forsaken.

But trust is crucial. The trust that a child and family place in those sent to sort out their crisis, whether they've met them before or not. Trust the surrounding adults place in those they've called in to do it. And the trust a therapist must build up over years with the community in which crises may occur. Which brings me finally to Hannah.

I often volunteered to be on call over Christmas. Nothing much happened and everyone was full of festive spirit, literally in most cases. But this time it was different. It had got to ten o'clock on Boxing Day night when I was rung about an emergency on a housing estate the other side of the city. I set off through driving rain, to be met by parents at their garden gate, wringing their hands with anxiety.

They were elderly, with a late marriage, and their sixteen-year-old daughter had always been a handful for them to manage. Hannah had serious learning difficulties, an excitable personality and unpredictable behaviour that was set off by the slightest obstacle. This time it was the wrong result on a TV talent contest. She was a pupil in a special school in the city, but the school was on holiday and there were no staff around to help.

I talked with Hannah in the back room, or I tried to. She raved on without making much sense at all. Even allowing for her learning difficulties, it was clear that she had become psychotic and should be removed from the situation, for everyone's sake. The last thing she needed was admission to an adult ward, where the florid state of older patients would have made her worse, and the adolescent unit was temporarily closed. But I had a brainwave. I rang the paediatric ward and told them about the situation.

'Do me a favour, you owe me one. Will you take her in and look after her for a couple of days? Until the school gets back or she calms down enough to go home. They can't possibly cope with her at the moment.'

'Actually we know Hannah. She's got physical problems too and we often had her in here when she was younger. She likes us and we've not got many others in.'

A year later, the same thing happened again. This time it was an unwanted Christmas present that had set her off and her elderly parents were as distraught as before. Once again, I rang the paediatric ward.

'Do us a favour . . .'

'OK, Mike. But don't make a habit of it.'

Emergencies are emergencies. But how they are handled depends on the goodwill built up long before. My banter with the paediatric ward over both Will and Hannah was a measure of the trust we had developed in each other. Their trust that my advice about Will was right, even though they were angry with what he had done. The trust I had in their ability to look after Hannah, when everywhere else was closed and she needed safety.

Underneath it all lay the trust that all parents have in the help they call upon in an emergency. The ability of parents to deal with a crisis will vary hugely: from young adults being held to emotional ransom by a confused little lad like Danny, to an elderly couple driven at length to despair by an adolescent girl as difficult as Hannah. But the crisis is for them to define and for us to help. No matter what we may feel about it from the privilege of our own position.

CHAPTER 15

THE DRUM MAJORETTES
PEER GROUP PRESSURE

Think about what people are doing on Facebook today. They're keeping up with their friends and family, but they're also building an image and an identity for themselves, which in a sense is their brand. They're connecting with the audience that they want to connect to.

Mark Zuckerberg, founder of Facebook

The opening quote is about as rosy a view as it is possible to get of peer group relationships and the role of social media as a vehicle for carrying them out into the world beyond the front door. One thing is certain: relationships with other people are a vital part of child and adolescent development, and a marker of how healthily they are progressing.

The seeds, as ever, are planted early on. Every parent will know that a baby smiles selectively at those it has come to recognise and trust. Confident in the first attachments it has made with its parents, the toddler will flourish in a mixed climate of encouragement and protection as it explores new relationships with the children it meets. And some of those will be within the family.

A great deal has been written about the bane and blessing of being an only child, and about the influence of birth order in larger families. About the responsibility of being the oldest, the freedom of being the youngest, and the difficulty of being a middle child struggling to establish an identity somewhere in between. About twins, the impact of fostered or adopted children, and the relationships between the offspring of two families coming together when parents remarry.

Some of this is well researched, a lot of it is old wives' tales, and most is common knowledge; but there is no doubting the importance of siblings to each other. Of course there are rivalries, when an older child's nose is put out of joint by the arrival of a new baby, or a younger child is resentful of an older child's privileges. Those rivalries are sometimes so deep that they fester into adulthood and infect relationships forever, but that is much rarer than you might think. Most brothers and sisters have a strong bond, however much they might fight on the surface.

And that experience is a training ground for what happens in the wider world. Children with good relationships inside the family are more likely to make good friends outside it. But friendship is an attribute that matures as the child develops. The short-lived relationships the young child makes with playmates are very much on their own terms. This is what I want and I'm going to get it; don't get in my way. True bonds come later, as the older child thinks less about what they can get out of the relationship for themselves, and more about a friendship that is mutually rewarding and more likely to last.

At first, such friendships may be quite judgemental and woe betide the friend who doesn't play by the rules. But by mid-adolescence we will have learnt to live with both the strengths and the weaknesses of those peers to whom we have grown close. They are not playmates, or sparring partners, or acquaintances along the way; but true friends.

Thus the scene is set, yet the plot is never quite so simple. The establishment of relationships with our peers is important, but some children and young people seem better at it than others. Some find it difficult to make them in the first place, some to maintain them happily thereafter, and some find them a nightmare that haunts their lives and drives them to despair.

To begin with, there are huge and natural differences in personality between children who are more gregarious and those who are happier in their own company. It's the difference that makes us all so fascinating. On top of that, there are disorders that make friendships very difficult indeed. I can think of no sadder sight than that young lad squatting by himself up there in the school playground on my Monday on call, or Mikey struggling to make sense of a world that wouldn't obey the rules as he saw them and being unable to see it from anyone else's point of view. Relationships for both of them were scrambled by their autism. I could teach them strategies to make life feel better, but I doubt I could show them how to make friends.

Parents have the job of making sure that the development of these relationships goes well. How they get on, or not, with each other is the model for their children. It's not much good trying to teach your child to have empathy for others if you're tearing lumps out of your own partner, the other adults around you, or the world in general. You can't expect a child who is shaky in its attachment to parents at home, to trust itself to those outside.

And that brings us to the nub of the issue. Opening ourselves up to peer group relationships can and should be immensely rewarding, but it also opens us up to all the peer group pressures that go with it. Some of those pressures are fleeting and do little harm. Others are much more long-lasting, and dangerous. Some children and young people are strong enough to withstand those pressures and learn about themselves in the process, but others are irreparably damaged. And we have invented all sorts of ways in which those pressures can be heaped upon our children's heads.

My first experience of the power of short-lived pressures on young people came when I was in charge of the accident and emergency department of my local hospital, on a hot afternoon in the middle of summer. A summer of fetes and festivals, of village shows and sports days, of contests in which some young people were eager participants while others cowered on the edge. And all of them were looking around to see what was expected of them, or what was not.

The first child came in at 15.58 (I checked with the log). She was fifteen years old, a drum majorette dressed in blue and white with gold buttons, a shako hat with a blue plume and golden eagle, and white boots with a treble clef embroidered on their side. And she vomited all over the front row of reception.

'It was the orange juice!' shouted her father, carrying her twirling stick in his hand. 'It's poisonous. You'll have the whole lot in here in a minute.'

The little town was dominated by horse racing. There was a single high street stretching uphill from the swimming baths to the hospital and a shopping precinct off to one side. Otherwise, it was all horses. Around midnight the stable lads would be back from the races, drunk, with their faces cut open where they'd glassed each other, and the odd stab wound. Wanting us to sew them up, body and soul.

Normally, Saturday afternoon was the calm before the storm. I could cope on my own and the seniors were free to play golf with their mates. But this was different. The father was nearly right; by teatime we were swamped and I'd dragged the consultant off the seventh tee.

There were over thirty of them, fresh from the annual regional gala at the recreation ground on the edge of town. The bands had been marching up and down for hours in the heat of the day, egged on by proud parents. Drum corps with their instruments slung over their shoulders, drum majorettes going before them, throwing their twirling sticks into the air, in uniforms of turquoise and scarlet, gold and silver, epaulettes and tassels, scarves and cloaks, sashes, heavy brocade, pleated skirts, and all in step.

By early afternoon they were flaked out and stopped to eat while the judges conferred. Most of them had brought their own supplies and sat around the plastic tables, their drums tossed into the grass. But some were tempted by great mugs of orange juice, home-made by the local mothers. Our fifteen-year-old fainted soon after her first drink and was carried off to see us.

The news spread around the drum corps like wildfire. Some of the girls threw up immediately, others passed out halfway through 'Colonel Bogey'. One or two felt queasy even though they'd never been near the orange juice. And now they were laid out in the hospital in rows. The early birds had beds, the rest were on trolleys or lay on the floor on travel rugs and blankets. Anxious parents fussed around them, holding sick bowls and mopping their brows. It was pointless trying to keep them out. And besides, they had been complicit in what happened.

A mysterious process. The fifteen-year-old who started it all off almost certainly had a stomach bug, and her drinking the orange juice was purely coincidental. But the rest was a peer group panic. The girls were already emotionally precarious, hot, tired and under intense competition. It needed only a trigger factor to set them all off, and the rumours about the orange juice were enough. They did everything in step, just as they had when they were marching before.

In later life, I would have moved amongst them like the Lady with the Lamp, whispering platitudes, reassuring them, calming them down. And it would have taken all weekend. This afternoon I could only marvel at the consultant's technique.

To those who had been sick, he gave a glass of clear fluid that I'd seen him drawing off from the sterile water dispenser behind the curtains. He told them it would wash away any of the remaining poison. The others he made sick with an emetic, then repeated the process with the water. No one questioned what he did and within hours they were back on their buses and away home. All except for the fifteen-year-old who we kept in for observation. Her youth made a welcome change from the little tonsillectomies and the aged grandparents with their hernias and urinary tract infections.

Peer pressure. It blew through the gala like a gust of wind and was gone again. Brief, dramatic and uncomfortable, but no harm done. By the time they got home, the orange juice, the hospital and the magician in the white coat would already have become a legend in the history of the marching bands. All the girls would talk about it for years to come, glad to have been part of the shared experience. But most peer pressure is much more insidious than this and capable of doing great damage.

Like self-harm. The news reports tell us that the incidence of cutting, burning and overdoses has increased by 14 percent in the last three years and reaches a peak in the mid-teens. The NSPCC has estimated that getting on for twenty thousand young people were treated in hospital during that period, in what Childline called an epidemic of self-harm. The worst aspects of peer group pressure could be found lurking in the background to many of these, and Seren was a case in point.

Seren was fourteen when I first met her on the hospital ward after she had taken an overdose. Her name means 'star' in Welsh, another misnomer. She didn't look like the star of anything, lying on her bed, face to the wall and a sick bowl clasped to her chest. She was part of the usual Saturday morning psychiatric task on call: doing the rounds of the local hospitals to see the young people who had been brought in with self-harm of one sort or another, had needed to be kept in for assessment and had been too sick to be seen the previous night.

Now, one or two of these each week were teenage girls who were following a family pattern of self-harm as a way of showing their anger. They had stomped off on the Friday evening on the back of an argument with a parent, fallen out with their boyfriend and come back in the early hours to another row. So they had swallowed the contents of the kitchen drawer, to pay everyone back. Few had any idea of what they were taking. Vitamin tablets, pain-killers and cold relief. If they were really unlucky, there would have been some of Grannie's old antidepressants in the cabinet and they would wake up in intensive care with an irregular heartbeat. Even fewer wanted to see me.

'Fuck off, Shooter! I've got better things to do.'

'Well, fuck off yourself. So have I. But you're not getting out of here until I say it's safe. Now, shall we go and talk about it?'

What I'd said, of course, was not strictly true. If they were old and fit enough, they could walk out of their own accord, whether I liked it or not. And they would never be safe as long as they kept on taking overdoses. Sooner or later, no one would be around to see what they'd done, until it was too late. This pattern was set in a family tradition rather than peer group pressure. Arguments were settled by retaliatory acts, not discussion.

Seren was different; she had been bullied into submission and she fitted the epidemic that Childline talked about. School is where social relationships are developed, which is one of the reasons I have been wary of children being educated at home. They may not miss out on academic learning, but they will miss out on learning about themselves. Yet school can be torture too. School bullies have often been bullied themselves and are on the lookout for those who are less self-confident and more vulnerable than themselves. Seren was an ideal victim.

She had what the paediatricians would call 'arrested hydrocephalus'. The drainage of the fluid that bathes the brain and spinal cord had been blocked at birth. By the time it had been noted and resolved, the plates of her skull had been eased apart and she had been left with a big head. A minor degree, they said, but not in Seren's mind. She was acutely conscious of it as soon as appearances began to matter and grew her hair to cover it up, willing herself to grow taller and more in keeping with its size. But the more she tried to disguise it, the more it stood out. And the more a potential victim she became.

There are many reasons why some children and young people become victims, and as far as Seren was concerned she had the lot. She looked peculiar, she behaved strangely because of it, and she had never developed the self-confidence to withstand the taunts thrown at her. Her parents were almost as desperate as she was. They had no idea of how to talk to her about how she felt, and they were loath to approach the teachers lest they make the situation worse. So they changed schools instead. The bullying went with her.

I have known intelligent young people who have taken a massive overdose, thinking it would just put them to sleep for a while. Seren took a couple of tablets, thinking it would kill her. But it wasn't for want of trying.

'You'll probably think this is a silly question,' I said, after we had talked about the misery of what she was going through. 'Because you won't know the answer.'

'I don't know the answer to anything,' she replied.

'How long have you been thinking about it? Killing yourself, I mean.'

Seren shrugged. 'Ever since I was a kid, I suppose.'

'But you weren't sure you meant it?'

'No . . . not until . . .' She stopped herself and stared out of the window, as if instruction would come winging its way through the ether. I waited for her to begin again.

'Until?'

'Until they told me I should do it.'

'And who are they?'

She seemed to make up her mind to tell me everything. She had been on the internet, in the loneliness of her bedroom, and she had found a suicide site. Anonymous. Gentle-voiced, she said, and apparently compassionate. They told her that what she was feeling was unbearable and that she had every right to kill herself, if that was what she wanted. It only needed one more taunt to push her over the edge, and she got it.

Seren was bullied directly in school and indirectly by the suicide site on the internet. Their words may have sounded understanding, but they drove her to the brink of death just as effectively as the name-calling in the school yard.

'Why don't we put a stop to them?' she said when we were discussing it later. 'Those suicide sites. Surely they're illegal.'

'Because they're run from organisations safely offshore,' I replied. 'Where our own country can't touch them.'

'But we could still say something about them, how we disapprove. They seemed so nice, but they caught me when I was at my lowest. There was no way I could resist.'

'Other countries have tried to get at them, but it hasn't worked. And it just gave them the publicity they crave.'

'So what's the answer, then? Just give in to them?'

'The answer is to stop people like you getting to that state in the first place.'

Seren was just one example of the peer group pressure that children and young people are subjected to, the way social media is fanning the flames of the situation, and how confused adults are about how they can douse the fire. To understand the situation, we need to think about how it has come about.

It is quite normal for young people to wonder about what other people think of them, to be inquisitive about alcohol, drugs and sex, and to worry that they may be left behind in a world where all their peers seem to be more knowing than they are. It is all part of the search for their own identity in relationship to everyone else. The more self-confidence the young person has developed in their family life, the quicker they are able to emerge from all that questioning with a secure sense of who they are and what to do with their life. The less self-confident they are, the greater the uncertainty.

But society has made it even more difficult. We live in an ever more competitive world. To the normal pressures of growing up are added the educational demands to pass more and more exams, a gloominess about the future and a loss of faith in political processes to put it right, private catastrophes at home and global catastrophes beamed in from all over the world, and a media that's in love with how to be popular, how to look attractive and how to be a success. Quite a list. No wonder that individual young children may feel a failure if they can't keep up, are ridden with guilt, and take out their unhappiness on their own bodies.

Social media has given them a ready vehicle for their uncertainty. The current generation of children and young people spend many hours a day online, posting images of themselves and checking on the reaction of their peers. Growing ever more desperate that they are missing out, that their own life is worthless compared to the photos which come piling in on Snapchat or Instagram, even though they may know that the person on the other end may be just as desperate for approval.

'Do you like what you see? Do you like me? Say you do. Please . . .'

Adults may see only a fraction of the problem or what their children and young people will admit to. Rather than the time they actually spend online in their bedroom before they sleep, the number of times they wake in the night to check the 'likes' on their phone, and the checks they make again as soon as they wake. Their lives are being smothered in an avalanche of online messaging.

The social media giants themselves would probably say that young people today are more connected than ever before. And so they are, on the end of the line. But they are becoming unconnected psychologically, from real people and from their true selves. According to those successive reports, our mid-teens are now less happy with their lives in the UK than anywhere else in the developed world. It is a joint responsibility to make them happier – or Seren will be just one more of that epidemic of victims that is spreading every year.

But whose responsibility is it? How can we help a young girl like Seren? Or Casey, a twelve-year-old who was dragged to see me by her parents. They had been told by an aunt and uncle that they had seen a semi-naked image of her on Instagram. Or rather their own children, Casey's cousins, had seen it and had told them about it. Gleefully, it seems, to divert attention from their own difficulties.

'You think we've got problems. Just look at this.'

In fact, given a private space to share her feelings, Casey was just as terrified by what was happening as her parents were. She had never felt able to live up to the success they had in their own careers and the expectations they had of her. And in her first year at big school she was struggling with both the academic work and how she might find any other way to make her mark.

She never seemed to get invited to the right parties, she said. She'd had lukewarm reactions to the selfies she had loaded online and in desperation had resorted to sexting, posting ever more suggestive pictures of herself and feeling increasing self-disgust at doing it. All sorts of men had contacted her as a result. She hadn't yet met any of them, but at school, in a back classroom during an evening social, she had sex with one of the older boys. A sort of sex. Fumbling, messy and incomplete. But he had boasted about it around his peer group afterwards.

'I feel dirty,' she said, through her tears. 'It's so unfair. He was just as bad at it as me. But what can I say? Without making it even more embarrassing?'

'Have you thought of telling your parents?'

'I couldn't. They'd be so angry. They'd probably have gone charging down to school, then everybody would know.'

'Like they do now?'

There are global measures that might help the Caseys of this world in future. Society has a responsibility to be less competitive and foster greater collaboration amongst its members. Education should place less emphasis on academic achievement and more on giving its pupils time to find out what they are interested in. The general media must rid itself of a hypocritical combination of lasciviousness and condemnation. And schools must encourage debate amongst young people themselves, training them in social media dangers and harnessing positive peer pressure from those who have experienced them and survived.

Lofty words, and the debate is welcome, in society at large and in the courses run in many schools on social, emotional and mental health. Where adults once thought that talk on difficult subjects like sex and drugs would spread bad habits, we know now that it is an essential way of sharing peer group opinion. However, it will be of little help unless the words are put into practice, and we need far more hard evidence of the dangers before policy makers in government, the press and education will change tack. But we have to start somewhere, and there are plenty of examples where attitudes have been changed in the past, in the face of narrow vested interests and a general pessimism about something so huge.

Meanwhile, social media bosses have a responsibility to police their own networks more efficiently. The technology exists to detect and filter out suggestive images, but those images shouldn't be circulated in the first place. Like most of the children and young people who post them online, Casey had no idea that she had signed away her rights to what she thought were private messages and pictures and that they could be sold on around the world for potential groomers everywhere. As ever, it would be more effective if the media companies were to put their own controls in place; if they don't, governments may have to legislate for them.

All of these approaches are essential, but all too easy to say and too remote from Casey's immediate situation. How could we help her and her parents in the clinic, with what they were going through right there and then?

'We need to talk, I suppose.'

It was a bald statement and her father said it with reluctance; but indeed they did. And they should have been talking together more closely all along. So busy had the parents been with their own careers that they had barely had time for their daughter, and she had come to the conclusion that they didn't love her. Her parents knew the dangers that might lie in wait for Casey on the internet but they had never taken the trouble to do anything about it, and she had come to the conclusion that they didn't care. Until it all seemed too late.

It's the parents' responsibility to be there. Not to steal their children's thunder by trying to be just as media savvy as them. It would probably be a fruitless task anyway, in a scene that is changing so fast. But there are many parents who use social media every day, as part of their job, their recreation and their social life, and may be unaware of the pressures their children are under. And there are many more who are only too aware, are frightened by the dangers and confused about what to do.

They need to be more exactly aware of what is going on, to anticipate the problems and to discuss with their offspring what to do about them. And if they feel it is all getting beyond their children's control, they should not be afraid of tracking what the children are up to and stepping in to control it. Those children may rail against their parents on the surface, but they may be secretly thankful that their parents have recognised the dangers and acted on their behalf.

And as always, the parents need to be there emotionally, in a much more general sense. To be interested in how their children and adolescents feel about the whole of their lives, to congratulate them on their successes, whatever they are, and to be proud of them. To increase their self-confidence, to foster healthy relationships with others, and to seek external help when it is needed.

It took a year of working with Seren on the adolescent unit, and many weeks of working with Casey and her parents in the outpatient clinic, to retrieve things. Services are having to adjust themselves to the impact of social media and its dangers, just like parents. But they are doing so, the help is there, and parents should not be afraid of calling on it. As they would with any problem of family life.

In other words, this may be a very modern problem but the dilemma for adults is the same as it is with any other aspect of childhood and adolescence. Deciding when not to intrude on their offspring's private world and when to intervene. Of course we need to worry; we wouldn't be good parents if we didn't. But we shouldn't panic. We have been through this before, with other strange ways of communicating that adolescents in particular have adopted as their own and been condemned by adults who do not understand them. And we must never forget that the internet, like them, is a force for good as well.

There can be no more poignant story than the rash of young people who committed suicide around a South Wales town a few years ago – boys, mostly, who hanged themselves or killed themselves in other tragic ways. The media were convinced that it was their contact through the internet that was spreading the infection. This despite the fact that it was the media who were most desperate to keep the story alive, ran blood-curdling headlines and paid potential contacts in their peer group to dish out any information they could, true or not.

There were many people trying to help, not least the child

psychiatrists and their teams in the local area. But when the dust settled and the media went away, the young people told us that what supported them most was an internet site set up by sixth-formers at a school that had more than its share of the tragedy. The site offered advice, sign-posted to sources of help, or just gave young people the chance to talk together about their memories of those who had killed themselves and the feelings left behind.

The young people had found their own path to help, peer group relations had rescued them from the deepest despair, and modern technology had enabled them to do so. As Mark Zuckerberg described it, they were indeed 'connecting with the audience that they wanted to connect to' and that audience had come to their rescue.

CHAPTER 16

RICKY AND HARRY
MANAGING EXPECTATIONS

Expectations are dangerous when they are both too high and unformed.
Lionel Shriver: *We Need to Talk About Kevin*, 2003

I sat in the GP surgery the other week, reading a seven-step guide to getting the most out of an appointment. How to plan everything you're going to say; how to tell your doctor what's wrong; how to tell the doctor what you're expecting to have done; how to write down everything the doctor says; how to ask questions about what happens next; how to fix the timing, length and content of every future appointment; and above all, how to read up fully on your condition before you go anywhere near the surgery.

Patients are experts in their own experience, of course they are. But if they were so totally in charge of their illness, diagnosis and treatment, one wonders what would be left for the doctor to do but write out the prescription under the patient's instruction and smile sweetly as they showed them the door. Fortunately, or not, depending on how you see it, expectations are never so one-sided in any branch of medicine.

Most patients entrust themselves to the doctor's expertise in the expectation of a good treatment. The doctor trusts the patient in the expectation that they will cooperate with the treatment prescribed.

And the manager of the health centre trusts that both of them will add to the expectations she has of patient numbers, the expensive medical facilities she has provided, and a successful outcome to treatment.

It's even less clear in psychiatry in general, and child and adolescent psychiatry in particular. All of us are caught in the triangle between what the patient wants at one apex, what the therapist thinks the patient needs at the second apex, and what the service has to offer at the third. Sometimes they agree: wants, needs and possibilities are roughly the same. More often they are not, and the tensions in the triangle are laid bare.

Richard came to see me with his mother at first. He was twelve years old and called Ricky for short. Except he wasn't short at all. He was very tall for his age, overweight even for his size, and hardly spoke in his mother's presence. And his parents were the sort that I dreaded – fellow medical professionals.

Both of them were health professionals in a town-centre practice; he full-time and she two days a week. She had referred other children and their families to me in the past, with a reasonable grasp of the sort of work I might do, but little idea of what the families needed. Her husband had no interest in child psychiatry at all, and he made it perfectly plain. When I had been invited to talk to their surgery staff one lunchtime, he half-turned away at the foot of the table, took out his mobile and began to scroll through his emails.

I say he had no interest – except, of course, when my influence was needed. It seemed as if he had sent his wife to give me the message.

'Ricky is having a terrible time in school.' She talked over the top of his head. 'He'd tell you himself, wouldn't you, Ricky? But he's very shy.'

'Shall I call you Richard or Ricky? What do you prefer?'

Ricky hung his head and his mother continued. 'It's Ricky, doctor. Everyone calls him Ricky.'

'What school do you go to, Ricky? You must be in your first year in the secondary school now.'

Ricky grunted and his mother jumped in again. 'I wonder if I should see you by myself, doctor. It's so embarrassing for Ricky to talk about these things.'

Frankly, it was Ricky who needed to see me by himself, away from his mother's inability to stop herself talking for him. But he looked as if he'd run off at the merest suggestion. Better to go with the flow, for now at least.

'What things would those be? And where?'

She told me that Ricky was being bullied by the other boys, despite his size, or maybe because of it. They had put the Year Sevens through all sorts of initiation tests in their first few weeks. The others had laughed them off but Ricky had come home crying every night. He was so upset by it all that it was interfering with his work. And he was such a bright boy.

'What have you done about it?'

'Well, we've comforted him, of course. My husband wanted to march down to the school and go round to see the parents of the ringleaders.' Ricky curled up, lower and lower in his chair. 'But it would just make it worse, don't you think? Just make him an even bigger target.'

'You still haven't told me which school.'

'Well, that's just it. He goes to the comprehensive in the town. And it's such . . .' She tailed off, slipping a glance at Ricky. He had his hands over his ears. 'You see what I mean. So embarrassing.'

'It's such what?' I tried to keep the challenge out of my voice but Ricky had heard enough. He went off to the lavatory to get out of the way.

'Such . . . a common school. Sorry. I didn't mean to use that word. But you know what I mean.'

'I'm afraid I don't.'

She came to the point. 'We've discussed it together, my husband and I. He . . . we . . . feel it just isn't the right school for Ricky. He'd be much better in that nice school over the border. Smaller, with such a good academic record. But he can't transfer schools without a good reason.'

'Which is where I come in?'

'Well, yes. My husband says you could write to the education authorities. We can't because we're his parents. But your opinion would carry weight. And you've seen what he's like.'

'I've had a brief glimpse of him. I'd like a session by ourselves next time. Just Ricky and me. Then I'd like to talk to someone at the school. Discreetly you understand. Before I can make up my mind.'

She wasn't happy. 'You mean you won't write the letter?'

'I might. If it turns out he does need to change schools. But Ricky might have bigger problems. If he does, his unhappiness would just go with him.'

I was prepared for an explosion of sorts, from Ricky's father. But I wasn't prepared for what happened. I had a holiday lined up before Ricky's appointment, and one of the health managers came to see me in the clinic when I got back. She was holding two cups of coffee and by the look of her, she had something difficult to get off her chest.

'Glad to see you've remembered where the outpatient department is, Mike.' She was referring to the way I spent so much time on the road.

'Clinic today. I've got a young lad coming to see me, and he needs the safety of four square walls.'

'Ah, Ricky. He won't be coming. Here. You'll need it.' She handed me one of the coffees.

'Why?'

'Ricky took an overdose while you were away. His mother's antidepressants. She's been depressed, you see, and she's under the psychiatrists. But you might know that.'

I didn't, but her depression wasn't a surprise. Ricky's overdose was. 'Was it a big one?'

'Not at all. But big enough to send the balloon up. I know his father. He's a good GP but he can be quite difficult.'

That was a euphemism-and-a-half. 'What happened?'

The manager told me that Ricky's father had complained and his mother's psychiatrist had written the letter for him, because the school business was adding to her depression. The education authority had agreed and Ricky was changing schools the next week.

'But he was my patient. Didn't anyone think of contacting me? Or waiting till I got back?'

'It didn't seem right, to interrupt your holiday. And it was an emergency.'

She left me to think about it. The letter that Ricky's parents wanted, the need that I thought might lie behind his problems, and the way the management had stepped in to save themselves any further hassle. Heaven knows what Ricky was feeling in the middle of it all.

It was no consolation when the manager told me, months later, that things hadn't worked out for him in that school either. He was now in a private school. The parents were paying through the nose, but told the manager that Ricky was doing much better. As they would. I tried not to feel justified, but it was difficult.

When I told the story to a colleague, he laughed. 'This is a bit of a shop, Mike. The customers can turn up and take what they like off the shelf, if it's available. You can advise them what's best, but you can't force them to buy what you want. And anyway, the management will tell you both what's on offer.'

That wasn't completely true. The important thing is what's best for the children, and in some circumstances it's the therapist who must act on their behalf to rescue them, whatever parents or managers might say. If Ricky had been really miserable in yet another school, I might have taken it further. But the school had a counsellor who was seeing him with the parents' permission and his involvement was obviously less of a challenge to their dignity.

I've come to expect the clashes of expectation. More often than not, I can smooth them out on behalf of the children and young people caught up in them and give them a role model at the same time. Life for them will be full of clashes between what they want and what other people want from them. The whole process of therapy is a learning opportunity: how it is set up, how we deal with the circumstances surrounding it, and how we cope with the threat of change. Quite apart from the content of the therapy itself.

But I am still taken aback when what I think is going to be contentious turns out to be to everyone's satisfaction after all. And that was the case with my radio programme and young Harry.

It was a daily programme that was a mixture of music, current affairs and expert discussion; and I had a slot on it every Monday morning. I would talk with the presenter about a different subject each week, parents and young people would phone in privately with their problems, and I would come back on air at the end to discuss the sort of reaction I had received. It was a success – it ran for seven years and it doubled the referral rate to our children's health service – but in the beginning I had grave misgivings.

Not the least was the fact that some of the more brazen listeners would phone in directly on air, while I was talking to the presenter. Like my mother, who disagreed with something I said about families, and then there was Mrs Prosser. Some of what we talked about was controversial; that's the nature of family life. I needed a moral conscience, a comment on what I might recommend, so I called it Mrs Prosser. And she became a sort of catchphrase.

'That's all very well, Mike. But would it satisfy Mrs Prosser from Pontlottyn?'

We were in the middle of a discussion on adolescent diaries, when the production crew put through a call from the other side of the glass. They were falling about laughing.

'Is that you?'

'It could be. This is Mike Shooter. What can I do for you?'

'I'm Mrs Prosser, from Pontlottyn. And you've been using my name for a year.'

I apologised to her profusely and asked myself round to tea. She was exactly as I had pictured a moral conscience might be. Small, bird-like, grey-haired and proper. She was rather flattered by becoming a catchphrase and phoned in regularly from then on to agree with me or express her indignation.

No problem there, then, but a greater worry was whether this programme was what my young clientele wanted or needed, or whether it was just an entertainment. Until I met Harry. He was sixteen and in local authority care. He rarely went to school and spent his mornings in bed, refusing to get up and listening to the radio. He phoned in to the radio programme when the topic was neglect. We talked in the private room.

'We were discussing neglect, Harry. Is that why you phoned in?'

There was a silence on the other end.

'Harry?'

And a reluctant answer. 'Harry knows what that's all about.'

'I'm sorry. Are you speaking for Harry? Are there two of you there?'

'Just Harry. He's speaking for himself.'

I was beginning to get worried. Was this someone psychotic who was speaking, someone who could flip backwards and forwards between different bits of themselves, or someone who found the immediacy of one-to-one talking just too threatening, even on the phone?

Bit by bit, Harry told me about his life of miseries. Or should I say that the voice on the end of the line told me about Harry's life, all in the third person. He had been brought up in a reconstituted family, after his parents were divorced and his mother remarried. Both his mother and her new partner had three children by their former marriages, so it was quite a crowd. There had been lots of skirmishes before the children settled down together and the parents sorted out their roles. But Harry had always been the odd one out.

He was the middle child of his parents' first marriage, and was the only one who was close to his father. They went fishing together and to football matches, and it was devastating when his parents separated. He kept in touch at first, but then his father got remarried too and he didn't get on with his new partner. Harry didn't fit in with his step-siblings in his mother's new marriage, and he didn't fit in with his father's new partner in his new marriage. Nowhere felt like home.

'Harry told everyone he was being neglected. He wasn't really – they looked after him all right. But it felt like it. They all had things to do together but Harry was left on his own. They just gave up on him.'

'Were there fights between you? Between Harry and the others, I mean.'

'At first. But then they stopped too. As if he just wasn't there.'

Harry was so unhappy that I suggested he should phone me again or come to see me in my clinic. Whatever he felt he could manage. He took it by stages. He did phone again, for several Mondays, and whatever the topic. Then he felt ready to come in person. When we met, it was as if he was reading a film script.

'Boy comes into the room. Boy sits down. Doctor asks him about his problems. Boy tells all.'

Except that he had retreated a few steps and told me little. But gradually he got more confident and we pieced together the last days before he went into care. He had decided that if he was going to be treated as if he wasn't there, he wouldn't be. He spent most evenings out on the streets, without telling them where he would be. He said nothing to anyone in the house and simply walked on by when they asked him a question. And he took to sleeping on the landing, by himself, instead of the room he used to share with two of the other boys.

'Perhaps Harry neglected them, not the other way round,' he said.

It was almost a relief when his step-father became so infuriated that he rang the social services and Harry was taken into care. Temporarily, into a group home, but there he had stayed. There had been no spontaneous contact between Harry and anyone in the family, despite the social worker's best efforts, and they had simply drifted apart. He had no idea whether he wanted to get back in touch or how he might do it if he did. And he imagined the family would just be glad to be rid of him.

I got Harry to record everything in writing and we examined the script together for the truth, like editors. Gradually the script became less important than the story it had to tell and he was able to own the feelings for himself, in the first person. His anger at his parents' separation, his uncertainty about where he fitted in to the new arrangement and his confusion. He had fallen down the crack between the old and the new, and was lost.

We worked together for several sessions and I visited both of his birth parents and their new families. Harry decided that it would be good to have contact with them all again and they were prepared to try it. Tentatively at first, and then more successfully. But too much water had passed under the bridge for him to live in either house. At sixteen rising seventeen, he left home.

That radio programme had been what Harry needed. It gave the right sort of distance from which to approach the one-to-one relationship that had let him down in the past and which he was frightened to recreate in therapy. On the phone at first, then face-to-face but in the third person, and then as himself. And there were particular parents and young people, I learnt over the course of the programme, who wanted to limit our relationship to the anonymity of their radio sets.

It satisfied their expectations, of what they wanted from me; and it satisfied my expectations, of what I felt they needed. But did it satisfy the expectations of my managers, that this was a legitimate part of my remit to the children, adolescents and families in our area? It looked good on paper, of course. The numbers of contacts with those who phoned in, and the increased referral rate of those who followed it up by asking to come in person, or who were persuaded to do so by professionals who had heard the programme. But I had never sought their permission.

Then I arrived early one morning for a meeting at our health authority's headquarters. Next to me in the urinals stood the executive whose possible reaction I feared the most. He spoke to me without turning his head, as if I was a fly on the wall.

'Michael. About that radio programme of yours.'

It felt as if the knife was hovering over my throat.

'Yes?'

'I was driving along the M4 last Monday and you were talking with that young woman who was wondering if it was safe to get engaged.'

'To the man who was jealous and kept beating her up, every time she looked at anyone else?'

'That's the one.'

'She was very brave, wanting to talk on air like that. Did you agree with what I said?'

'How do I know? You were just about to tell her when I went under the bloody road tunnel. What did you say, man? I was telling my daughter and she's dying to know.'

It didn't seem to matter, after all. The managers' expectations were satisfied too.

CHAPTER 17

DAVID

THE MYTHOLOGY AND STIGMA OF MENTAL ILLNESS

> For those he caught he did this lesson teach,
> To keep aloof from out a madman's reach . . .
> Among the rest he takes one by the heele
> And with his head knocks out another's braine.
>
> Ludovico Ariosto: *Orlando Furioso*, 1516

I have made no secret of my own depression. The resolution I made after my first major episode and its treatment was to talk about it openly. Wherever and whenever I was able. By doing so, not only would it help me but it might encourage others to talk about their mental illness too, to get help, and to lessen the stigma that surrounds us. But I made one big mistake.

'Dad, you told everyone about your problems and what they're about.' One of my sons had plucked up the courage to challenge me over a pint. 'But you never told us. We were only little when you got depressed. We had no idea what was going on. And it was horrible.'

By trying to spare my children, I condemned them to being angry, frightened, guilty and confused in secret. Unable to share their feelings openly with me, they were prey to all the worst aspects of their imagination and the overheard snippets of neighbours and friends. They may have thought that my depression was their fault. And I denied myself the support that even little children can offer their parents in return.

I was reminded of his words when I went to visit the family of a young man, David, who had slipped into a psychotic episode. Slowly and frighteningly for all the family. Verbal aggression at first, shouting at his wife and children, then sinking into a heap and tearing at his clothes and hair in his misery. Physical threats at the last, preparing the house against attack and trying to involve the family in his delusions.

David had been admitted to hospital under a section of the Mental Health Act. The adult team thought he was still too fragile to cope with family sessions, but he gave me permission to talk to his wife and children in the interim, to see how they were feeling. Not surprisingly, their emotions were all over the place.

His wife, Carrie, wanted to talk to me by herself at first, to see if I could be trusted to talk with the children. In fact, she had so much to get off her own chest that she didn't want them around while she did so. She had packed the oldest two off to school with the neighbour and we sat around the kitchen table. A baby slept in a cot beside her but woke and needed attention whenever she got to a difficult bit. Or so it seemed.

'They've been through so much already. They've lost their father. The last thing they need is to see their mother flaking out too.'

There was so much packed into that short statement that it was difficult to know where to start.

'You say the children have lost their father. Do you feel you've lost him too?'

The baby woke and needed changing. It was some time before she was able to pick up the thread.

'We've lost everything. David was depressed off and on for months before this happened. He struggled to stay at work for a while. He's a long-distance lorry driver, you see, but he couldn't concentrate. It was dangerous and eventually he had an accident. A minor one, but they laid him off.'

'You must have had to do without him a lot of the time before that. When he was away driving.'

'Funny, that. When he was driving to the other end of the country, I always thought of him as being with me. He used to phone us, wherever he was. And we looked forward to him coming home. We did all sorts of things together at the weekends and on his time off. It was fun.' She looked wistful. 'But after he lost his job and he was home all the time, it was like he wasn't here at all. For me or the kids. They must have felt he didn't want them any more.'

'What about treatment? Didn't he get help?'

'Typical man. He refused to see anyone for ages. Said he could cope, even though it was obvious he couldn't. Finally, I got him to see the GP. She said he was depressed and gave him tablets. I didn't see her myself so I don't know what they were.'

'Did they work?'

'Not much. But I'm not sure he took them regularly.'

'And finally, how did David end up in hospital?'

'It all seemed to happen so quickly. He got stranger and stranger. Kept saying there were people after him. Closed all the curtains and told the kids to hide upstairs. The next day, after they'd gone to school, he locked all the doors and started barricading us in with tables and chairs.'

'And you, Carrie?'

'I lost it, I'm afraid.'

'What did that mean?'

'I shouted at him not to be so silly.'

The baby woke again and needed a feed. This time she persevered.

'I shouldn't have done it, I know. But it was just like all my feelings came out at once. Everything I'd been bottling up. I screamed at him and he hit me. Then he just sort of crumpled up. I climbed out of the back window with the baby and ran for help. The police came and the GP on call. And . . . well, you know the rest.'

'What about the children?'

'They were still at school, thank goodness. They would have been terrified. When they got home, it was all over and he'd gone.'

'And the baby?'

'I don't think she'll remember anything.' She finished feeding her and put her back in the cot. 'Strange, isn't it? David lost all his urges right from the start, if you know what I mean. The only time I got him to do it, I fell pregnant.'

Carrie agreed that I should return in the late afternoon, when the children were back. I could have given them all an appointment to see me in my clinic, but it was important to see them at home, in their own territory, while she was still open to talking. If I delayed it, she might clam up again and the children would follow her lead.

There were two older children: Sam, who was eight, and Millie, who was five. We told them that I had come from the hospital to see how they were, which was the truth and they accepted it quite happily. More than that, they were excited to show me their toys and we went upstairs to their bedrooms while their mother made them tea.

Many of the toys had been bought by their father, for Christmas and birthdays, and it wasn't difficult to get them to talk about him. Some of their feelings showed the difference in their age, but both of them were still very confused about what had been happening to their father, where he'd gone and when he would be coming back. If he ever did.

Sam had thrown his schoolbag under the bed and I asked him if he had much homework to do.

'Not much at the moment. My teacher says she knows things are difficult, with my father in hospital. She knows that I've got to be the man about the house and everything.' His language sounded curiously grown up, as if it reflected his new job.

'Why do you think your father has gone to hospital?'

'Because he's ill.' He looked wary of saying any more in front of his sister, but she went off to the lavatory and I had a chance to explore it a bit more.

'What sort of illness has your father got?'

'Something called depression.'

'And what does that mean?'

Sam looked as sad as his mother had done earlier. 'I overheard one of the adults whispering in the playground. To one of the boys in my class. She said my Dad is mad, and . . .' His lip was quivering now and his adult-like defences were cracking round the edges.

'What did she mean by that?'

'That . . . that my dad is mad . . . and mad people are violent . . . so my dad must have been violent too . . . and he's been locked up.' He was crying openly now but there was more to come. 'She said madness runs in families and that I might get mad too. So . . . so best to avoid me. The boy won't play with me any more.' He could barely speak. 'See . . . see what my dad's done.'

Millie had come back while we were talking and ran across to her brother. I held them together, as any parent would when they were comforting their children, and waited until they were calmer. Then I explained what had happened in words that I thought they could understand: their father's depression, how it had changed him for a while, the treatment that he needed, and that he would get better and come home.

'Was it my fault, what happened?'

Millie had the typical thinking of a five-year-old. There were times when she had been so frightened by her father's behaviour that she'd wished him out of the way, secretly, in her heart of hearts. And her mother had told her to be quiet for her father's sake, or it would make him worse. But she hadn't been quiet, and he did get worse, and now he was gone. Just as she had wished. So she must have caused it all. Magical thinking. Not true, but terrifying in itself.

Thankfully, I have never been admitted to hospital in psychosis, like David. But I have come close and my periods at home with depression were once just as confusing for my own wife and children. They had the same feelings. My wife felt frightened and angry, like Carrie, and left out somewhere on the edge of my treatment. Trying desperately to protect the children but bottling up both them and herself in the process. Until she, too, exploded.

My eldest son felt that he had to be grown up and look after his mother and sister, egged on by well-meaning but misguided teachers. Underneath, he was as angry with me as Sam was with his father, but he couldn't express it. Mad people are angry, and angry people are violent. And it runs in families. His young sister felt as guilty, and as frightened, as Millie. And they were all full of the mythology that surrounds mental illness and the stigma that goes with it.

I was admonished by my son over that pint many years later and it stood me in good stead. What Carrie and her children needed was to share their feelings with each other openly instead of trying to protect each other by keeping those feelings to themselves. Both Carrie and her children needed to be told exactly what was happening lest they fill in the gaps with a mythology that was worse than the truth. And they needed to be involved in David's treatment, in a way that was appropriate to their age and status in the family, rather than feeling excluded.

We talked together over several sessions at the house. I brought messages from David to his family and from them to him. If he had been at home, he would have been included in all these discussions from the start. As it was, I brought Carrie, the children and the baby in to see him as soon as the adult team said he was stable enough. This enabled them to make contact again with the husband and father they thought they had lost, to understand that the hospital was neither a prison nor a punishment cell and to see how well he was doing there. When at length he was discharged, we continued the sessions all together at home.

One of the most worrying aspects to David's story, and to the story of most people with a mental illness, is the assumption that they will automatically be violent to those around them. It hangs over them like an accusation. It was there in the whispers of the parent in Sam's school playground. And it is proved in the minds of public, press and many politicians every time an adult with a mental illness is involved in a serious incident.

It would be foolish to ignore the fact that this can happen. Every now and then the sad stories crop up in the newspapers, of Good

Samaritans who tried to tackle psychotic patients or just happened to be there, at the wrong time, in the wrong place. On an underground station platform or in a deserted park. And it's of little comfort to their families that the attacker was driven to it by voices from another world.

But such incidents – tragic and spectacular – are very rare. However good our treatment, we would struggle to prevent them completely, except by locking up all patients with a serious mental illness and throwing away the key. I've no doubt that many of the public would like us to do exactly that, but thankfully we live in a more humane society and the vast majority of mental illnesses will never reach anywhere near that state. The depression of someone like David, disturbing though it may feel, will be treated perfectly adequately at home or in hospital, like any other illness. And family, friends and colleagues will be comforted if they are able to talk about it in the way that I did not at first with my own children.

More worrying still is the fact that people with a mental illness are far more likely to be violent to themselves than to the people around them, and they may get precious little sympathy for what they do. We can include here all the young people with mental health problems that I met on those Saturday morning rounds, who took overdoses out of their misery, or who regularly cut themselves as a way of easing tension.

'It's like the badness is all draining out of me,' said a fifteen-year-old girl, when I asked her why she did it so often. 'I can feel it building up, until it's unbearable. Then it goes again, as soon as I see the blood.'

Children and young people who do harm to themselves, like Seren, are becoming all too common. Those who succeed in killing themselves – like Lauren who fell over the cliff-face and the boys in the South Wales town who hanged themselves – are desperately sad but uncommon. As are those who are left in the wake of parents who do serious harm to themselves or commit suicide.

For several years, I nurtured an interest in trying to help the children of parental suicide. There were not many, but each was part of a common pattern. It was almost always the father who had killed himself, and most often by hanging. Their suicide came as an abrupt shock, but it was usually the end result of a personal and family conflict that had dragged everyone down into a sense of hopelessness, no matter how unprepared they were for what happened.

The surviving adults had tried to shield their children from the misery, both before and after the hanging, but the children usually knew far more than they were given credit for, were often in the vicinity when the hanging happened, and may even have found their father's body. They wanted to share the tumultuous feelings with which they were left, not least because their fathers had often killed themselves on a date that was significant to the family in happier times – Christmas, the birthday of one of the children, or the anniversary of the parents' marriage – which made it all the more bitter and difficult to understand.

But this was exactly what the adults least wanted. Grief-stricken and often still seething from the arguments that had torn them apart, the surviving mother would protect her own feelings by refusing to let the children explore theirs. The children's feelings emerged in their behaviour, and then they were referred for help by teachers or their GP, but getting behind the behaviour required patience, tact or serendipity of some kind. The mothers were as fragile as their children and needed great care.

Take, for example, the children of two different cultures. Zoe, fifteen, and her sister Hailey, twelve: the daughters of a self-employed, Irish sales representative. And Kabir, eleven, and his brother Parvez, six: the sons of a Pakistani self-employed businessman. The details of their stories were different, of course, but the pattern of what happened was similar and their needs the same.

Zoe and Hailey were referred to me by their GP within a week or so of their father's suicide. He described the girls as seriously depressed, which said more about his own anxiety about the situation than their real feelings, but it needed a rapid response. I saw them together with their mother in the immaculate front room of their house.

Kabir and Parvez were referred by their head teacher and the educational psychologist at their mother's request, because of their behavioural problems in school. It was just one year after the suicide of their father and I saw them in my clinic, together with their mother and their maternal grandmother.

There was a strong family history in both stories. The maternal grandfather of Zoe and Hailey had also committed suicide, when their mother was just fifteen – the same age as Hailey. Kabir was the child of his mother's first marriage, which had split because of her first husband's depression. He had returned to Pakistan, and was reported to have killed himself there. 'I've lost two Daddies,' Kabir said.

In both cases, the fathers had been mentally precarious for some time and the children had been trying to make them feel better, believing that they could rescue their fathers from their unhappiness.

The father of Zoe and Hailey had been increasingly depressed since his own, elderly father had a fall and broke his hip. In hospital, it was clear just how demented he had become and his son began to regret the trials and tribulations of their relationship, too late to repair. He retreated into an armchair, eating and drinking little and untouched by the GP's antidepressants. The girls tried desperately to show him how much he was loved, and he seemed to have got a little more lively the week before he killed himself. He had even taken them to school.

The father of Kabir and Parvez was already working flat out when the family took the decision to buy a second shop some twenty miles away, all in the middle of the wedding celebrations for their mother's younger sister. The father was increasingly tired, trying to watch over everything as the head of the household. He was working into the early hours then finding it difficult to get off to sleep because of the worry. His anxiety developed into full-blown panic attacks and the boys persuaded him that it was dangerous to drive. The mother drove him to the shop each morning on the way to school.

In retrospect, it would have been possible to see the catastrophes lurking just around the corner. But everyone had convinced themselves that the fathers' symptoms were improving, or were distracted by happier, family events. When the suicide happened it was a devastating surprise, and the children in both cases were involved to different degrees.

'It was Father's Day,' said Zoe. 'We had a special tea with toast and doughnuts. Dad got tired so he went upstairs to have a nap. So he said. Maybe we shouldn't have let him out of our sight.'

'It wasn't that so much,' added Hailey. 'We went round to visit friends, and then there was homework and TV. We shouldn't have left him so long.'

'And how do you think I feel?' blurted out their mother, looking increasingly miserable in the background.

Eventually, she and Zoe had gone upstairs to wake him and found him hanging in the bedroom. Zoe could remember every detail and the image of him hanging flashed unbidden into her mind whenever she stopped concentrating on anything else. By contrast, Hailey stayed downstairs and had been stopped from seeing him. Her mother refused to give her even the barest detail, and she had filled in the gaps with an imagination that was just as lurid.

Kabir and Parvez still had a vivid recollection of their father's suicide, even though it was a year ago. It was no accident that they had been referred on the anniversary of his death, and the mother and grandmother who came with them were clearly full of their own grief. The behaviour that had got them referred was hardly mentioned.

'It was early closing and we drove up to collect him from the other shop,' said Kabir. 'After school. There was masses of traffic and it took ages. Mum's not a very fast driver.' He took a glance at her, but she was deep in her own memories.

'We had tests at school,' said Parvez. 'I was top and I had my workbook to show him.' He looked as excited then crestfallen as he must have been at the time.

'His work's gone downhill since then,' added the grandmother. 'Not surprising, is it?' She looked to the boys' mother for confirmation, but she was too sad to speak.

She and the boys had found the shop locked up and could get no reply when they shouted through the letter box. Kabir went round the back and climbed in through a window, getting increasingly anxious at what he might find. His father had fainted once or twice in his panic attacks. He unbolted the back door and he and his mother searched until they found him, hanging in a storeroom. Parvez had stayed in the car.

How on earth could children be helped to cope with such events? There are no magic wands to wave over them, of course, but perhaps the first thing to say is that they should be allowed not to cope. None of the children had a psychiatric illness, but it was all too easy for GPs to call them depressed and treat them with a tablet, rather than allow them to experience their grief, with all its disturbing emotions. This treatment might be more comfortable, but it is misguided and ultimately fruitless. The feelings will come out in some form, either at the time, or at an anniversary reminder.

And the feelings shared by the children in both families were certainly both natural and disturbing. They swung backwards and forwards between guilt and anger. Guilt at whether they should have prevented their father's suicide: 'Didn't we tell him we loved him often enough?' Anger at why he should do it to them: 'Wasn't our love enough for him?' And fears of all kinds. Fear that they might not see it coming again if things got difficult, fear that someone else might kill themselves too, like their mother, and fear that they might kill themselves one day. After all, it runs in families, doesn't it? Look at ours. These feelings needed to be aired openly, not hidden under the blankets.

It was natural for Zoe and Hailey to be wary of going upstairs alone, and for Kabir and Parvez to refuse to visit the new shop. It was natural for the children to be sleeping poorly and running into their mother's bedroom with nightmares. They didn't need the GP's offer of sleeping tablets. But it was natural too for the children to be concerned about the day-to-day aspects of living. Zoe had already got back to school and exams, just weeks after her father's suicide, and little Parvez was anxious whether someone would still give him his pocket money now that his father was dead. Getting back to routine is important for children; it doesn't mean they don't care.

We should accept that the children will have a detailed memory of what happened, and let them know how things will be planned now that the fathers are not around. We should share the emotions openly with them. We need to include them in the rituals of grief. And they need to know, too, that suicide is not inevitable. Yes, there may be a genetic vulnerability to mental illnesses like depression. There may even be people in the family who have killed themselves in the past. But help is ready and available to stop the children and young people ever getting to that state. The pattern does not have to be repeated.

The mother of Zoe and Hailey had learnt from her own teenage experience, and took them to see their father's body in the chapel-of-rest and to the funeral. They wrote poems to their father and placed them in the grave, together with presents they had given him, like his favourite aftershave. They were already visiting his grave to put fresh flowers on it, and had filled a memory box at home with photographs, a rugby programme, beer mats and odd bits of stuff. Odd, but filled with love.

Kabir and Parvez were saved by their Muslim culture. At first, their mother had tried to be so strong for the children that Kabir thought she didn't care enough because she didn't cry. Either that, or it was wrong, and therefore wrong for him to cry too. And Parvez was protected by everyone because he was so young. But the culture demanded that everyone should go to the funeral, including small children, and that there should be an extended forty days of mourning afterwards. Together they prepared a photograph album of the ceremony to send to those members of the family who couldn't get over from Pakistan.

The two families have long since got back to their routine. It will never be the same without their father and they will still be pitched back into grief at important anniversaries, but that will be expected. They are welcome to my further help if they need it, but they probably won't. And I have stopped seeking out the experience of such families.

I told myself that it was because I didn't want to become typecast, but I have a feeling that it was something more. When I first became depressed, I too contemplated suicide and the families' experience was so close to the bone. I encouraged them to be open with their children. I owed it to my own children to be as open with them now as I was not at the time. Even if it cost me another pint or two.

CHAPTER 18

SIMON AND KERI
DEALING WITH AGGRESSIVE CHILDREN

I distrust the incommunicable: it is the source of all violence.

Jean-Paul Sartre: '*Qu'est-ce que la littérature?*'
in *Les Temps Modernes*, p. 106, July 1947

'Random events aren't random. Sometimes they cluster.'

I was chatting to a statistician at the end of a long day. I was tired out and was having trouble following his argument, but the day had been a perfect example of what he meant. Normally, my work would be a living textbook of everything that could go wrong in families. I hardly knew what was just around the corner and it was the variety that I liked, distressing though much of it might be. Today had been different. Every child was an aggressive child. And the first two were typical.

Simon was five, a little emperor brought in to see me by his mother. He was hitting her whenever he wanted to get his way, hard, angrily and painfully, and she showed me the bruises all over her arms to prove it. She could see it coming each time, but seemed powerless to prevent it.

Keri was fourteen and I saw her at home with both her parents. They had been shocked when her teacher told them that their daughter was the school bully, but they might have expected it because she was hitting her little sister at home too. Slyly, when she thought they weren't looking. Two aggressive children with the same sort of symptom – but what different causes.

Simon was already telling my secretary what to do when I went down to meet them in reception. His mother was fussing ineffectually round the edge. 'Simon . . . Stop interrupting . . . I'm sure they've got far too much to do already . . . But he's so old for his years, don't you think?'

It seemed to me that Simon was trying to rule the clinic in the same way he did at home, and we should start off by establishing just who was the real parent. I asked him if he would tidy the waiting room for me while I talked to his mother; I would come down and collect him shortly. He looked at me suspiciously, afraid to be left out, but the mess in the room was too attractive to complain.

In the short time we had together, Simon's mother told me that she had separated from his father a year ago. He was an angry man, angry about everything, she said. He hated their house, hated his job, and hated her. Marriage had put paid to everything he'd ever dreamed about. Then Simon had been born and that was that. Except it wasn't. They came back from visiting her parents to find him gone; he had moved in with another woman. He saw his son occasionally but against his partner's wishes. Now Simon was the man about the house and they had to make the best of what they'd got.

After ten minutes, she began to fret and Simon burst in through my door. It was almost as if she had shouted for him to come up. He demanded to know what we had been saying and his mother began to tell him, in a roundabout sort of way. I stopped her.

'That's grown-ups' business. You and I can have some time together next time.'

I'm not sure whether I handled that well or badly, but it did the trick. Simon raised his hand to hit his mother and I caught it in mid-air. I turned him round so that I could look him in the eye. I spoke to him, firmly but gently.

'We don't hit people to get what we want. If there's something you want to tell me, that's all right. You can say it now. I'm listening.'

Simon tried half-heartedly to hit me too, but his struggles subsided and I was able to hold him closer for a while. He cried a little, then got away from me and cuddled up to his mother. A healthier start.

Keri absented herself when I arrived at their house. She sloped off to her room as soon as her parents opened the door, despite her father calling after her.

'Keri! Don't be rude. This man has come all the way to see you. The least you can do is tell him what's wrong.'

I doubt that Keri had a clear idea of what was wrong herself, and she certainly wasn't going to tell me in front of her parents if she did.

'That's OK. Keri can join us if she wants, but there will be plenty of other times. Meanwhile, perhaps you can tell me a bit about yourselves.'

They told me that they had tried for years to have a baby, but failed. The mother dropped her head at the word, as if it had been her fault. They had fostered Keri and then adopted her, as her unruly behaviour settled down. They had treated her as their own in every way they could, said her father, and she had taken their name. Then the miracle happened. The mother became pregnant and their natural child was born. The mother picked up a photograph from the table top and handed it to me. A grinning child looked coquettishly at the camera, her head on one side. She was nine and safely at school.

'And one other thing,' added the mother, as if it was an afterthought. 'The social worker has contacted us again after all these years. Keri's birth mother has crawled out of the woodwork and wants to see her. Keri doesn't know yet and we're not sure what to do.'

There was a slight noise on the landing. It could have been the cat stretching itself, a draught coming through the open window, or nothing at all. But it confirmed my suspicions. Keri had been sitting there, listening, on the fringe of things. Just as she saw herself in this family. If she didn't know about her real mother before, she did now. And there would be lots to talk about when I saw her next, wherever she felt safe.

As always, the first task would be to make sense of what was happening. What was the meaning of the aggression that Simon and Keri were showing and how might it fit into the dynamics around them? Jean-Paul Sartre was right in one way. Children and young people who find it impossible to communicate their deepest feelings may be driven to violence. But their aggression is a form of language. It's telling us that something is wrong, and we must work out what it is.

Aggression isn't all bad. Anger is a natural part of our human make-up. There are differences between us in temperament that mean we are more or less likely to fight back when we are cornered. But it is probably inherited in our genes, a built-in protective mechanism, and not something we would want to change. Thus the toddler in his terrible twos, as we have seen, may react to his frustration by biting, scramming and hitting out at those who are trying to hold him back. All very normal, but it is usually the poor parent who gets in the way.

This sort of primitive reaction is governed by specific areas of grey matter in the brain, called the amygdalae. As the brain matures, these areas are modified by the pre-frontal cortex. The child learns to express what he wants in more constructive ways, with all the sophisticated emotions they entail – empathy with the views of others, a sense of what is right and wrong, fairness, guilt, and a wish for reparation. And his coping strategies are maturing too.

There are disorders, like those on the autistic spectrum and ADHD, that make such developments very difficult. Hence the aggression with which boys like Mikey still react to their frustration. But we also need to remember that not all is sweetness and light in the normal adolescent's world. The new processes are not yet fully bedded in, quite literally if brain research is to be believed. The influence of sex hormones within, and the jealousies of peer group relationships without, mean that teenagers are tetchy much of the time and likely to explode when you least expect it.

'Why the hell should I?' shouted one adolescent when he was asked to tidy his bedroom before he went out for the evening. 'It's my room. I'll do what I want with it.'

He slammed the front door so hard that the glass panel fell out and shattered on the garden path. And he was referred to me because of his adolescent behaviour, like many young people before him and since. His emotions were simply out of control at times, and he was as disturbed by them as his parents were.

Unlike Simon and Keri, he never actually hit anyone when he was angry. (At school, he punched a hole in the woodwork instead of his form teacher. And at home, he backed off when he squared up to his father and his mother got between.) Which was just as well, because he was a big lad and very intimidating for the people with whom he was angry.

'Sex hormones again,' said his father, half admonishing and half proud of his son. He may well have been right, but his son needed to have firm boundaries put around his behaviour as well as an understanding of what was causing it. For his own sake as much as that of the adults.

None of that gets us very far with Simon and Keri. If they were reacting aggressively as a one-off, to a particularly threatening situation, we would probably congratulate them on their courage and pass on. In fact, they would not have been referred in the first place. But their aggression had become habitual. We have to ask with what emotions they were struggling, why they had never learnt more mature ways of dealing with them, and why they chose the targets for their aggression that they did.

Simon was an insecure little lad from the start. His father was a poor role model, angry about everything and violent to his wife. Even lousy relationships might have been better than nothing, but when the father walked out on the marriage it was the end of them too. Simon had been stuck in the middle of his parents' rows and when they separated it must have seemed that it was his fault.

Now his father didn't want anything to do with him and his mother was giving him mixed messages about his role: you're just a child, but you're the man about the house.

In his confusion, Simon was recreating his parents' marriage. He was violent to his mother, just as his father had been, and she was just as submissive to him as she had been to her husband. Whatever the misery he felt inside, Simon was outwardly her angry and authoritarian pseudo-partner. The relationship was built upon their mutual needs and both of them would have to change. She to be a firmer and more consistent parent, and her son to be relieved of his parental role. I decided to work with them on the mother's territory, in her own house, where she might be more confident in her adulthood and less abashed by whatever role modelling I might give her.

Keri had been just as insecure from the start of her own life, and her worries were based on hard fact. She had been taken into the care of the local authority as a small child and had disrupted several foster placements with her behaviour. Every failure proved that she was not wanted and her anger was directed at those who obviously were – the happy, secure, younger classmates at her school. It would have been difficult for the adoptive parents to counteract her insecurity, no matter how hard they tried for over a decade or more. Then the two further events made it impossible.

The parents had described the birth of their natural daughter as a miracle, and the rows of photographs showed just how proud of her they were.

'She's a such a sweet child,' said her mother. 'Always smiling, but no thanks to Keri. She takes her feelings out on her poor little sister.'

'Keri thinks we don't notice,' added her father, 'but we do. It's all we can do not to get angry, but it would only make things worse.'

'Your younger daughter takes a very good photograph,' I said. 'But where are the photographs of Keri?'

'Oh, Keri doesn't like having her photo taken, so we don't push it.'

I could imagine just why Keri didn't. She was a rather dour, scrub-haired teenager and could never have competed with the younger, more attractive girl who smiled at the camera with the confidence of someone who knew she was loved for her own sake, however she behaved. It was a reflection of how Keri felt in general and it wasn't surprising that the aggression she was showing at school was directed at that perfect little sister at home too. If she carried on like that, would the parents reject her just as so many others had done before, her worst fears come true?

The reappearance of Keri's natural mother was the final straw. I have known the most secure of adoptive placements to be shaken by this: the natural parent's wish to recontact their child, the child's wish to recontact natural parents, or both. The important thing to remember, as ever, is that it is the child who has the right to decide things for herself and the adults who have the obligation to go along with it.

Many adopted teenagers do harbour a wish to find out more about their past and that may indeed mean trying to contact their natural family. It is part of the search for their identity that all adolescents will go through at some stage. But it does not mean that their love for the adoptive parents is being undermined. On the contrary, the happier they are to support their teenager's exploration, the stronger their relationship will become.

In Keri's case, there was no security to build on. The children she had bullied at school would have wanted to hit back in any way they could and the rumours about her natural parent would have been a perfect weapon. She almost certainly would have known, no matter how secretive her adoptive parents had tried to be. They would need to talk openly about it, but it was almost too late. For Keri, it was the final proof that they would be only too glad to give her up.

It seemed best to work with them separately: with the parents at home to explain what was happening and how they might try to put it right, and with Keri by herself in my clinic. She needed a private space to talk about the feelings that would have been too dangerous for both her and her adoptive parents to discuss together.

Two aggressive children, each with clear reasons why they should be so, and directing their anger at the expected targets. They needed a different approach, but with lots of common features in how that should be done. Only connect, the saying goes, but what does that mean? In Simon's case it meant physical holding, the sort of all-enveloping care that a five-year-old in a temper tantrum would welcome, though he might squirm a bit at first. That would not have been appropriate for me to do with a teenage girl like Keri, but soft, warm and empathic words were just as good.

No blame, no shame. It was easy for a therapist to see what was happening in these two families, looking in objectively from the outside. But the emotions inside were so raw that they might have been only dimly aware of it, if at all, and certainly not able to do much about it. If they had been, they wouldn't have needed my help. The last thing that either the parents or their children needed was to be blamed for how they were behaving and the shame that would go with it. They needed to know that it was misguided, but that it was understandable and could be put right.

It would also have been easy for me to offer glib advice: to tell the parents to praise their children's good behaviour and not punish the bad. It would be important for them to offer the children a different, positive model and not to reinforce the negativity of all the anger and violence that had been flying around. But that would have to be done slowly and carefully, with parents who had been doing the best as they saw it and needed help with their own feelings before they could change tack.

All of them had become so used to the old ways of doing things, distressing though they may have been, that it would have been naive to expect them to try something different, simply because they knew now that it was possible. They needed educating, in its broadest sense: to be shown some more mature coping strategies and to be helped to try them out with each other in the safety of the therapeutic setting.

'You mean we should never get angry with each other again?' asked one set of parents I was seeing, incredulously.

'No. That wouldn't be natural. Parents and children will always make each other angry at times. It's part of being close; of showing that you care.'

'So you can be angry and still love each other?'

'Of course. It's the most important lesson families will ever learn. But next time you get angry, don't hit each other, don't say cruel words, don't stomp off to your room and sulk. Try something different. Try talking about it instead.'

Finally, and most important of all, what Simon and Keri needed was security. So often, the aggression of the children at the centre of these families is a product of their insecurity and the lack of self-esteem that goes with it. And it was certainly true of these two children.

Simon needed to be reassured that he did not cause the break-up of his parents' marriage, that we would try to establish contact with his father on a regular basis, but that he was sure of his mother's love, whatever happened. Of course he would have a say in what went on in their future life, especially as he got older; but she was the parent, caring but firm. And he should not be trying to take over.

Keri needed to be reassured that she was every bit as important to her adoptive parents as their natural daughter. They should intervene when they saw Keri hitting her sister and it would not make it worse. It was Keri's choice as to whether or not she saw her own birth mother. But her school teachers should stick to their anti-bullying policy even if they had sympathy for why Keri was angry. Understanding is not an excuse for inaction, and teenagers need the comfort of boundaries to their behaviour.

In other words, both Simon and Keri needed to know that they were loved, whatever their behaviour, but there were better ways of testing it out than being angry. And their aggression would decrease when they learnt the message.

'Thank you,' said Simon's mother, when we were saying goodbye after our final session at their house. 'I was terrified that he was going to grow up into a monster. You read such terrible stories in the papers. Maybe we were going to be one of those stories too . . .'

'I've decided not to see my mother,' said Keri, in our final session in my clinic room. 'My natural mother, that is. Maybe one day. But right now it's enough to hear that she's still around if I ever want to. I know who my real parents are. And my sister. Even if she is a little pest sometimes . . .'

So some measure of aggression is a normal part of child and adolescent behaviour. It is built into our genes as a reaction to danger and is modified as the brain matures. There are people who are quicker to anger than others, but their flare-ups are usually brief and to the point. And they are accompanied by contrition afterwards if they go over the top, provided we give them an opportunity to rescue the situation without losing face.

Sometimes a child's anger threatens to get out of hand, is disproportionate to what has triggered it, or becomes a habitual response to being thwarted in any way. It is natural that parents should be worried, even jump to the conclusion that their child will end up in prison for harming someone, and be confused about how to stop it happening. But children and young people like Simon and Keri can be helped with understanding, firm handling, and by building up their sense of self-esteem, long before they get to that state.

Without such help, they will never learn a different way of managing difficulties and will continue to meet them by lashing out. The fantasies that Simon's mother was harbouring are usually just that. Fantasies. But rarely, they may come true.

CHAPTER 19

FREDDIE AND ELLIE

EXTREME BEHAVIOUR AND
THE CONCEPT OF EVIL

*Those inquiring whence Evil enters into beings, or rather into a certain order
of beings, would be making the best beginning if they established, first of
all, what precisely Evil is.*

Plotinus: *Enneads* I, 8, 1

My father was a chapel organist and he insisted I go with him,
through the wind and weather, to isolated outposts of the Methodist
circuit. As a child, I listened to many a sermon on evil without
being sure what it meant, other than what he and the Bible said
was right and wrong in the world out there, beyond the end of
the street. As a teenager, with new sexual urges and magazines
stuffed under the bed, it came nearer home.

'I smell sin!' exclaimed the lay preacher, coming down from his
pulpit like an avenging angel to throw me out for reading one of
the magazines on the back row. The evil was not out there after
all; it was in me and there was nothing I could do to get rid of it.
Better hide it under the bed with all those pictures.

Now we use the word for almost everything, from the everyday
evil of weather and hangovers to major catastrophes in the newspaper headlines or on TV. 'He's evil, this one,' said a young parent,

pushing her five-year-old up the clinic stairs. He'd been caught shoplifting, an ordinary sort of misdemeanour, but he was branded all the same.

The nature of evil has kept philosophers busy for thousands of years and we could get lost again here in a thicket of ideas, but there is a common point to much of the discussion. We describe as evil the things that we don't understand, that are beyond reason, and for which we have no other word. If it is out there, in people and events, we are not to blame. If it is part of ourselves, we are duly horrified, look for it in others and punish them for it. The scapegoat of the Old Testament, sent out into the desert with the sins of the world on its back.

Many groups of people have found themselves ostracised in such a way. And children and young people who commit serious crimes, especially those who kill, are a prime example. We tend to have a firm idea of the sort of person we are talking about, but they can come from surprisingly different backgrounds. Here are just two.

Freddie was over-indulged from the moment he was born. He was the only boy in a family of three older sisters, all of whom adored him as much as his mother did, and pandered to his every whim and fancy. His father was a self-made businessman who had climbed to the top at the expense of anyone who got in his way. He had worked hard for his money but the rewards had become more important to him than the way he achieved them.

'Never do to yourself what you would do to others' became the father's philosophy, and Freddie absorbed it in the way he ran his own life. At home, he was showered with toys as a child and priv- ileges as an adolescent. He dressed immaculately in designer scruffs and expensively tousled hair, and was given a new car as soon as he was able to drive. He loved the trappings for their own sake, but even more for how they enabled him to lord it over his peers.

So much for the surface story. What nobody outside the family could have known was that Freddie was regularly beaten by his father, for minor transgressions or for nothing much at all, alternating with an almost pathetic assertion that his boy could do no wrong and showering him with gifts as a way of saying sorry. It left Freddie confused about his own self-worth and hardened in his attitude to those around him. His mother and sisters were too cowed to admit to what was going on, let alone intervene.

He was a bright boy at school, both academically and in his personality. His light shone out of the crowd, but he was a bully to those he saw as lesser mortals and gathered around himself a coterie of shallow-minded peers who were in awe of him, afraid of him, or both. He boasted of his sexual conquests, even those he had made up, and seemed inviolate to criticism. There were teachers, he claimed, who were secretly jealous of him and others who despised him but were wary of saying anything lest his father come running to the attack.

'Just because your father thinks he's above the law, it doesn't mean you are too,' said one of the braver teachers. 'Carry on like this and you'll come to a sticky end.'

A bit of a cliché, perhaps, but it was wise and it got a predictable response.

'Carry on like this and at least I won't end up in a dead-end teaching job like you.'

Neither Freddie nor the teacher could have predicted just how quickly the words would come true. Freddie and his mates became notorious around the city-centre clubs and pubs for their behaviour. They drank heavily and bought designer drugs that were as exclusive as the rest of their image, then took them back to the house and watched pornographic films for the rest of the night. Freddie had been to at least one illegal dog fight, hidden in a quarry in the hills.

On a Saturday night they beat up a bouncer who refused to let them through the door without a ticket, but the police turned a blind eye because the bouncer was a well-known thug, and besides, he was black. There were increasingly racial overtones to everything Freddie and his mates said and did, and they tuned in to the racism in the family and community around them.

For a while, even Freddie respected the drink-driving laws. But he was inviolate, wasn't he? He began to carry carloads of his drunken friends around the city, marginally sober himself at first, and then well over the limit. It needed only the right combination of circumstances for the calamity to occur, if right could possibly be the word to use.

They were rowdily drunk as usual on a Bank Holiday Monday and left the pub before the landlord could call the police. A similarly drunk old man staggered around the car park in front of them. They whistled and jeered when he gave them the V-sign, and decided that it would be fun to nudge him around. But he fell under the front wheel and was run over. Freddie drove off, one of his mates screaming from the back seat that the old man was seriously hurt and that they should stop. The same lad who gave evidence at their trial.

Freddie was convicted of causing death by dangerous driving and sent to prison. His family tried vainly to claim that he was innocent of anything more than an accident, but the sequence of events was so deliberate and so heedlessly inevitable that you could almost call it murder. Not the usual image of a young person who kills, but becoming all too common.

Ellie's case was much more archetypal. She was born with a host of minor physical problems and an IQ that hovered on the edge of being a learning disability. Perhaps these would not have been crucial if she had grown up in a loving family environment, where she was cherished for what she was rather than what she might have been. But the reality was very different.

Her father left almost immediately after she was born, convincing her in later life that it must have been her fault. 'He took one look at me and did a bunk. Don't blame him really,' she said.

That was only the start of her story. Her mother wheeled in a string of men, who got more unsuitable every time. The last was a Schedule One sex offender, when Ellie was just eight years old. He had already been convicted of abusing young girls in at least two other families, but there might well have been more that the law didn't know about.

Ellie was abused by him too. She was afraid to tell anyone because he told her that he would leave if she did so, and she knew how much her mother depended on having him around. She convinced herself, instead, that being wanted for her body was better than nothing, even if it felt very wrong. But it made no difference; he left anyway and her mother blamed her, as she always did.

In her misery, Ellie's mother became addicted to crack cocaine and was almost certainly prostituting herself to get the money to support her habit. None of it was spent on her daughter, who looked increasingly ill-fed and unkempt on the irregular occasions when she turned up at school. The teachers were worried enough to call in the educational psychologist, but all his efforts to contact the mother were rebuffed and he gave up. Ellie was transferred to special education because of her unruly behaviour and effectively disappeared from school altogether. At ten.

'No one wanted me. My father ran off. My mother was too interested in getting things for herself. So I started drinking with any money I could thieve from her purse,' she told the psychiatrist when she was assessed at the end of it all. 'I got fat. So no one wanted to pay for my body either . . . I had to give it away for favours.'

'What favours?'

'Drink, mostly. Drugs. And more drink . . .'

A year later, Ellie was picked up off the streets and taken into local authority care. Despite the best efforts of a succession of short-term foster parents and social workers, Ellie burnt them all off and continued on her race to the bottom of the pile. She began sleeping rough in sheds and barns with other young girls and older men. Drinking, taking drugs, having casual sex, and watching violent films on their mobiles.

Ellie had always had a violent streak to her nature. Her mother called her a psychopath because she tortured small animals for fun, dropping cats from as high up as she could manage and slicing insects in half to see if they would grow new parts. At school, she twisted the arms of smaller girls and laughed when they cried. And in the sheds and barns at night, she took apparent delight in creeping up on the other dossers in their sleep and burning them with cigarette ends on their hands and feet. There were many in school and social services who had called her evil.

Her reputation made her a prime target for even tougher girls, looking for partners to share their fantasies and convert them into hard fact. Ellie was being led into ever more violent crimes, fuelled by alcohol and curiosity, more brutal each time, less thought out and with no reward other than the thrill of inflicting pain and the determination to do it again as soon as possible. It had become a drug every bit as addictive as any other.

Ellie and an older girl intercepted an eight-year-old lad, walking home from school when his parents failed to turn up to collect him. They took him to a waste lot, plied him with alcohol and drugs, sexually abused him and were beginning to torture him in other ways when they were disturbed by a man hunting rabbits with his dogs. They were arrested, tried, convicted and sent to a secure unit on an indefinite sentence. The media were agog with the evil of their crime.

Freddie and Ellie, from very different family backgrounds, but whose stories both ended in the most serious of crimes, with common antecedents to the crime they committed. Both were called evil for who they were, how they behaved and what they had done. And in order to understand them, the questions we have to answer are clear.

Is there something qualitatively different about those children and young people who commit such crimes, or are they just the end products of what has been done to them? Are their crimes the understandable acts of evil children, or evil acts done by understandable children? Are they off the wall, or just one end of a spectrum on which we all sit somewhere?

To answer those questions, we only have to look at their history. To begin with, both of them had little self-esteem. Ellie obviously so, undermined from the beginning by her physical and learning problems, and compounded by every rejection along the way. Freddie less obviously so, but his surface bravado hid a hollowness inside which he tried desperately to fill with behaviour designed to show what a superior being he was.

Both of them had a lousy upbringing, with role models who were about as bad as it gets. They emerged with the shakiest idea of right and wrong, and as little appreciation of the effect their behaviour might have on others as their family had of what they did to them. Ellie was repeatedly slapped down by the adults in her family, and Freddie can have got little real joy from the strange inconsistency in his father's behaviour towards him, and the women's fawning adulation.

On top of all that, both of them were abused. Ellie was sexually assaulted by a known offender, and Freddie was physically abused by his father. In neither case were they able to do anything about it but grit their teeth, endure it, and take out their feelings on weaker victims later. It is no surprise that both the abused became abusers in their turn.

The services offered little rescue. School did nothing to change the behaviour of either Ellie, who was effectively rejected from education, or Freddie, whose school was a fertile ground for his antics, around which the teachers failed to put any sort of boundaries. The local authority stepped in belatedly, to take Ellie into care, but the care was equivocal at best. And they would have felt that they had no remit with Freddie at all, despite what was happening to him.

That behaviour was fed on a diet of drugs and alcohol, pornographic films, smart phone games, pubs, clubs and dog fights. Together, they gave Ellie and Freddie a vicarious satisfaction but increased their need for further thrills. And so on, in a self-perpetuating cycle of violence. In their heads, the borderland between fantasy and reality must have become very hazy indeed.

Looking back, it's easy to see an escalating pattern of harm in their actions, but it should have pressed the alarm buttons at many points in their lives. Instead, their behaviour seems to have been indulged, ignored, or given a static and unchangeable label like psychopath, or evil. If it's unchangeable, there would be no point in getting involved. Or so people would have thought. And so it continued, until the end became an inevitability, in which no one could feel themselves blamed for not stopping it, except Ellie and Freddie themselves.

That end came near when both of them found partners in crime. Freddie as the leader of the pack, egged on by his peers, and Ellie as the junior partner led by the nose. All it then needed was a ready-made victim and an opportunity, and there we have it. An old man dead in a pub car park and a lone eight-year-old scarred for life.

Reading through that list of antecedents in the short history of Ellie and Freddie, and the very similar list in the history of most children and young people who commit serious crimes, there can be no doubt about the answers. These are not evil people. Their acts may be described as evil, for want of any better word to describe something so terrible. But they are the understandable culmination of everything that the family, services and the community have thrown at them. In effect, society has groomed them for what they do. We are all responsible for the end result.

And that, of course, begs another question. What can be done about it? If it was evil, then it would be unchangeable and we would have neither the responsibility nor the ability to do anything. But if not, we have a job on our hands.

We shouldn't panic. The constellation of factors in the lives of these children and young people is very rare. The vast majority of children with difficult behaviour will never go on to be like Ellie and Freddie. But few though those who do may be, they raise hugely important issues for us all.

Firstly, the matter of balance between the victims of society, as I believe Ellie and Freddie were, and the victims of their crimes. However much we may sympathise with how those crimes came about, it will never compensate the family of the dead old man, the traumatised eight-year-old, or his parents, agonising forever as to why they didn't pick him up on time. The children's behaviour may have been understandable, but that is not to say that it should be excused. At the very least, their victims needed to see justice done through the courts.

But we live in a society where punishment should be tempered with rehabilitation. Other countries are far more enlightened than the UK about this, with their age of criminal responsibility set higher and the serious consequences of poor upbringing seen as an opportunity for treatment, not imprisonment. But an attempt should be made, at least, even with children and young people as damaged as Ellie and Freddie. And if rehabilitation is successful, the young people should be released with a guarantee of anonymity. They should not be hounded forever for what they have done.

All this is like shutting the stable door after the horse has bolted. How much better it would be to keep the horse in the stable, eating more contentedly, in the first place. No easy task, but it should surely not be beyond services, working together, to prevent people like Ellie and Freddie from reaching the ultimate catastrophe. And nowhere in either of their stories were child and adolescent mental health services mentioned at all.

Here I have a confession to make. The reason I know so much about Ellie and Freddie is partly what came out at their trial, partly the notes I have been able to read from other services, and partly because my own services were involved, briefly and unsuccessfully, though not myself in person. This may have been due to the resistance of the young people, but more I suspect to the lack of motivation of the services themselves. It would have been difficult to pin a diagnosis on either of them, and without it they would have washed their hands of such an overwhelming problem. Our services have a lot to learn.

So have the public. If we are to help, it will depend on a change of attitude to the whole concept of evil, to the stigmatising of children and young people for the way families and society have affected their behaviour, and to the wish to lock them away out of sight for good. An enormous task, epitomised in the way the media treated Mary Bell.

As an eleven-year-old, Mary had killed two little boys in the Scotswood district of Newcastle. She was the daughter of a prostitute who specialised in violence to her clients and had several times tried to kill Mary in her infancy. But the press knew Mary forever as 'The Tyneside Strangler', found her, exposed her to the public, and ensured that there should be no rest for the wicked – for those regarded as evil and not like us.

Of course it is right that those children and young people should be given a second chance. But we may also require a change of attitude on the part of children and young people. Many of those whose parents have committed serious crimes are convinced that they must have inherited evil. And their lives continue to be wrecked because of it.

Neal's parents had been fighting each other for years. The husband hated his wife and her family hated him. It was a toss-up who killed who first and the five-year-old was trapped in the middle. In the event, his father found her in bed with another man, chased her into the garden and hit her across the head with an iron bar. She died instantly, in front of Neal, who was playing in the sandpit.

I have been involved with a score of such children over the years, where one parent has murdered the other, and there has always been a race for custody of the children afterwards. Invariably, the dead parent's family have won, and I use the word advisedly. Because it has still felt like a battle between the two sides, with the children as the spoils of war.

In all the turmoil, no one has thought about what the children might want for themselves. It has invariably come as a shock to discover that the children still harbour positive feelings towards the murderer, usually the father, and that they should have regular access to information about him, letter contact and visits if these can be arranged. But the children are confused about their own inheritance, and the whispers of friends and neighbours don't help. I have heard them myself, when I have been trying to carve out space for the children's wishes.

'That's the lad whose father killed his mother, you know,' said one. 'He was evil, that one. No child should have anything to do with him.'

'Poor little mite,' said her companion. 'God knows what'll become of him, when he grows up.'

'With all that stuff inside him,' said the first. 'Evil will out. Especially if you insist on him seeing his father in prison.'

I had no permission to work with Neal as a child, once the visits had been organised. But I saw him again when he was eighteen and living independently in a remote valley town. He went to his mother's grave once a year, alone, and had heard nothing from his father for ten years or more. Now he had been persuaded to seek criminal injuries compensation and I was asked to prepare a report. We went for a walk on the moor nearby, as we talked.

'You often come up here?' It was an observation rather than a question. Neal knew every stick and stone along the way.

'Each weekend. And most evenings in the summer.'

'That doesn't leave much time for anything else.'

'There isn't anything else.'

'No friends? No girlfriends?'

'I can't have any girlfriends.'

'Why not?'

'Because of what my father did, because he was evil . . . And he might have passed it on to me . . . I might kill someone too.'

Neal got his money. Ostensibly he had done well. He had a job and a flat. But emotionally he was still very damaged. The concept of evil lived on in his mind just as surely as it does in much of the public. The whispers were in his own head now.

'I know you might be right,' he said as we came down off the moors. 'It might not be true, what I feel.'

He stopped for a moment and stared out to the east, towards the prison where his father might still be held. There were tears in his eyes that might have been the wind, or the sadness untapped for over a decade.

'But I can't help it. Every time I get angry, I feel it inside me. The same evil as my father. Best to avoid getting close. Just in case.'

CHAPTER 20

OLIVER, JAMIE, LOC AND OFURE
GIVING CHILDREN THEIR AUTONOMY

The public buys its opinions as it buys its meat, or takes in its milk, on the principle that it is cheaper to do this than keep a cow. So it is, but the milk is more likely to be watered.

Samuel Butler, English novelist, in *The Note-books*, Ch. 17, 1912

Whatever age my patients are, therapy must start from them: what are the problems they are trying to deal with, and how can I help them to find their own solutions? The power to make decisions should lie in their own hands.

However, many children and young people do not have the autonomy to make such decisions. They are at the mercy of health managers, who decide what sort of problems we should be involved with and where to tackle them, and of adults in their family, who decide what those problems are about and how we should view them.

In other words, I must use my own power to carve out a space to see those children and to give them the help they need, for as long as is necessary, and wherever it is most likely to succeed. I must use my own autonomy to establish that of the child. Oliver, just six, and Jamie, seventeen, were two patients at the opposite ends of my age range. But the issue was the same.

I'd set off early to see Oliver's family, knowing the house would be hard to find, somewhere in the maze of lanes along the banks of the river. And my satnav wasn't working. This edge of the county was in my patch and I had assumed it was rich agricultural land, but no one had ever been referred to me from its villages and it was just as poor as the mining valleys on the other side.

By the time I crossed the town bridge, steam was rising from the river and frost hugged the throat of hedges. In each of the villages that I drove through, the women were herding their children towards the school gates. I stopped at one and asked the way, but the women shook their heads and waved me on. They were too preoccupied or didn't know the way. Or perhaps they just didn't like strangers.

In another ten miles, I arrived at an estate that might have been the one I was after. But it was full of run-down social housing, huddled round a circle of beaten grass, with a single crab-apple tree in the centre.

An old woman was washing pots in a kitchen at the far end, and there was no one else about but a postman; dressed in shorts, despite the cold. What he told me was not what I wanted to hear.

'Sorry. I'm new to this area. But I'm pretty sure the place you want is back along the river. The way you've come.'

He must have spotted my sagging shoulders. 'Don't worry, it's a nice day for it. There's a supermarket just by the bridge over the river. Ask in there and they'll put you right.'

The women were ambling back from school now, or standing around in groups with dogs and babies muffled against the wind. I found the supermarket all right but the young Bangladeshi girl behind the counter was about as helpful as the postman.

'I don't know any estate by that name round here. Wait a minute, I'll ask my dad.'

Her father emerged from the back, the remains of a sandwich in his hand. I told him about the directions the postman had given me.

'Know it well. Ten miles back along the river. You must have been close when you asked the postman. Students on work placement – they don't know their arse from their elbow!'

The remaining women turned at their gates and looked bemused as I passed by them for a third time. The postman had gone, but the old woman was still at the sink on the estate with the crab-apple tree in the middle. She came to the door when I knocked, drying her hands on a tea towel.

'That'll be Doctor Shooter, I said to Wyn when I first saw you. Come to see us about our Oliver. But he's gone off again. Don't know why.'

'So why didn't you knock on the window?' I tried to keep the frustration out of my voice.

'Because round here we believe in people finding things out for themselves.'

Typical of the area, I was to learn later. Especially from two elderly grandparents, born and bred there. They had looked after Oliver since he was two years old. When his parents split up, the father went to prison for beating up Oliver's mother, their daughter, and she disappeared on to the streets of London.

A boy like Oliver can spring up in the most unlikely places, even from a family living in a threadbare home like this. I had already seen him in his primary school, which fed a few pupils each year into the public schools in the next town. On scholarship, to make up for their lack of money. Oliver was bright enough, but he had big problems.

'I want you to colour in green everything on your card that begins with the letter "C". I'll be along to look at them in a bit.'

The form teacher had been playing for time while she dealt with one of the younger class members at the front, who was feeling sick. Oliver looked puzzled and went up to her, pointing at his card. He couldn't wait.

'What did I say?'

'Colour the "Cs" in green, miss.'

'Well, do it!'

Both Oliver and the teacher were running short of patience, and open warfare was imminent. It wouldn't be the first time. He was one of her brightest pupils but sometimes he seemed incapable of the simplest task, and he wasn't rewarding her with what she felt her teaching deserved. This was what had got him referred.

It was obvious what Oliver's problem was, when I called him over to where I was sitting at the back to observe what was going on. Amongst the pictures on the card was a cow. It might begin with the letter 'C', but Oliver knew that cows are not green. His classmates were following the teacher's instructions to the letter, literally. But Oliver was incapable of compromise.

He could not see round the problem or to ignore one criterion for the sake of another. He could not use his imagination to pass the test. And watching him over a longer period, even to a diagnostic sceptic like me, it seemed that Oliver lay somewhere on the higher functioning end of the autistic spectrum.

At the very least, he was going to need more careful handling of his needs in the classroom. The teachers would have to understand the particular cognitive deficits that an autistic child like Oliver was born with and appreciate that he was not being pig-headed. Deficits that they were just beginning to rub up against and which they would have to make allowances for and work around, despite his intelligence.

The grandparents would need to know about the social difficulties that would emerge as Oliver got older. The pedantry, the obscure interests and the fights with other village children, who were less bright but less rigid in their outlook. They would need to teach him strategies to deal with his frustration that relied more on practical results than vague moral values that would just seem unfair. And they would have to adjust their expectations for his future.

How could I help with all that if I hadn't been there, to see things at first hand? How could I help if I wasn't there to advise them when things got rough? I would need to travel along that road many more times, to work with the teachers who hadn't the time to come to a clinic, and a family that hadn't the means. To coordinate the work of all of them together, in their own environment, for as long as it took. Despite the warning of my health service manager, with her figures for the throughput of patients and how much each one cost.

Jamie was almost the opposite, but the principle was the same. His father rang me at home one weekend. I've no idea how he got my number.

'I need you to see my son.' His voice was imperious and his orders came out like bursts of gunfire. 'Up at the house. Next week would be good. After that I'm away on business.'

'What's wrong with him?'

'He won't do what I tell him to. Keeps saying he wants to go to art school. He's not very bright but he should go to university. I could arrange it. But he's in with the wrong crowd. Drugs. Drink. Staying out late. That sort of thing.'

'And is he happy with all that?'

'How can he be?'

'Lots of teenagers would be. Even if you aren't. How old is he?'

'Seventeen. Old enough to know better.' He was beginning to sound like my father.

'Well, tell Jamie he can make an appointment to see me if he wants to. At my office, in town. You can give him my number. And he can come on his own at first; it doesn't matter if you're away. I can see you later if necessary.'

'But what's your waiting list?'

'It depends on how urgent it is. In Jamie's case, about three weeks.'

'This is an emergency. I'll pay you to see him earlier. Here. At the weekend or in the evening. As much as it takes.'

'I don't do private practice.'

'The head of the health authority is a friend of mine.'

'Or give in to threats. Tell your son he can come to see me for free. On the NHS. Like everyone else.'

Rather to my surprise, Jamie rang up and booked an appointment. What's more, he turned up alone, on time and reasonably tidy. He had a letter from his father. I gave it back to him unopened.

'I don't need that. I've talked to your father on the phone. I know what he feels. Now tell me about things yourself.'

All of Jamie's surface anger was directed at his father. His own behaviour excited and scared him by turns and I'm sure he didn't really like his wild friends, the drink and the drugs, any more than his father did. He would have been happy to give them up if only they weren't such a useful weapon to beat his father with. He was far brighter than his father gave him credit for, of course, but pointed out that art school was what he wanted and no reflection of his IQ. Nevertheless, he would have been happy to discuss his future, if his father could do so with an open mind.

So far, so routine. Like many other adolescents with domineering parents, he was lashing out at his father's business, his money, and his lifestyle. It took me several sessions to get at the particular distress that I felt might lurk underneath. Where was the mother in this story? She was nowhere in my telephone conversation with Jamie's father, and nowhere in my first few sessions with Jamie. And yet she was everywhere, made all the more important by not being named.

I have learnt the hard way not to trick adolescents into revealing too much too early; that way you can end up with rich material and no patient. But it was frustrating going at Jamie's speed, and when the revelation came it was almost by accident.

Thinking it was way beyond his appointment time, the receptionist assumed I must have finished with my previous family and sent him up. Jamie arrived outside my door just as the family were leaving. Two children and their mother, her arm around them as she shepherded them away. He was quiet for some time after they had gone.

'You look sad, Jamie.'

He was on the edge of tears and I thought I had earned enough of his trust to find out why.

'Was it something about that family that upset you?'

'They looked so happy. The children, with their mother, I mean.'

'And you don't have a mother. To look after you.'

The lid was off now and the emotions swirled around like the evils escaping from Pandora's Box. His mother had grown tired of her husband's business life and the constant trips abroad. She'd had affairs, which Jamie knew more about than the adults guessed. His father had tried to buy her back with ever more expensive presents, holidays and a new kitchen, but this had only served to alienate her further. Eventually she left, when Jamie was twelve years old.

Jamie had sporadic contact with her, against his father's wishes, until she developed cancer. In his usual way, his father got her into the most advanced private treatment that money could buy, when all she wanted was love and comfort. She died and Jamie and his father were left to a life of friction. Now Jamie was planning to go too, like she had done five years before.

But just like Pandora's Box, curled up in the corner was a message of hope. Uncovering Jamie's feelings about his mother might release his attitude to his father. If I could do the same with his father, it might release his attitude to his son. Together they might grieve their loss and come closer in the process. And they did.

Jamie was able to face up to how angry he still was with his mother for leaving and how he had lumped that on to his father for making her do so. His father was able to say how scared he was by emotions, how he found money much safer and how he had tried to buy everything – his wife, her life, and now their son. And how angry he was that it had been rejected. Together they were free to mourn the mother's death; and how would they ever have found the space to do so, unless it had been created for them?

Two very different families, but the same principle: how to use my strength to protect and nourish the autonomy of the child or young person at the centre. And perhaps that is the very essence of therapy. How to hold the patient in the palm of our relationship, nudging and nurdling around the edges, while the patient finds their own feet. But there is something worrying me about all this.

Yes, I had to work against the will of some very powerful people. My manager could have pulled the plug on Oliver, insisted on my seeing him briefly in my clinic or referred him to a specialist team elsewhere. I must have been the only person that Jamie's father had not been able to buy. What a significant role model that was for both of them, even if it was scary to maintain at first.

But there are groups of children and young people who I have barely been able to help, where our power to make space for them is minimal. Not because of money, of managers with economics on their mind or parents trying to bully their way to what they want. But because of the attitudes of state and public and the way they conspire together to keep their problems out of sight.

Psychiatry has often called itself the Cinderella of the NHS, and child and adolescent services the Cinderella of psychiatry. But these groups of children and young people can't even get into the kitchen, let alone go to the ball, no matter how we might try to shoulder open the door. And there is no more desperate example than those trafficked halfway across the world to work in cannabis factories and prostitution in the UK and the rest of the West.

Loc lived in poverty on the streets of Hanoi, in Vietnam. His father was killed on a building site when he was five years old, leaving his mother to look after a family of seven. A man describing himself as an 'uncle' offered to take Loc off her hands and transport him to a better life in Europe; she leapt at the chance.

It took another five years to smuggle Loc through one of the trafficking routes. He tried to escape on many occasions but he was caught, beaten and threatened with reprisals. If you don't behave, we'll kill your brothers and sisters back home. He arrived in the UK in the back of a lorry from the continent when he was just ten.

Loc spent the next two years as an unpaid skivvy for a succession of eastern families in houses across London, maltreated and told that he had to work to pay back twenty-five thousand pounds of debt incurred in his passage. When he did manage to escape their clutches, he slept on park benches and ate scraps from rubbish bins. Until he was picked up by a Vietnamese couple who made promises but sold him into slavery again.

He was made to water the plants in a cannabis factory in Wales.

He sprayed them with toxic chemicals by day, was locked in at night, and was beaten when he got upset. The factory was raided by police as part of a major operation to curb triad crime, but the owners had been tipped off and fled. Loc was discovered alone and terrified. And was arrested.

Loc had little English, no one to vouch for him, and not even a translator to guide him through the maze of controls. He protested in vain that he had no idea of the countries he had been through, the names of his captors, or even the identity of the plants he was looking after. No one believed him and he was sent to a young offenders institution on remand.

There Loc festered until the authorities were persuaded that he was telling the truth and he was given asylum. He had been deeply traumatised by the way he had been handled by his traffickers, by those who had enslaved him in the UK and by the services who should have helped but had imprisoned him instead. One on top of the other. And he was frightened that this was not the end.

He was right. Before we could do any useful work with him, another 'relative' turned up at the local authority's door and took him away. We have not heard of him since.

Ofure Funmilaya's story was similarly brutal. She was born into another poor family, in war-torn northern Nigeria, where she was sold to local traffickers who prey on the villages with money and promises. Because she was a girl, Ofure would have had little value to anyone except through sexual exploitation. At thirteen, she was taken to Benin City, the capital of the trafficking trade, and spent the next two years being passed around the beds of prominent businessmen and politicians.

She was transported by boat to Morocco and then on to Europe by a larger gang, along with other West African girls. Many of them died around her, through physical beatings, rape, starvation, dehydration and disease. Barely alive herself, Ofure was escorted into Wales by people claiming to be family members, on a false passport. She was forced into cleaning a nail-bar during the day and prostitution on the streets of a Welsh city by night.

There was as little chance of escape for Ofure as there had been for Loc. Her papers were held by her captors, together with any money she earned to pay back the huge debts they said she owed them. She was submitted to strange religious rites and was convinced that her family back in Nigeria would die if she told anyone what she was going through.

Eventually, Ofure was spotted soliciting by a charity agency and taken into a foster placement. Psychological help was sought for her, but after only a few weeks she recontacted her traffickers with the mobile phone they had given her for the purpose. She disappeared from the foster home and has been seen on the streets of other big cities in England. No doubt being passed around again for sex, just as she was in Nigeria.

These are two equally terrible but all too typical stories. For one reason or another, we were prevented from giving any meaningful help to either Loc or Ofure, and I have had to piece together these accounts from the services' fleeting contact with them, from newspaper cuttings and from the stories of thousands of children and young people just like them. Much as their own lives were scattered across the trafficking routes of the world.

It will remain so as long as the public wish to remain unaware of the problem on their own streets, border controls are both prejudiced and inefficient, governments have little investment in changing the situation, and services are powerless to help. More than that, they represent the extreme end of a whole spectrum of children and young people whose problems are felt to be too difficult to reach.

I had to work hard for the needs of Oliver and Jamie to be recognised, and to work with them in the way that they needed in the teeth of professional and parental threats. But it was just about possible for someone with the clout to do so and the determination not to be bought off. For those on the margin of the margins there is as yet much less chance of such an autonomy.

As will be evident by now, I am struck by the meaning of names, especially by those that are about as inappropriate as it could get.

Loc means good luck in Vietnamese; Ofure means peace in her local Nigerian tongue. For them there was no good luck and no peace. And unlike Cinderella, no happy-ever-after.

CHAPTER 21

LITTLE PEETY
SEEING THE PROBLEM FROM ALL SIDES

Being in a band is always a compromise. Provided that the balance is good,
what you lose in compromise, you gain by collaboration.

Mike Rutherford: Guitarist, singer, songwriter.

Founder member of Genesis

Most of the time I was a lone wolf, prowling around my patch, doing
things the way I thought they ought to be done. The advantage was
that I could be quite experimental, even iconoclastic, ignoring the
rules for the patient's benefit. The disadvantage was that I was always
seeing the problem from my point of view. Try as I might to put the
patient first, I got in the way at times, making the problem more
obscure, not less.

There are many ways of guarding against this and one is supervision. I reached for a supervisor whenever I was confronted by a
difficult patient, in a difficult situation, with a problem that threatened to overwhelm me. Not because I wasn't skilful enough to
handle it, but because it was so close to my own experience that
I might lose my sense of perspective.

'Michael,' said my supervisor one day, peering over her half-moon
glasses. 'I think you're trying to treat your mother.'

My patient's mother was a cut-glass lady with a blue-rinsed perm and a faintly disapproving air. My supervisor was right. The patient's mother looked exactly like my own mother, she behaved like my mother, and I was doing as badly as I did with her.

Another was group work. I was trained in a hospital that frowned on anything secretive. Each day on the acute wards began with a group session for the patients; there were groups for the ward staff later, to work out what happened in the patient groups; and all the medics were gathered together every Friday morning for groups of their own. I learnt pretty quickly that you could say anything in those groups. On good days, my words were an inspiration; on bad days, they sank to the floor. From where they stared up at me with baleful eyes, like fish.

While I had mixed feelings about their value, I have often used groups since. I ran groups on the adolescent unit and down in the outpatient clinic. I ran groups in the hospital ward and in social services homes. I ran them in schools. Groups of young people, all with their own problems, who could swap insights into each other's lives and ideas about what might work and what would not. And sometimes the young people found a better solution for the distress of one of their members, like Becky.

But by far the best guardian of objectivity is the multi-disciplinary team. Colleagues from many different walks of professional life – doctors, nurses, psychologists, occupational therapists, physiotherapists, teachers, social workers and the rest – working together in a hospital or clinic, can talk to each other about their patients and exchange views on an equal level.

They have almost become a mantra for practice these days, but there are still some who don't like them, who pretend to be part of them but who are just as controlling at the centre. And it's the most autocratic of consultants who fear them most. I met one in the supermarket.

Now there are fellow consultants with whom I would happily spend an hour, talking tactics and grumbling about the state of the nation. And there are others who I would try to avoid if I saw them out shopping. This one caught me hiding from him behind a pyramid of lager.

'Mike, you work in teams, don't you?' His tone was friendly enough, but he was clearly out to challenge our way of working.

'Yep, same as you. Lots of different people, as well as psychiatrists like you and me.'

'But you have a system of open referral?'

'Right again. Referrals come in to the team. We share them out on numbers, special interests and so on. It doesn't have to be me who sees them first.'

'But that can't be safe.'

'Why not? I trust everybody and we all trust each other. We meet every week to discuss what we're doing and we can always call on each other in between, if we want advice. And right now we have no waiting list. How long is yours?'

'Three months, actually, but that's beside the point. Supposing one of the non-doctors misses a brain tumour in someone referred because of their behaviour.'

'The waiting list isn't beside the point. Anything could happen in those three months. And how many brain tumours have you picked up, as a doctor?'

'None. But it might happen. How many have your team picked up?'

'One. And you know what? It was a psychologist who first spotted it. Not a doctor.'

The consultant left for the check-out, looking disgruntled. And I went home, thinking about Little Peety and his pituitary tumour. And about how the views of the multi-disciplinary team had helped at every stage of his illness.

The symptoms first. Peter was his real name and he was aged six. He had been referred to our team by his GP with a whole array of background problems. Preliminary investigation had shown up nothing of importance, so the only explanation, the GP thought, was a behavioural reaction; and there was plenty to react to in Peter's family.

His father had been off work with depression since the death of his own mother, with whom he had a very tempestuous relationship and who had left him full of guilt. Peter's mother was holding everything together as best she could. She had always had an anxious personality, but now her worries were flowing over in all directions; and understandably so. Peter's older brother seemed to have escaped the problems scot-free, leaving Peter to carry them on his fragile shoulders. In the middle of it all, the father had developed secondary diabetes.

I'm not sure at which point he had become Little Peety, but the nickname suited him. His parents said he had always been small for his age, but even at six he seemed tiny. He was miserable and sleepy a lot of the time, which the family put down to the worries that kept him awake. And he had started to complain about headaches and blurred vision.

'I can't see what's going on,' he said, and the metaphor seemed striking.

A teacher at his primary school had called in his mother to suggest he have an eye test. 'He doesn't seem to cotton on to the things I write on the blackboard. But maybe that's just a lack of concentration. He's so sleepy . . .'

The family was seen by a psychologist on the team and he used his gentle skills to tease out all the issues they were struggling with and put them together again in terms of Little Peety's behaviour. The family were quite prepared to believe that their youngest son was expressing the unhappiness for all of them. That this was the role he had been given in life. I think that many family orientated consultants would have thought so too and settled down to relieve him of the role, but to my colleague it didn't seem to fit.

He got me to see the family too and I shared his suspicion. The family dynamics were just not enough to account for his symptoms. With their permission, we presented them to the multi-disciplinary team, to get their all-round perspective. And they agreed as well. It was like putting together a jigsaw of very familiar pieces, only to find it didn't quite look the same as the picture on the box.

We told the family that we had all come to the same conclusion. Leaving aside the family problems, there was something physical going on that might be causing Little Peety's behaviour. We should refer him to the paediatricians for their opinion. The family respected the weight of our argument and agreed.

This was one of those occasions when the mutual respect built up by years of liaison between the two teams paid dividends. The paediatricians were as prepared to act on our suspicions as we had always been to work with their patients. An eye test showed that there was an increased pressure inside Little Peety's skull, which could have caused his headaches, and he was just beginning to lose some of his peripheral vision.

Blood tests revealed a complicated mix of abnormal levels of hormones from his adrenal and thyroid glands, and of those responsible for growth and sleep pattern. In short, the only possible explanation that would fit all this was a disturbance of 'the master gland' that controls all the body's hormonal functions and is locally invasive in the brain. They ordered CT and MRI scans and at length they found it. Little Peety had a pituitary tumour.

And so to the diagnosis, explaining it to the family, and working with the consequences. The pituitary is a tiny, pea-sized body, sitting in a depression in the sphenoid bone at the base of the brain. It may be small, but it is vital. From it come a range of hormones that act directly on the body, and others that stimulate other organs to produce their own hormones in turn. Tumours of the pituitary are not common and usually occur in the young, like Little Peety. The vast majority are benign and will not spread to other parts, but they are a big problem nevertheless.

They may either over- or under-secrete their hormones, which would account for his complicated pattern of behaviour. And they pile up in a confined space, just below the optic nerve which carries information to and from the eyes, hence his headaches and sight loss. Little Peety and his family understood the implications, and it presented them with huge challenges.

In the hospital, they would be faced with a formidable range of experts: an endocrinologist, expert in hormones; a neurologist, expert in diseases of the nervous system; a neurosurgeon, expert in operations on the brain; an oncologist, expert in cancers; and specialist nurses. All of them with high status and not always able to bring themselves down to the level of a six-year-old child. They would need to explain things in language that a child would understand, and to see what they proposed from a child's point of view.

One of the functions of non-medical members of our team was to sit alongside them and ask the doctors to rephrase things that I might have accepted without a second thought, and the family would have been too scared to challenge. And a team that was used to individual and family dynamics could also work with the sort of impact that a diagnosis would have on a child, his parents and his siblings.

Little Peety's perception of himself was intimately bound up with his brain. The first drawing that he produced for one of the team was a big black spider eating away at the base of his skull. It was destroying not just tissue but his very being. The emotional reaction to the news of his tumour was all but overwhelming to his and his family's life.

It so confirmed the sick role that Little Peety already had in the family that it was difficult for him to be positive about anything. His mother became even more anxious, to the point where it began to interfere with her ability to hear what was necessary. Her husband sank into his depressive position and absented himself even further from any decision-making. The well brother became peripheral to events. It was proof of our assertion that all diseases are psychosomatic. In the sense that emotional disorders have physical repercussions; physical disorders have huge emotional components. We had to work hard before they were in any position to think about the treatment.

The implications were bigger than anything the surgeons might imagine. To put it bluntly, surgery would entail an endoscopic transphenoidal resectomy, a bit of magical jargon which they produced like a rabbit from a hat. A thin tube would be manoeuvred up Little

Peety's nose towards his pituitary, with a camera at the end for the surgeon to see where he was going. The aim would be to cut out as much of the gland as necessary, followed by radiotherapy. It was almost certain to be successful in someone of Peety's age, they said. But what on earth would he make of that?

All sorts of questions tumbled over themselves in his six-year-old head. He was well aware of the schoolchild's warning that the surest way to kill yourself is to stick a pencil up your nose and bang your head on the table. Wasn't the surgery that they were proposing to do just the same? The doctors had told him that the progress of his tumour meant that he would almost certainly go blind if he didn't have the operation, but they had also told him that the optic nerve was so close to where they were going to do the cutting. So might he not wake up blind anyway? On the one hand, the treatment sounded horrific; on the other, was it really necessary at all? Little Peety had the typical magical thinking of a child of his age. *If I ignore it, it will go away.*

With the help of the team, consent was eventually given by Peety and his family; or rather Peety and his mother. His father said nothing and the brother was nowhere to be seen. But that wasn't nearly the end of the story. Peety needed extensive follow-up: scans to make sure the tumour was not recurring, replacement of the lost hormones and regular blood tests to check their levels. The impact on the family of his struggle back to health needed just as much work, long after the surgeons had done their job and moved on.

And we could have predicted what would be our final involvement. Like so many young people with a chronic condition, Peety chose to fight his adolescent battles with the weapon nearest to hand and most calculated to make the adults nervous: by messing around with his follow-up treatment, just like Will and his nasogastric tube. Once again, the task was to help him find a safer way of showing his feelings, and I doubt whether the paediatricians in their clinics, which had changed hands many times since the operation, were even aware of it.

Just one case, but it could have been hundreds of others. A

physical disorder, but it could have been countless families with emotional problems. And all of them needing the all-round vision of a multi-disciplinary team to help them through the tangle of issues that might have defeated a single therapist, consultant or not.

If they are so vital a part of therapy, and so popular with patients, why are such teams still under attack? As long as the person they are seeing is warm, empathic and readily accessible, the children, young people and their families couldn't care a toss who they are and what hat they're wearing. We've reached the ridiculous point where cash-strapped managers are investing what little they have in traditional, consultant-based psychiatric clinics with specialised services and long waiting lists, while successive inquiries show that the patients want just the opposite.

'Why did you ring our helpline?' I asked a young person who had contacted one of the voluntary sector organisations for whom I was doing some work. It had been besieged with calls from children and parents as soon as it was set up.

This fifteen-year-old had told me about an awful family background. Her mother had died when she was little and her father had brought in a whole succession of women in her place. Not quite the wicked step-mother, and she was hardly Snow White, but near enough. They didn't like her and she didn't like them. The brother she loved had reacted so badly to his father's new partners that he had been sent to live with their maternal grandmother. And she was alone.

'Because I couldn't get help from anywhere else,' she said. 'Are you surprised?'

'Not much, but I'm interested all the same. What about your local children's mental health service? I know there's one in your area.'

She snorted down the phone with a sort of strangled laugh. I could almost picture her on the other end, her eyes rolling heavenward in disgust.

'Some of the team are all right. My friend got to see their psychologist. She was lovely.'

'Why couldn't you?'

'Because they said I had to see someone called the consultant first, a psychiatrist, and that could take ages.'

'What about your friend?'

'She cut her wrists so it all got speeded up. I don't want to do that. And I haven't got another diagnosis to get me in.'

'How about the GP? And the counsellor in school?'

'They just referred me to the consultant. Same thing. Round and round in circles.'

She was like so many other children, young people and parents, enmeshed in the red tape of formal attitudes, who seek help in their desperation from the voluntary sector. She took me back to that conversation at the beginning of the chapter, to that old-style consultant with his three-month waiting list and a team he didn't trust.

Of course there can be problems with the multi-disciplinary way of working. They pride themselves on their skill-mix, but the skills have to be there in the first place. There is always the danger that too many cooks will spoil the broth and no one feels able to make the final decision. Particularly if it is risky. And the members of the team do not always trust each other enough to share the responsibility for what happens. But the real problem is still one of attitude.

I went to the government to discuss psychiatry's problems in recruitment. The answer, I suggested, was the multi-disciplinary team. Consultant psychiatrists might still see the patients with the most complicated problems, but they should be no more powerful than other members of the team, who could receive direct requests for help and share them amongst themselves. Morally that would be right, practically it would relieve psychiatrists of the numbers, and it would increase the speed with which patients could be seen. Everyone would be a winner.

'That's a good idea,' said the senior civil servant I was talking to. 'We'll call it New Ways of Working.'

Actually, it had been around for a long time where I was working with children and their families, but we wrote up the idea and

toured the country to publicise it. Patients loved it, but we ran into
a storm of protest from psychiatry. Junior psychiatrists thought we
were selling off the family silver before they could get their hands
on it. And the senior psychiatrists who shouted loudest were those
who had grumbled most about their workload.

Not my problem, I can hear the children and families say. But
it is if they are trapped in the Catch 22 of traditional ways of doing
things. Like that fifteen-year-old on the helpline, unable to see
anyone for help. Anyone, no matter what they might be called.

CHAPTER 22

MAX AND LAURA
CHILDREN AND LOSS

No defeat is made up entirely of defeat – since
the world it opens is always a place
> *formerly*
>> *unsuspected.*

William Carlos Williams: *The Descent*

No matter how much you learn about therapy, no matter how well you plan what you're going to do, it's sometimes serendipity that counts. The off-chance. And you'd better grab it when it comes.

Our outpatient clinic had a cat. I've no idea where it came from, but it was in reception one morning and there it stayed. The secretaries fed it when they arrived first thing, and again before they left at night. In return, it allowed itself to be stroked by the children, calmed them down and kept them occupied while they were waiting to be seen.

Max was a six-year-old lad who came to me from his school, because he had been hiding under the desk and biting the teacher's ankle as she passed. That would get you referred pretty quickly to any service. He was sitting in the waiting area with his mother and twelve-year-old sister, Laura. The mother looked unhappy and distracted, and the children were playing with the cat.

I had spoken to the school beforehand, and they filled me in with what they knew about the background story. Several months ago, the father had suffered a fatal accident. He was a born-again biker and had wrapped himself around a tree on a country road that was notorious for similar deaths. He survived for a while in intensive care but he never regained consciousness. His wife had sat patiently beside his bed throughout, but he was so mutilated that they decided the children should not see him. He died three days later.

The children came up to my room chattering excitedly about the cat, their mother following heavily behind.

'Have you got a cat too, at home?'

'Yes. No. We had one,' said Max.

'He means our cat got run over,' added Laura.

'That's very sad. What was his name?'

'Sammy,' they answered together.

A light went on inside my head, but there was no need to rush it.

'What kind of cat was Sammy?'

'He was a ginger nut.'

'They're mostly males, ginger cats.'

There was a pause. It was time to go for broke or the chance would be lost.

'Was Sammy killed straight away?'

Laura looked too sad to speak, but Max was off and running.

'No. He was badly injured, though. Our neighbour found him and Mummy took him to see the vet.'

'And did Sammy die there?'

'I think so.' His mother nodded, sitting quietly at the side.

'Did you manage to see him before he died?'

Another, longer silence. I was beginning to put into words what they were all feeling now.

'We couldn't. The vet had already helped him die,' said Laura. She was crying. 'To stop him suffering.'

'That's a bit like what happened to your father, isn't it? He got badly injured and had to go to hospital too.'

'He died,' said Max, taking over from his sister.

'And you weren't able to see him, before he died. Just like Sammy.'

'They wouldn't let us.'

'I expect they thought it would upset you too much. They were trying to protect you. So you could remember your father as he was, before the accident.' Now the children were nodding too.

'Were there things you would have said to him, if you had seen him? To say goodbye?'

'I wanted to ask him what it felt like on a bike. To go so fast,' said Max.

'I wanted to tell him about my report,' said Laura. 'I came top.'

I asked them if they would like to say those things now, if we pretended, and they jumped at the chance. Their mother said nothing, and I took it to be her agreement. So we put two chairs together like a hospital bed and I lay on them. The children sat on either side and chattered away about things at home and school and about the pipes and charts and machines in the hospital ward. I answered as best as I could, in the way that I thought their father would have done, if he had been able.

They fell silent at last and I was wondering how to bring it to a close, when their mother came forward from where she'd been watching at the back of the room. She took my arm, the tears running down her face.

'I never found out . . . whether you knew . . . that I loved you.'

The children hugged her. She tried to explain why she had made the decision, because she thought it would be for the best. She knew now that it was a mistake, that it had stifled the children's grief and her own in the process. Max had been angry with her for doing so but couldn't tell her because everyone was so upset; so he had directed it at the teachers instead. And no doubt he was as confused about why he did it as they all were.

It didn't matter now. They were all released and could begin to grieve the father's death together. The children were able to tell their mother how it had felt, knowing that their father was seriously injured but excluded from what was happening. And their mother was able to tell them how difficult it was for her, sitting with him in hospital while the children were with friends and neighbours at home. They asked her about intensive care, she told them all about it as far as she could, and I filled in the details about equipment and routines. They laughed and cried about their memories of their father and family life. And Max no longer had to show his anger by biting the teacher's ankles at school.

I stayed involved with them until I was sure that they didn't need me any longer; as an interpreter, a mediator, an observer, whatever roles I had performed. It took several weeks of intense and sometimes harrowing effort to help them share their grief, but that is a very short time compared to the life of unresolved friction that they might have had to endure without it.

This story illustrates everything I have come to believe about children and loss and how to handle their bereavement. The theories culled from the work of experts, the experience from my own; the trust that has to be built up before many patients are able to say how they feel; and the happy accidents that offer an immediate opportunity for others, if you are prepared to grab them. Like that cat in reception. But it was a tough journey and it had begun in Duluth, Minnesota.

Duluth is a one-moose town. Tucked under the Canadian border, at the extreme western end of Lake Superior, it was once the home of more dollar millionaires per head of population than any other place in the USA. It was built on iron ore, shipping it out through the Great Lakes to foundries and car-makers and shipwrights all over the world. Now it squats at the centre of the continent, rusting and redundant, like the iron it once helped to produce.

I had gone to Duluth for two reasons. To begin with, it was hosting the annual conference of an association devoted to death: educators and counsellors, researching and practising on grief-stricken families. Ordinary death, if there is such a thing, and sometimes in the most horrendous situations. When one partner had murdered the other, when a grandfather had backed over his grandson on the way to work, when a depressed mother had driven off the freeway and drowned herself and her baby.

My managers couldn't make up their minds whether bereavement was part of their remit, or what we should be doing if it was. So they sent me to the conference to find out. I'm sure it must have been a relief for the delegates to get away for a while, but they were happy to share their expertise and there was a lot of it about.

And I was also there to see Robert Coles. I had read a whole library of books by the early pioneers in bereavement work, but I still wasn't sure what I was supposed to say to a young child facing up to death, to the loss of a parent, a sibling, or himself. Then I came across Coles's books, sitting incongruously in a junk shop, filled with the lessons he had picked up in a lifetime of listening to children and young people where they lived. Back-street kids in Belfast; Cambodian boy-soldiers, slaughtering their families to order with machetes; rich kids with a terminal illness that money couldn't cure; and ordinarily bereaved children everywhere. He was giving the opening speech.

He arrived late. A tiny man in a scruffy anorak and sneakers who could barely see over the lectern. I thought it was a janitor come to tell us he was stuck somewhere, but it was Coles himself, Professor at Harvard University, and for an hour and a half he held us spell-bound. I took him for coffee afterwards and asked him about his life, how he had made the choice between poetry and psychiatry, and what I ought to do about my own career.

When Coles was a medical trainee, he had been writing a part-time thesis on the work of William Carlos Williams, who just happened to be my own favourite poet. He went to see Williams, himself a doctor–poet, whose father and grandfather had been doctors too. Between the three of them, they had served the poor people of Rutherford, New Jersey, for over a third of the life of the American nation. Williams met him on the doorstep and thrust a doctor's bag into his hands. 'Follow me.'

For three days, they tramped up and down the tenement blocks, talking about life and death and poetry as they went. And each evening they finished up with an old lady in an attic room. She was dying, he said, but she and Williams seemed to have a relationship of loving hostility. On the last night, he finished examining her and packed his instruments in their case.

'Well, old lady,' he said at the door. 'I don't expect to see you again.'

'Don't be so sure, Williams,' she replied. 'I'm going where you're going. Straight to hell.'

They could hear her cackling after them as they went down the stairs. 'Fuck you, Williams! Fuck you, Coles!'

'At that point,' said Coles. 'I knew I wanted to be a psychiatrist.'

I wish I could say that I had been struck by a vision on the road to my own Damascus, but I have remembered what Coles taught me about children and bereavement all my clinical life. Listen to what the children say, not what adults say about them. The course of bereavement is not as smooth as the books suggest; it may not be your fault if it feels all wrong. Be open to surprises and use them when they come. And above all, he confirmed what I have always believed, with all my patients, not just in bereavement: follow what your gut tells you, not your head.

When we talk about bereavement, we usually mean death; but there are many other losses in children's lives. Some of them could be a training ground, like the death of Sammy. We should be careful not to underestimate children's grief about the loss of a pet. Let them talk openly about it and have a proper burial ceremony. The bottom of my own garden is a cemetery to dead cats and dogs and white mice.

Some losses are even more complicated for children than death, like divorce, where the dead body will not lie down and go away and relationships must be maintained in the midst of anger and guilt and parental opposition. And remember, magically thinking young children may believe they've caused it, especially if they've been dragged into the arguments on one side or the other. For adolescents, the loss of a girlfriend or a boyfriend can be cataclysmic; right at that moment there just aren't any more fish in the sea, whatever you say to comfort them.

Many families will be dealing with multiple losses, either because one bereavement is churning up the unresolved feelings from an earlier one, or because these losses coincide. Like the mother and her daughter, Philippa (Pip for short), who I saw in the middle of their mutual frustration.

'I've no idea what's going on with her,' said the mother. She was separated from Pip's father, had custody of Pip and her younger sister, and was trying to cooperate with the divorce court's ruling about contact and the demands of a full-time job. All at the same time.

'Here I am, trying to cope with everything at once. You'd think she would give me a bit of a hand sometimes. But all she does is moon around the place as if she's got the cares of the world on her shoulders.'

'Perhaps she has,' I replied. Pip said nothing. She wasn't going to give me a bit of a hand either.

I saw her for a session by herself, away from the pressures that her mother was feeling and that she was anxious to share with her daughter. Pip was unhappy about her parents' divorce, but had weighed up the pros and cons in quite a mature way. Life had not been good for a couple of years beforehand and at least she was relieved of the arguments that had raged over the children's heads.

'And we see him pretty regularly. He's got a new girlfriend now. She's nice; I like her. I can talk to her about things I can't share with my mother. Not at the moment, anyway. She's got too much on her mind.'

'And what sort of things would they be?'

Pip thought for a moment, while she wondered whether she could trust me too.

'My boyfriend. Or my ex-boyfriend. He's gone off with another girl.' She looked thoroughly miserable.

'Was that sudden? How long had you been going out together?'

'A year. He wanted sex, but I wouldn't give it to him. Lots of girls my age would. But I thought it was wrong.'

'And the other girl jumped in?'

'Yeah. Jump's the right word, I suppose.' She still had a wry self-confidence somewhere inside. More than her mother, perhaps.

'I think you should risk talking about things. Both of you are going through a separation, and you need to share how it feels. You losing your boyfriend; your mother losing your father. Would you like me to suggest it to her for you?'

I did so, and they talked together about their losses. It was difficult, but they managed it openly. And having found a mutual appreciation of their unhappiness, they were able to share the everyday tasks of running the family too.

Deaths may be sudden and unexpected, or prolonged and give opportunities for things to be said and done before they happen. The father of Max and Laura never regained consciousness, but he lived on for three days and the children would happily have talked to him. Who knows whether he would have heard them or not. The important thing is that they should have been allowed to say them. And while we're in intensive care, my experience is that children are more curious than frightened by what they see there. They will want to know what the tubes are for and where they're going. It's the adults who are more likely to be squeamish.

Once the death is anticipated or has occurred, the experts follow it with the stages of grieving: a linear progression from shock to acceptance. But that is far too ordered. The emotions are much more like a washing machine, slopping around in circles, and some of them can be very disturbing. Max was clearly angry – angry at his father for dying, angry at his mother for stopping him seeing him, angry at the hospital, angry at the world. Unfair, you say, but death never seems fair to a child. We need to give them an open outlet for those feelings, not try to dampen them down, or substitute targets like teachers will feel their bite.

At the other end, there is no final resolution to grief. Yes, we may find a way of coming to terms with what has happened, sufficiently to get back to work, and children are quicker at it than adults. I have known them be back at school within days of a death, playing with their peers and welcoming the routine it gives them, whilst parents are left floundering amongst the emotional chaos at home. But important anniversaries like Christmas and birthdays are quite natural occasions for re-grieving, long after the event; and it may be a chance sight, sound or smell that ambushes us when we least expect it.

Some of the phenomena involved can be scary. I'm not at all surprised that Max and Laura took so readily to the role play in my room. It was real enough to carry their emotions at the time but artificial enough to leave behind afterwards, and they were happy with the distinction. Many children still talk to their dead parent at nights, when they miss them most. They may even see them and not be disturbed by the experience, while adults would feel that they were going mad and keep it secret. They would not be, and I think it would actually be stranger if all our senses of someone with whom we have lived for years were cut dead with their loss. Just ask that lady in my Bene't Street clinic, cuddling her husband's jacket in bed at night.

Families, as I've said many times before, have their own way of doing things, handed down unchanged through the generations. And nothing is more idiosyncratic than the amount they are prepared to share with their children in a crisis like bereavement.

Such sharing can mean many things. Sharing the emotions of grief with your children rather than trying to be strong, like the mother of Max and Laura, and sharing the rituals of grief. Asking if they would like to go to a funeral or cremation, and honouring their wish. Even if they blurt out the most innocent questions at impossible moments and cry when everyone else is trying not to get upset.

'There, I told you,' said one of a little lad's aunts at a funeral I went to recently. 'You should never bring a child to a funeral like this. He's only going to weep and wail.' As if that isn't exactly what funerals are for.

It also means sharing information. Telling the children what's going on, even if you don't fully understand it yourself. Repeating the explanation, even if you've given it a hundred times before. Expressing it in language that a child of that age might use and not resorting to vague euphemisms that cause confusions in the child's mind.

'Where's Grandad going?' said the same young lad as the coffin was lowered into the ground.

'He's gone on a long sleep,' said his father. Later he might wonder why his son wouldn't go to bed at nights. The last time his grandad had gone to bed, they put him in a box and buried him. Better to stay awake as long as he could.

And finally, bereavement can strike at the most surprising moment, at events that are supposed to be times of rejoicing, not loss. Like pregnancy and childbirth. And like the young couple I saw in my clinic at the request of the obstetricians, who already had a five-year-old son but had had a stillbirth after years of trying for another.

Even normal childbirth can be a loss for the older sibling. They may feel sidelined by the little bundle of joy that their parents have brought back from the hospital and over which everyone is making such a fuss. Which is allowed up at all hours, while they have to go to bed. And which is cuddled when it makes a noise, while they are told to shut up. Their status is threatened; they no longer have their parents' undivided attention and life will never be the same again.

The young couple had recognised the danger. They had included their five-year-old in what was happening, let him stroke his mother's swelling belly, put his ear to it and feel the baby kicking in response. He helped prepare its room, was promised that he could join in looking after it when it arrived, and that he would be given special privileges to show how much older and more responsible he was. It was going to be his baby too and he could be as proud of it as they were.

The stillbirth was a bereavement for all of them, and the couple struggled to describe it in my clinic. It was the anniversary of the baby's death and the emotions were as raw as if it had only just happened. Their son was at school. He was six now and doing well in year one.

'We were so happy,' said the mother. 'I wasn't really prepared for the sickness and how uncomfortable I was. It was so hot. But I didn't really mind. I was having another baby and that's all that mattered. To any of us.'

Her husband took her hand while she drank a glass of water and I waited for her to go on.

'And then?'

'Then it stopped. Right at the end. I only had a few weeks to go and she stopped kicking. She used to kick him in the back and wake him up. Then one night she didn't do it and we slept right through . . .'

She sobbed for a while in her husband's arms and I refilled her glass. It was some time before they were able to tell me more. About their panic visit to the GP, the telephone calls and the ambulance journey to the hospital.

'I knew. Everyone rushing around and no one looking me in the eye. My baby had died inside me.'

'You said she. Was your baby a girl?'

'Yes.'

'And how was your son in the middle of all that? How did he cope with losing his little sister?'

Things had altered since we had campaigned for a change in the way stillbirths were swept under the green sheets and out of sight. They had all been encouraged to hold her, to talk to her, take photographs of her, give her a proper burial, and give her a name. Cerys. And their son had been included all the way through.

I only needed one session with him, at home, just to check. He told me how frightened he'd been at the time. He didn't know what was happening at first, then he thought his mother might die too. And perhaps it was his fault. The night before it had happened, he had got into trouble for prodding his sister too hard and he'd run off to his room and wished she'd never existed.

But he'd been reassured. Cerys still existed. She was part of the family and would always be his sister, even though she was dead. He showed me her photographs and the memory box he had helped to collect with his parents. A lock of her hair, the wristband she'd worn in hospital, and part of a mobile he'd bought with his pocket money for her cot.

He had been overwhelmed by it all at the time, but his parents had helped him despite their own grief. And the routine of school had helped. He understood why his parents should be upset on the anniversary of Cerys's death, and perhaps they would be every year. But he was doing his best to help them too.

It was a lesson in how children can sometimes comfort the adults, like Max and Laura helping their mother to share her grief. And the eight-year-old lad I saw with his mother, whose own mother had died and who was desperately trying to smooth over their unhappiness. I have said how important it is that we talk to children in language that they will understand, but they are capable of a surprising metaphor, which is even more exact than words.

He picked up a snow globe from the toy box in my room and shook it. The snow swirled around so that it was impossible to see the village inside it. Then it settled and the globe was clear.

'Look,' said his mother. 'Everything's back to normal.'

'No, it isn't,' said her son. 'The snowflakes have all come down in a different place. It's not the same as before. But it will still be all right.'

CHAPTER 23

QUEENIE AND LEANNE
CYCLES OF HARM

The thing that hath been, it is that which shall be; and that which is done is that which shall be done: and there is no new thing under the sun.

Ecclesiastes 1: 9

I was sitting in my clinic, waiting for a young child and her teenage mother, Queenie. Her name rang a bell.

The few details she had given my secretary on the phone didn't much help. 'Just tell him he's in for a big surprise,' she'd said. It must mean I'd seen her before somewhere, but try as I might I couldn't place her. Except for a dim memory of another young woman, with a girl of four, who I had gone to see on the estate where they lived. A little girl who was running rings around all the adults at home and in nursery school, and who she affectionately called 'my little queen'.

Whoever she was, she was late. I began to think back to some of the other patients who had come to see me over and over again. Or who had passed on their problems to the next generation for them to come in their turn. Cycles of harm, in individuals and in families. And it had begun in my first six-month attachment, in the early days of my psychiatric training.

My consultant was planning my future. 'You can either stick with me for another six months, or you can move on.'

'I'll stick with you.'

'Good. I hoped you would say that.'

And I hoped it was because he thought I was so good that he wanted to hold on to me for as long as possible. But it wasn't.

'If you left now, you'd get the wrong picture. Patients develop a mental illness, they come into hospital, you treat them, and they are cured. Never to be seen again.'

I wasn't that naive, but I understood his point.

'Stay another six months and you'll see them all come back again. Stay forever, like me, and you'll see the cycles get shorter and shorter. Until it becomes a way of life.'

It was possibly one of the most depressing things anyone has said to me, and he was a depressed man. Nearing the end of his career, young hopes long since gone, burnt out by sitting in his clinic day after day like Canute, trying to keep the tide of mental illness at bay.

And it was only half true. Many psychiatric conditions are not curable, in the way that a broken leg can be mended or an infection wiped clean with antibiotics. Many of them are recurrent, my own depressive disorder included, and we have to treat each episode anew. Some of them have an almost continual effect on their sufferer's life. But that is no different from a physical disease like diabetes and no more cause for his pessimism.

The watchword now is recovery. How can we space out the episodes and shorten each one when they occur? What new treatments can we find to lessen the effects of mental illness, even if we can't eradicate the cause? How can we help someone to spot the earliest signs of relapse and head off the full-blown episode at the pass? And how can we ensure that every patient makes the best use of life in between, despite the illness?

Adult psychiatry has done much to answer those questions in research, in training and in patient education, but I left to work with children, young people and their families. Where early intervention could make an even greater difference to people's lives; or so I thought. Yet the same negativity exists here. The assumption that this family is disordered because the generation before it was disordered and the generation afterwards will be too. What will be, will be. Our job is to guard against the worst of the consequences.

I looked at my watch again. Queenie was getting even later. I wandered around the waiting area, sympathised with a muffled young lad sitting outside the dentist's door, and made myself another cup of coffee. Then got back to thinking.

Only a few weeks ago, I had been at a child protection meeting. I knew everybody around the table except one, the recently appointed director of a nearby social services. He was tall, urbane and very smart. And I recognised him from somewhere in my past. He came up to me when the meeting closed.

'The last time we met was in court,' he said, seeing the look of vague recognition on my face. 'I was the social worker for a little girl who had been neglected by her mother. The mother had been in our care in her own childhood, and now she was shacked up with a Schedule One offender.'

The pieces were assembling in my head. A child of five or six, with strawberry blonde hair done up with pink ribbon, who I had talked to at a neutral venue. And her mother in black tights and her hair in bunches, hunched angrily in the back of the courtroom. Both of them with bad teeth.

'You were a young child psychiatrist and our expert witness. We took her into care, largely on your recommendation. And guess what?'

A feeling of inevitability had come over me like a wet blanket.

'I'm the director now and that little girl is sixteen. And we've just taken her baby into care too. You know what they say, there's nothing new under the sun.'

He was cheerful enough and I'm sure his service is stretched to the limit, rescuing children from abuse of one sort or another. But it was the pessimism inherent in what he said that grated. The cycles of harm that my first consultant had hinted at all those years ago, and was somehow still the rule in families. And that I had become complicit.

I was getting angry, and I had a feeling that Queenie was not going to lighten my mood. She was walking up the outpatient path from the bus stop, pushing a baby in a buggy and stopping every now and then to chivvy up an older child with a grumpy face. She waved when she passed under my window and saw me peering out.

'Sorry about that, Mike. The bus was late.'

She settled herself in the clinic chair and looked around the room, oblivious to her young daughter prodding the baby in the background.

'This place doesn't change much, does it? You came to see me at home, because I was behaving badly. Then I came here with my mum and dad, to sort out why. I was only a kid then, but I remember it all. They called me a little queen and the name just sort of stuck.'

I remembered her too. 'How did it work out?'

'Not very well, I'm afraid.'

'What sort of not very well?' I could see the young girl getting fractious but it would keep a minute.

'My parents split up soon afterwards. That's why we stopped coming. Me and my sister swapped homes between them. Backwards and forwards. And that didn't do us any good either. Then my dad got sent to prison – burglary or something – and we lost touch with him.'

She was monopolising the session and her daughter prodded the baby so hard that it cried.

'I think your daughter is trying to get your attention.'

Queenie picked her up, sat down again, and continued. All in one move.

'I've been in trouble myself, you know. And it's difficult to find a place to live when you're a single parent like me. Especially if you've got a record. And their fathers haven't been much help. Either of them.' Her daughter squirmed around in her lap. 'I'm living in social housing now, but it's pretty crowded and I haven't got the money to fix things. Anyway, enough of me. Can you do anything about this one? She's as bad as I was.'

I was wondering where to start when she spoke again. 'Oh, by the way. I almost forgot. My mother sends her regards. She would have come too but she's on the psychiatric ward again. She spends most of her time there these days. She gets depressed, you know.'

Cycles of harm in the patients and cycles of psychiatrists trying to break the chain. Anyone who has worked with families would have similar stories to tell and there is a steady accumulation of evidence to prove what they say.

If treatment is denied, is ineffective, or is truncated as in Queenie's case, children who have problems will grow up into adults who have even more problems; and the adults are likely to pass them on again to their own children. Either because there is a thread running through them of a mental illness like anxiety or depression, the majority of which we know becomes evident in childhood but the vulnerability to which we can reduce if they are caught early enough. Or distorted patterns of upbringing are handed on from parents to children and so on, in a vicious circle of unlearning. Or both. Like Queenie, her mother, and now her own daughter in turn.

But we shouldn't be pessimistic about that. To begin with, it has provided the evidence that politicians have needed for early intervention services. From educating pregnant mothers about the effect their lifestyle can have on their unborn foetus, through perinatal services for parents and their babies, to parenting programmes for disruptive toddlers and young children, and on to school counselling for emotionally distressed adolescents.

Spend money at the beginning and you will save six times as much further down the line: in the greater emergence of mental health problems; in relationship breakdown; in days off work and unemployment; in drug and alcohol abuse; self-harm and suicide; and in crime and punishment. Put like that the message is irrefutable but it requires a leap of faith on the part of those who hold the purse strings; the services that will reap the benefit are not necessarily those who will have to find the money in the first place.

Underneath it all is the most important and the most optimistic message of all. Children, young people and their families can be helped to learn new ways of relating to each other and to change their perception of themselves and the outside world. No matter how unpromising their start. And you don't get much more un-promising than Leanne.

By the time I came to child psychiatry, I was already a family man myself. Three of my children were at school, but one was still a toddler and needed looking after at home. My wife was dipping her toe back into education via an occasional fill-in teaching job, and I stayed at home when she did so. Her supply posts were usually planned and we could make arrangements in advance, but sometimes they came as an emergency at the breakfast table when we were fussing over coats and a car that wouldn't start. This was one of those mornings.

I waved them all goodbye and rang the adolescent unit to tell them I wouldn't be coming in. On one side of me sat a pile of notes that needed writing up; on the other was a two-year-old who needed entertaining. It was almost a relief when the unit rang back to remind me that it was my turn on the emergency rota and let me know that they had just had a breathless call from someone in the docks. A young teenager was trying to throw herself out of a window in one of the tower blocks. Leanne was her name and they gave us her address, but nothing else.

There was nothing for it but to order a taxi, strap our two-year-old in the back and head for the community centre in the docks. I handed him over to the friendliest nurse I could find and ran to the tower block. This area was once a thriving community, but the heart of it had been ripped out to make way for new, poor quality housing, full of dispirited families and dispirited lives.

I climbed up the stairs through pools of rain-water and old vomit; the barriers on the landings were broken and gaping open. In a third-floor flat, a large man was sitting on a young girl in the middle of the sitting room floor, surrounded by a ring of women who were smoking and exchanging bits of gossip. They had reached an impasse and now everything was curiously calm, as if this was a daily occurrence. I was not calm.

'For Christ's sake, what do you think you're doing?'

'Stopping her throwing herself out of the window.'

'Don't be ridiculous. Get off her or you'll suffocate her instead.'

He did as he was told and the young girl ran for the window as he had predicted. I caught her when her belt snagged on the window latch and led her back to the sofa. The women shrugged their shoulders and gave each other told-you-so glances. The man looked smug. And they all left us to it.

Leanne was trembling and so was I. We both needed a moment to calm down.

'Is this your flat, Leanne?'

She nodded, moving away from me to the other end of the sofa.

'How old are you? Do you live here by yourself or are your parents out somewhere?'

Too many questions all at once, and I gave her some breathing space while I looked around. There was a wheelchair in the corner and the whole room smelt of stale urine. Someone had been trying to vacuum the carpet, but it was threadbare and still soiled. Through the kitchen door, I could see piles of plastic trays from takeaway meals.

'Fifteen.' Leanne had found her voice. 'My mum's gone to hospital.'

'And your father?'

'I haven't got one. At least, I don't know who he is.'

'Is your mum ill?'

Leanne had begun to tremble again, and she was near to tears. I fetched a blanket from the bedroom and wrapped it around her shoulders.

'She's got multiple sclerosis. I've been trying to look after her, I really have.' She was crying now and the words came out in bursts, tears and snot dripping on to her lap.

'I'm sure you've done a great job. But has nobody else been helping?'

'There isn't anybody else. I don't really know anyone round

here . . . My auntie calls in every so often, but she isn't really interested . . . She's got her own problems.'

'What about school?'

'They know my mum's ill and I've been looking after her, so they make allowances . . . I'm not there very much.'

'And the hospital?'

'They know who she is, but we haven't kept the appointments . . . Mum was scared that they'd take her away.'

'And now? Why has she ended up there anyway?'

It sounded far too final and I wished I had put it differently. Leanne could barely look at me.

'She got really bad . . . wouldn't eat or speak . . . so I called the doctor and he sent for an ambulance.'

'What did the hospital say?'

'They said she was real bad . . . She won't be coming out again . . . She's going to die.'

It was another hour or so while we talked. I persuaded Leanne that she should come back with me to the adolescent unit, where we could look after her instead, and begin to sort things out in her life. We couldn't cure her mum of multiple sclerosis, or stop what was likely to happen, but we could help Leanne through it. She didn't raise much of a protest. I rang for a taxi and it had arrived by the time she had packed her bag and made sure everything was locked up.

At no point did either of us mention the window and her trying to throw herself through it. I'm not sure whether she would have done it or not, and I doubt that Leanne would have really known herself. But it was certainly a measure of how desperate she had become as a young carer, trying to do everything for her sick mother. Feeding her, fetching her painkillers, even wiping her bottom and clearing up the mess. And how she felt she had failed at the last. I was only too glad that the man who tried to stop her had seen what was happening through the open door.

Leanne stayed with us on the unit for over a year. Her mother did die but we helped her through her grief. We liaised with her teachers, and she settled in the school on the unit with the work they sent her. Above all, freed from the task of caring for her mother, she was able to look at her own life and its future. She found a new self-confidence in her relationship with the staff and her peer group there, worked on her own problems, and helped others to find strategies to cope with theirs.

She was discharged at length to another flat and a job as a waitress in one of the dinky new wine bars in the docks, within sight of the tower block where I had first met her. To people like me, the wine bars were the end of a romantic nostalgia for the pubs and clubs of old, but to her they were a source of work, security and a hard-headed view of her everyday needs. And she was right.

I heard later that Leanne had got married, had a baby and moved up north with her husband. Not necessarily in that order. It was many years before I was contacted by her again. By then, I had moved on too. But I had done some work for the radio, and she was able to track me down.

'There's someone on the phone called Leanne,' said my secretary, peering round my door. 'She says you'll know who it is. You helped to treat her years ago. Shall I put her through?'

She did. Leanne sounded just as bright and breezy as when she left the unit, and I wondered why she had gone to so much trouble to find me again. We chatted on about old times, about her native city, which she never visited these days, and about her life in her new town. Then it came.

'I suppose you're wondering why I rang?'

'It had crossed my mind.'

'I thought you'd like to know.'

'Go on.'

'I've been married for years now and I've got a son. He's the same age as I was when you took me in. But he's a pain in the arse.'

'What's the pain about?'

'He gets so upset about things. He's not very bright. A bit like me, I suppose. He hates school and he bunks off quite a bit. And he doesn't get on with his dad. Neither do I.'

'What does your son do when he gets upset?'

'He threw himself out of the window once. But he'd forgotten we live on the ground floor. He sprained his ankle.'

She must have heard my muffled laughter, because she began to laugh too.

'You don't sound very fussed about it,' I said.

'I'm not. I know it sounds like history repeating itself, but it isn't. It's different this time. That's why I rang.'

'How different?'

'We talked about it. He told me why he was unhappy and I told him what happened to me. How I'd been so miserable, and how I'd been helped. So we got some help for him too. And it worked.'

'How did it work?'

'We talked to his teachers and we got things sorted out at school. He was being bullied. His dad and I decided to separate. Best thing we ever did. My son's much happier living with me and seeing his dad at weekends. Less arguments. And he's got a girlfriend.'

'And you? How are you feeling?'

'I'm just happy it all worked out.'

Leanne rang off. With my number in her pocket, she said, if she ever needed to call. But I have never heard from her again. She was a standing example of a young person in a desperate state, whose life had been saved by a window latch and a year spent on the adolescent unit.

Yes, she had got into difficulties in her marriage and her son had reflected that and the bullying in his behaviour. But they had sorted it out. The cycle was broken. Not because there would never be any more problems. Life isn't like that. But because they had learnt how to deal with them when they arose.

CHAPTER 24

BILLY
THE NATURE OF HOPE

Ever tried. Ever failed. No matter. Try again. Fail again. Fail better.
                              Samuel Beckett: *Worstward Ho*, 1983

For several years I was asked to sit in with a consultant from the genetics department of our district teaching hospital. Her job was to help the families who had a strong history of genetic disease, counselling prospective parents about the likelihood of their next child being born with the disease, and helping to treat those who were. My job as a child psychiatrist was to deal with the emotional consequences of both.

It taught me many things, and the greatest of these was about the nature of hope. I never ceased to be amazed at how families could react so differently to the same piece of news. Some saw huge hope where there was little; others saw little hope where there was a lot. And the first two families in one morning clinic were a perfect example.

Both parents in each couple were carriers for an autosomal recessive disorder caused by a faulty gene. That is to say that they were unaffected by the disorder themselves but could pass on the faulty gene to their child. In order for the child to have the disorder, it would need to receive two copies of the faulty gene, one from its carrier mother and the other from its carrier father. And the chances of that happening were one in four. None of the parents had had the remotest idea that they were carriers until they had been devastated by the birth of their first affected child.

The first couple we saw that morning were immigrants from an Ashkenazi Jewish community in Poland. Their daughter had been born with Tay-Sachs Disease. Because she lacked a vital enzyme, fatty substances had built up in her nerve cells in early pregnancy. Her brain degenerated rapidly after her birth and she died when she was just four years old. There is no cure and the outlook for each subsequent child with the disorder would be grim. We explained the chances to them.

'Only one in four chance of getting it,' exclaimed the father. He hugged his wife, who was weeping with joy. 'That's marvellous news.'

'I know I'm crying,' added his wife. 'But I'm so happy, I really am. I thought we could never risk having another baby. Now I know it will probably be all right.'

The second couple were born in the city and their first child had cystic fibrosis. Patients with the disorder secrete abnormal body fluids, including a thick and sticky mucus which clogs up the lungs, interferes with the function of vital organs like the pancreas, and leads to chronic infections. The life of children with cystic fibrosis has been immeasurably improved in recent years, and young people like Will, the teenager I saw with his naso-gastric tube, are likely to live well into adulthood. But our explanation came as another blow.

'That's terrible,' said the mother when she'd found her voice. She and her husband had seemed frozen by the news. 'I don't know if we could ever take the risk. Of having another baby.'

'Not with that hanging over us,' agreed her husband. 'Those aren't the sort of odds that I would be prepared to risk.'

Such huge variation in their hopes, and neither the consultant nor I were much good at predicting which way the patients would jump. Some of the other professionals that I worked with were just as bad at it, and teachers especially so. Many of them hoped that I could resolve an intransigent problem; others felt that what they were doing was hopeless, even though they were achieving great things in a child's life. Lewis and Tommy were perfect examples of what I mean.

Lewis was fifteen and he hadn't been to school for a year. Badly behaved children annoy most teachers but those who refuse to come to school annoy them even more. Frequently, they get suspended for it. Lewis's teacher had called in the educational psychologist and he led me halfway up a mountainside above the town then turned his car around.

'You're on your own now, Mike. I'm not welcome round here. Good luck.'

I crunched across the gravel in front of the house, watched by a slim, baseball-hatted man who slouched against the doorway. He pointed a double-barrelled shotgun at my chest.

'You from the social?'

'No, I'm a doctor. Come to see about Lewis. Can I come in?'

He was prepared to defer to a doctor, even though he must have wondered what was wrong. He ushered me in and waved me towards a stool on the earthen floor, then went to the fridge to fetch milk for tea. There was nothing in it except alcohol. Dog muck lay around everywhere. In a corner was a huge TV set with a Harris hawk perched on top, brooding, eyeing my every move. A litter of entrails and small bones were scattered across the floor beneath.

Several other young men joined us, with a woman who looked old but turned out to be their mother.

'These are my sons,' she said. 'I never had any daughters, but it wasn't for want of trying.' She laughed. 'My husband's dead now. Killed when a load of old cars fell on top of him, out in the yard.' She jerked her head towards the back door. 'Anyway, why are you here?'

I came clean about who I was and they didn't seem to mind, now that I was established.

'About Lewis. He hasn't been to school for a year. Where is he?'

'He's doing his lessons,' said the man who had met me at the door. 'Every day he does them. At home, like. Me and his brothers, we were never ones for school. Dad used to thrash us if we didn't make the effort, mind. But he gave up with this one. Then he died. Do you want to see him? Our kid, I mean.'

Lewis was in the back room, the only one carpeted in the house. He was reading from a book he'd snatched from three wooden crates next to his bed; it was upside down. All the books looked new, many of them not yet opened. Encyclopaedias, teach-yourself manuals, picture books and adolescent novels. On top of one of the crates was a garishly coloured atlas of the human body. He couldn't have got through them all if he'd read a couple a week for years.

'Sorry, I didn't hear you come in,' said Lewis, making a half-hearted attempt to push an air rifle further under his bed. 'I've only got another hour, then I can help my brothers in the yard.'

'What about school? Why haven't you been going?'

'School was horrible. The teachers were horrible. And so were the other boys. I can learn just as well here.'

His tone sounded final, and so did his older brother when we left him to it.

'He won't go, you know. And I'm not going to thrash him into it. I had too much of that from our dad. Anyway, he's fifteen; it's a bit late, isn't it?'

And so it was. Whatever the teachers might want, it wasn't going to happen. Lewis would refuse to go to school on his own account and no one in the family was going to make him do it. It would be pointless fining them in the courts; they just wouldn't pay up, and who were they going to imprison for that? The only possibility would be to take him into care, but the local authority would struggle to find the grounds. And in less than a year he could leave quite legally. They had false optimism.

Tommy's situation was the opposite. Where Lewis's house was as remote as his chances of ever going back to school, Tommy's family lived in the middle of town and he went to my wife's school. Regularly but destructively. He had multiple minor physical problems, his brother had a long criminal record, and his mother an even longer string of partners. Tommy was eight and he deserved much better, but the future seemed bleak. My wife came home one night crying.

'It's Tommy again, isn't it?' She nodded and I made her a drink. 'What happened this time?'

'His teacher sent someone to my office, to tell me. Tommy was wrecking her lesson. He wouldn't shut up or sit down. And he kept knocking things over and thumping the girls next to him.'

'So what did you do?'

'I went down to the classroom and I picked him up, kicking and scramming and yelling, and I carried him back along the corridor to my room.'

'And then?'

'Then I plonked him down on a chair next to my desk. I told him to sit there quietly because I had to make some phone calls. Then we would have a pot of tea and talk about things.'

'And Tommy?'

'He sat quietly, like I asked him. And we drank tea. And we talked about what happened in the classroom. And . . .' She took another swig of her drink. 'And he told me about his family. How awful they were and how he really wanted to behave but he didn't know how. And I sat him on my lap, and he cried.'

'What did you do then?'

'Then Tommy felt better. And I took him back to the class and he was as good as gold. All day.'

I told her that what she had just done was wonderful. That it was more than a child psychiatrist like me could have achieved in months of therapy.

'So why are you crying?'

'Because tonight he's gone home, to the same family and the same mess, and tomorrow we'll have to start all over again. And again. And it's no use.'

We talked about hope. 'You have to believe,' I told her. 'As a teacher or a social worker or a health visitor or anyone trying to help children like Tommy. That when he gets older and he's in trouble again with some sort of authority, that he'll remember you and what you did. That someone treated him differently, worth knowing, as a person in his own right. And he'll feel enhanced.

'Just one relationship, that's all it takes. You can't alter the whole picture; it's too big and you would give up. Just do the bit you can, as best as you can, and hope that one day the bits will all join up and things will change. You have to hope. What you had was false pessimism.'

False optimism with Lewis; false pessimism with Tommy. They got me thinking about the nature of hope, its meaning in therapy, and where we put the dividing line between a reasonable hope, false optimism on one side, and false pessimism on the other. And how I have been guilty of both.

'How can you promise me that?'

I was working with a young woman whose husband had died of cancer earlier that year. I had been asked to help the children, but they wanted to get back to school and their friends, as usual. They sighed with relief when I opted to see their mother by herself; to explore the grief they all felt but with which she had become stuck, to the exclusion of everything else. I was still feeling my way with bereavement then and poured hope all over the place.

'Trust me, one day you'll feel much better.'

'No, I won't. I'll always feel like this,' she retaliated. 'And why should I trust what you feel? It's my feelings that matter.'

It was a cutting remark that went right to the heart of what I was doing. It was impossible to get close enough to treat people's problems without tuning in to their feelings, and them tuning in to my feelings at the same time. Their unhappinesses came home with me, and my unhappinesses went with me to work. How was I to survive without collapsing under the accumulated miseries of my patients and my own recurrent depression, if I didn't pretend that all would be well?

In my defence, I was not alone in peddling false optimism, in psychiatry or any other branch of medicine. Drug companies stood accused of duping doctors by publishing only the positive findings of their research and burying the bad. Doctors were accused of duping their patients by dishing out millions of unnecessary prescriptions every year for anxiety and depression without tackling the cause. And we were all accused of duping ourselves, because we liked it that way. False optimism.

I would like to think that I have learnt enough now not to need it; not to keep my patients at a safe distance with a dodgy diagnosis and a pill and a smile on my face. That I have developed the confidence to get out from the comfort of a clinic desk and into the community. To face up to managers who would have me behave like a proper doctor. And to be able to take risks with patients like that bereaved young widow.

'Sitting where I am, I think that one day you might feel well enough to get back to work like your children. But right now I don't expect you to believe me. You're right in the middle of the tunnel and you can't see the light at the end.'

To validate what she was going through, and to let her experience her anger, her misery and her worst fears, within our relationship. Not to promise false hopes, but to get into the blackness of the tunnel beside her.

The danger is, I suppose, that I might sometimes have swung the other way: from false optimism to false pessimism. Politicians may talk about how to pick up those who have fallen off the bottom of the economic ladder, while their policies seem designed to keep them on the floor. We see many of those people and they are called 'heart-sink' patients, because our hearts sink when they walk through the door. Better to blame them for being what they are – too fat, too lazy, or too feckless to live on anything but a 'sink' estate.

I have chosen to work on those estates. To sit on earthen floors; to supervise contact sessions with an estranged father in run-down parks with broken slides and rubble in the road; to have a shotgun pointed at my chest and a pitchfork driven through the bonnet of my car. And there are times when I wonder whether all that work could possibly make anything better in such an economic climate, when one in three of the children live in poverty and families have gone three generations without a job. Better to put a placard in their hand and march with them to Downing Street.

But I have to remember that young girls like Leanne have problems that are every bit as deserving of help as those of anyone else, and that Nathan showed exactly what can happen if we don't give it. That the woman who came into my clinic with her son Jake was living proof of what a difference that help can make to a family from the most unpromising background. And that I should stop being so falsely pessimistic.

It is a fine balance to strike with many groups of patients, and nowhere has it been more difficult than working with physically disabled children living in poor families in the once thriving mining Valleys of South Wales. They have challenged my hope of helping like no other, but they have given me the greatest rewards. And the best of these was Billy.

It wasn't his real name, but everyone knew him as Billy. Most out of affection; a few out of cruelty, after Billy Whizz, the *Beano* character who could run incredibly fast. This Billy was wheelchair bound and couldn't run anywhere at all. He had a progressive neuro-muscular illness for which the doctors in the hospital had done all they could. At the age of eleven, he was living at home in a tiny ex-mining village at the top end of one of the Valleys. The very top, where the two trains a day were just enough to keep the rust off the rails. But the people had no jobs to go to and no money to shop. So the trains were mostly empty.

I was asked to visit Billy at home to check on his emotional welfare, and I dreaded the prospect. How could I possibly help a young lad with a medical illness that was beyond treatment, in a community where everyone was materially poor? I pictured him in his wheelchair, in his terraced street, like a spider waiting to gobble me up. And I drove to meet him as slowly as I could, through the pouring rain and the wet and cracked-paved streets, past chip-shop queues and waste tips with their 'Keep Off' Coal Board signs flapping in the wind.

He was at home with his older sister and his parents, none of whom was employed. Every curtain twitched as I parked the car and walked down the row. No doubt they would all have something to say if I asked them, but the family were enough.

'He should thank his lucky stars we had him,' said his mother. 'I could have had him aborted, you know. We knew what he was going to be like.'

'We've all got our problems,' added his father. 'Mary with her legs and me sacked from the darts team.'

'Then there's his uncle Ron next door with his diabetes. He do piss every half-hour, that one.'

Billy sat in the middle, in a Manchester United bobble hat and scarf, his sister standing quietly behind him with one hand on his shoulder.

'Billy just wishes he could piss at all,' she whispered to me. 'And didn't have to rely on a catheter and bag.'

'Shall we go for a walk?' I suggested, and wished I'd put it differently the moment the words were out of my mouth. Billy didn't seem to mind; he was glad to get away from the house.

I pushed him over the railway tracks to a coal yard on the other side. An old man in a moleskin waistcoat told us that it had once been full of good Welsh coal, waiting to be taken down to the ports on coal trains twice an hour. Now the mines were closed and it was all foreign muck, he said, and not a patch on what came out of the Rhondda.

'Still, there's always the pigeons,' he said, nodding his head towards the lofts higher up. 'But nothing's right there either. Two pairs of peregrine falcons from up the top. Fastest birds in the world. They can hit a pigeon at a hundred miles an hour. They don't stand a chance.'

I looked at Billy. His eyes were shining with excitement and I knew now the grounds on which we might meet. I pushed him as far as the lofts, then carried him higher up the hillside. He weighed nothing at all. We sat against the rocks, watching the pigeons come and go below us. We examined the dead crows, hung in pairs on the barbed wire fence, like gloves. And we were startled by every flapping noise.

In truth, we never saw the peregrine falcons; but it didn't matter. Up there on the hillside every week we talked about what it felt like to be disabled and the sort of things he could still do with his life. His love for his sister, and for his parents. Despite the sort of things they said.

At the last, I gave Billy a bird book and a pair of binoculars. He gave me a handshake. But what we really gave each other was much more. He had found a greater sense of self-respect and a surer idea of his importance to the family. His future was no longer tied to the wheelchair, even if that was the only way to get around. And what he gave me was a new optimism, that I could do something to help.

I drove a mile or two down the valley, then stopped the car to look back at the hills around its head. An empty train went past, its lights full on in the late afternoon.

As I stood there, I felt something swoop low over the horizon and seize me with a fierce hope. True hope. That things might be better, even for someone like Billy. And I could be a part of it too.

CHAPTER 25

ROBERT
THE MEANING OF SEPARATION

What is that feeling when you're driving away from people and they recede on the plain till you see their specks dispersing? — it's the too huge world vaulting us, and it's good-bye. But we lean forward to the next crazy venture beneath the skies.

Jack Kerouac: *On the Road*, 1957

There is nothing more painful in life than endings. The end of childhood; young people leaving home. Coming to the end of a session; the end of a relationship between patient and therapist. Losing a job, retirement, the end of life itself.

My life has been full of endings, both personal and professional. As a teenager, I devoured all the classic novels of separation and discovery, like *On the Road*, and danced around jukeboxes to a hundred records of lost love. In the words of Bacharach and David, breaking up is hard to do.

As one of my colleagues once observed, all attachments contain the seeds of loss. The moment we commit ourselves to a relationship, we commit ourselves to losing it. Some people cope with it by clutching a memory of what they've lost to help them across the gap. Some people cope by clinging on long after they should have let go. Some people cope by never forming a relationship in the first place. Few people are able to pass on to the next crazy venture, like Kerouac, without a pang of regret.

Robert was my last patient in the particular clinic where I was working at the time, and he was the most difficult I saw before I moved on. Or maybe he was the most difficult because he was the last. I'm not sure; but the issue for both of us was separation.

He was seventeen when I met him and coming up to leaving care. His life was full of botched separations and here was another. His relationship with his mother was strained from the start when she developed cancer soon after his birth and was hospitalised repeatedly during his childhood. He was angry with her one minute because she was nowhere around when he needed her most, and guilty the next because he might have caused her relapses by his behaviour.

'You'd better be well behaved or you'll be the death of her,' said his father. And Robert reacted with typical magical thinking when the prophecy threatened to come true.

Robert's mother had so many last gasps that he must have wondered if she would ever die. For his father, this lingering death was more than he could bear. At first he began to withdraw from her emotionally and then found solace in an affair with another woman. It was a surprise to both of them when she finally did die. Robert was eight at the time and had been persuaded, against his wishes, to go on holiday with a school friend and his family. When he came home, not only was his mother dead but his father had swept away all sign of her.

There was no funeral and she had been cremated with no grave. Her photographs had been taken down and her wardrobe emptied. Robert was not allowed to discuss his mother's death, he had been denied a role in any of the rituals surrounding it, and the lid had been fastened down securely on everyone's emotions. There was no way that Robert could say his goodbyes.

His grief was compounded when his father brought a girlfriend into the house within months of the mother's death. Robert did what he had always done. He swung between paranoia, in which he felt persecuted by the bad bits of his dead and inviolate mother, and depression, in which he was convinced that he had killed her by going off on holiday to enjoy himself when she was at her most frail. Some psychoanalysts might have loved this psychopathology, but no one else did.

When he was at his most paranoid, he reacted angrily towards his father's girlfriend, his female teachers and any other woman who dared to come close. It was the stuff of fairy tales: anger at his mother that he could no longer express directly, foisted on to the ghosts of her that haunted his life. Eventually, he threw a plateful of hot food at the girlfriend, smashed up his room when he was sent to bed, and was taken into local authority care as an emergency. He never went home again.

Robert's behaviour destroyed a whole string of foster family placements. I say it was his behaviour rather than Robert himself, because I doubt whether he was ever conscious of where his outbursts came from. He was loath to commit himself to any sort of settled relationship with his foster families lest it let him down as it had always done before; he tested it out soon after he arrived and was partly gratified, partly demoralised, each time his expectations came to pass.

More out of desperation than good judgement, the local authority paid through the nose to place him in a small, privately run group home where there were many staff to carry the load. Such was their turnover that there was no opportunity, and no obligation, to develop a close relationship with anyone, negative, positive, or a mixture of both. And that was the bit of distance that he needed.

Without the pressure of expectation, Robert settled enough to try a further placement. The new foster parents had seen all this before. They placed firm boundaries around the worst of his behaviour, rewarded the better bits and let him explore his relationship with them at his own speed. In other words, they were the good-enough parents that he had never had in his family of origin. For the first time in his life, Robert began to trust his feelings for people close to him, but a sword of Damocles was hanging over his head and the adults were so delighted by his fragile improvement that they failed to draw his attention to what was sure to happen.

Local authority care is supposed to be as close to good family care as possible, but it has been riddled with arcane rules that have no grounding in need. Anyone who has been a parent will tell you that children grow up sufficiently to find their own feet in the world, but they rarely truly leave. Even if they go off to university, get married, buy their own house and raise children in turn, they are still part of the family and visit it to reinforce the ties and receive their support – though it might be disguised as a bag full of dirty washing or a Sunday roast. All of this has been complicated by economic hardship, the lack of jobs and affordable housing for young people, and their need to stay at home long after they would formerly have left.

But those in care have had little choice. Formerly, they were thrown out at a given age and all ties were severed. It may have been managed a little more delicately than that, but there is no doubt how it felt to young people who were just beginning to develop relationships only for them to be snatched away by stupid rules. By Robert's day, government initiatives had tried to put it right, with more rules. They were to be allowed to stay on in foster placements until they were more ready to leave, and better supported afterwards. But reports showed that the young people still felt 'Lost in Care'.

When the issue of leaving was tentatively broached with Robert, his new-found faith in humanity collapsed about his ears, he refused to listen to what might be on offer, and he became as upset as ever. It is difficult to get angry with rules and the anonymous officials who make them, so he took his feelings out on those around him. Even his long-suffering foster parents found it difficult to cope with his behaviour and the GP referred him to me for therapy, as if it was his fault.

That was a heavy baggage to bring to our appointments and I decided that it would be safer for him to be seen in a consulting room in the hospital, where he could express his feelings and leave them behind with me as he wished. I was rather surprised that he agreed to come at all, but not that he sat sullenly uncommunicative for most of the initial sessions.

I have used the framework of therapy wherever it has suited – the beginning, the middle and the end, the earning of trust and the careful use of it once established. But like Robert, I can be exasperated by rules and have ignored them whenever they have seemed less important than what I feel instinctively is right. Intuition, you could call it, but with a lifetime of experience underneath. This was no exception.

'Sometimes, Robert,' I said in frustration, 'I wonder if you really want me to help. Or perhaps you just want to criticise me for not helping.'

I could imagine Robert's mother saying something similar to him in his childhood, knowing she hadn't been there for him because of her illness, realising how angry he was about it, and trying to get him to talk about it all. He retaliated in the same vein.

'The trouble with you,' he said, 'is that you're jealous. You want to be me, but you can't be. You're too old. And you're going to die . . .'

It was a risk, but it got us closer, and more quickly, to the pathology that had dominated his life: the anger towards his mother that he was unable to express and his anxiety that he might have been the cause of her demise. I could work with the anger which he transferred on to me in the sessions and with his worries that it might have killed me off. This showed in the way he rang my secretary between sessions, ostensibly to check on appointment times, but really to see if I was still alive. But my feelings were involved, just as much as those of Robert. And my baggage was full of separation anxieties too.

I was due to move on from this clinic in six months' time. That sounded quite long enough for the normal run of patients, but what about Robert? Could we work our way through his problems in six months or would he be left in a sort of limbo, with his pains exposed and poorly patched up, like an open wound?

If that happened, would I keep to my schedule and leave him to it, or would I shelve it and continue until the wound had healed? And how long might that take, once Robert knew that he had the power to keep it going? I was well aware of how, in the early days of therapy, he would produce the most important material just before the end of a session; wouldn't that happen to the whole course of therapy itself?

Should I keep to the timetable in my head and work towards it in secret, or should I make it explicit? If we talked about it openly, would he withdraw again, wary of another separation, or would it help us to explore the separations that had ruined his life – his mother's death, his father's desertion, and the artificial rules about leaving care? And, of course, where did my own problems with separation fit into his?

Happy the therapist who works within a brief and acknowledged timetable. Six sessions of CBT and that's all you get, both doctor and patient tailoring the depth of their commitment to the time available. A sort of Parkinson's Law of therapy. But what can that achieve with the Roberts of this world, with a lifetime of pathology to uncover and a commitment that would need far longer to develop, if it wasn't to repeat the problem?

And what would that mean to a therapist, feeling guilty about selling a patient short, guilty about the direction of commercial pressure in medicine, guilty about an impending move? Both of us facing up to leaving the care we had grown used to, in our respective worlds? Maybe Robert's jibe about my age wasn't far off the mark.

A therapist can easily become bogged down in rumination like this, while the patient skips out of the consulting room free of the mud that he has left behind. For a while, I had a room that had windows out on to the path down to the car park. It took about five minutes for patients and their families to get from my room to their car. After one session, I sat miserably contemplating the agony of what had been revealed and how crass had been my attempt to lift the family to a point where they could go home without killing each other. Only to see them pass under my windows, arm-in-arm, laughing and joking as they went about the realities of life.

Other patients, aware that therapy was coming to an end, would get the boot in first and fail to turn up for their last appointment. Avoiding the face-to-face pains of saying goodbye, but leaving me with the frustration of things I had yet to resolve.

And as it happened, my worst worries were unfounded. Yet another set of analysts would have gone to town on the separation anxieties that Robert had been struggling with when he first came to me. He had never internalised a stable image of his parents, sufficient for him to explore his natural independence, secure in the knowledge that he could allow himself to attach to future people, to things, and to circumstances, and survive their loss without disaster.

Instead, he had alternated between an insecure 'ambivalent' attachment, clinging on whilst acting out his distress, and an insecure 'avoidant' attachment, denying that the losses meant anything to him at all. Both of them would have made separation in therapy very difficult indeed, even to the point of the attenuation I had considered. It wasn't necessary.

I never made the six months explicit, but it proved enough for Robert to face up to his grief and all its anger, its fears and its sadness. As he did so, he built up a more secure relationship with his lost parents, became more confident in his own autonomy and left care, comforted that he had inside him a happier experience of parents, foster parents and therapist, and that he could call on those of us who were still around if he ever needed to; but he never did.

Meanwhile, I too found some sort of resolution to my own separation anxieties, comfortable in the knowledge that my therapy with Robert had been difficult but had gone well. It represented all that had been satisfactory in my clinical career so far, made up for the trials and tribulations along the way, and allowed me to leave that clinic, sad but secure. As ever, it was therapeutic for both sides of the clinical fence. I had left Robert, and more importantly, he had left me.

A few years after we separated, I met Robert again. By accident, not design. The end of my latest batch of work was in sight and I decided to use the time to write a series of down-and-dirty, violent and probably unpublishable detective novels. I had reached the point where I needed to find out more about the drug scene in the area where they were set.

I went down to the roughest pub I could find on a Friday night, armed with a list of runners given to me by an undercover friend from the police. The bar looked like a scene from Hieronymus Bosch. I navigated my way around the drunken stag nights and the hen parties, down for a night of drugs and debauchery, ordered a pint and handed my list to the barman.

'Any of them in?'

'He usually is,' he said, pointing to the top of the list, 'but not tonight. His son is, though. You could talk to him.'

I followed the jerk of his head and there was Robert, a few years older but unmistakeable. And he recognised me too. He was mystified by what I was doing there, if I didn't actually want to buy any of the stuff. And I found it hard to understand why he was working with his father, when he had hated him so much.

'I thought you and your father didn't get on.'

'We didn't. But what you did for me changed everything. I could see things differently, I suppose. I forgave my mother for dying, and I forgave my father too. Poor sod. It must have been just as horrible for him. Anyway, what are you doing these days?'

'This and that. I took your advice and decided I was too old for full-time clinical work.' I told him about the posts I had held during the rest of my time, about teaching, about my charity work and the books.

'Oh, I see. When you got too old to do it all the time, you tried to show others how to do it instead.'

I said nothing, but squirmed in my seat.

'And when you got too old to teach all the time, you started to sit at home and write about it.'

Not quite. Working directly with children, young people and

their families has remained important for me all the way through. You can't teach about them, or write about them, if what you're saying is not refreshed by what they tell you to your face. That's what makes clinical work so exciting.

But he was right about one thing. He had once called me jealous, and so I was. I was jealous of the way our work together had helped him to come to terms with his father, in a way I had never been able to achieve with my own father before he died.

For Robert, separation from therapy had helped him to heal the relationships in his past. For me, the separations from my own family were still raw. Like Kerouac, I could lean forward to the next venture, but saying goodbye to the old ones was painful. Breaking up is hard to do.

EPILOGUE

SORTING THROUGH MY FATHER'S BOOKS

In books lies the soul of the whole Past Time; the articulate audible voice of the Past, when the body and material substance of it has altogether vanished like a dream.

Thomas Carlyle: *On Heroes, Hero-Worship, and the Heroic*, 1841

This book has been full of stories, just like therapy.

Therapy is the chance for children, young people and their carers to explore their story, to work out where it went wrong, and to put it right wherever possible. It is the job of the therapist to encourage them to reveal their story, to listen to it, and to help them find a better outcome. Without that chance, the same story will be played out again and again, from one generation to another.

It's a tough lesson, one that medicine is in danger of forgetting amidst all its technology, and one that I had to learn in my own life. For this has been my story too. The lessons that children and young people have taught me, as much as the lessons I have passed on to them. And above all, that families in trouble must get help as early as possible.

Long before I was thinking about writing this book, my mother died. Almost exactly a year later, my father died too. I had always had a distant relationship with him, and it wasn't helped by what he did on my mother's deathbed.

My mother was an old-time dancer, a big woman but light on her feet. She had a friend who was equally big and they danced together for forty years. Despite their friendship, they never called each other anything but Mrs S and Mrs B. They were formal ladies to the last. But Mrs B had a younger sister, who was always called Mavis, as if she was a child.

Every Thursday night, I met them in the park on their way home from the dance. Mrs S and Mrs B, even rounder in their overcoats, with Mavis supported askew between them. Tall, thin and drunk, in a long dress and a hat with a feather on top. They came towards me like a percentage sign.

When my mother was dying in her hospital bed, I persuaded the doctors to put her on a morphine drip, to dull the pain; but it dulled her senses too. My wife and I raided her wardrobe and hung her room with sequinned dresses, fur stoles and court shoes, and she drifted back to the dance nights of her youth. All it needed was the ghosts of Mrs B and Mavis to come waltzing through the open window, to Mantovani's Golden Hits. It was too much for my father; he took everything down.

Unlike many of the families in this book, I had no reconciliation with my father. He died as distant from me as ever, as we pushed him around the village in his wheelchair and in stony silence. Did that matter? Of course it did. Like all therapists, I have been as affected by my past as my patients have been by theirs. It is impossible for therapists to cope with their patient's feelings without learning to deal with their own feelings as well. And if I hadn't got help to face up to mine, I would have gone through life kicking my father in the crotch.

I did get that help. Too late for our relationship together, but it broke the cycle of resentment in my life and stopped me passing it on to my own children. It freed me from treating all authority figures as if they were my father, and relieved me from the label of being angry and subversive. The labelling process with which so many children and young people will be burdened, if they don't get similar help. But there was more work to do.

When my father died, I inherited his book collection. The bibles he'd won at Sunday school, farewell gifts when he went off to university, dusty hardbacks of the lives of scientists, Latin classics and maps, delicately dissected and glued on linen cloth. So involved was I still with his memory, that I couldn't bear to part with a single one. I raged at them and cried as I took them out of the packing cases, just as I should have done with him when he was alive. And they sat on my shelves, frowning down on everything I tried to do.

I hope that the lessons in this book will be heeded by many people. By children, young people and their families, about the need for help. By professional colleagues, about the importance of listening to their patients' stories. By politicians and the law, about the sort of policies that are in our children's best interests. By the public and the press, about the mythology that clings to mental illness. And by all of us, about our vulnerability. But for me it has meant much more. It has helped me to come to terms with my father's memory.

Talking about his novel *The Citadel*, A.J. Cronin said: 'I have written all I feel about the medical profession, its injustices, its hide-bound unscientific stubbornness, its humbug. The horror and inequities detailed in the story I have personally witnessed. This is not an attack on individuals but against a system.'

I feel much the same. The individuals I have railed against have been as much the victims of the system in which they work as my patients have been of their lives. And I have tried to forgive them, as I have forgiven my father, trapped in his 1930s straitjacket of Methodism. But I will not forgive the system, or its rules, which impose on children, their carers and those who try to help them, a generalised formality that has nothing to do with their individual needs.

So where does that leave me? Sorting through my father's books. I have taken many of them down to the second-hand shop, passed some on to my friends, dumped the least interesting and kept the few I value most. In other words, I have been sorting through our relationship and keeping what reminds me of the good in him; the rest I do not need. I am free at last to do with my days what I will.

Exciting and a little frightening at the same time. As it is for all those patients who are freed through therapy from the expectations of the past and into a future where they can be themselves. A future whose days will be full of their self-discovery. Of new relationships. Of a chance to reassess their place in the world. For where can we live but days?

> Ah, solving that question
> Brings the priest and the doctor
> In their long coats
> Running over the fields.
>
> > Philip Larkin: 'Days', in
> > *The Whitsun Weddings*, 1964

ACKNOWLEDGEMENTS

Two years ago, my doctor told me to rest for six weeks. I am constitutionally incapable of doing nothing, so I decided to write instead. This book is the result, and I have a lot of people to thank for it finally seeing the light of day.

Firstly, the daughter-in-law who persuaded me that it was a good thing. And all my four children, their partners and my grandchildren, whom I must have bored silly in the process with my constant search for reassurance.

My agent, Jane Turnbull, who helped me knock the first draft into shape. She has held my hand and fought my corner ever since, metaphorically and through innumerable trips round the pubs of London. Thank you for the wisdom of your experience.

Rowena Webb, Maddy Price, Ian Wong and the publicity staff at Hodder have taken me through the publishing process with infinite care. Thanks also to the wonderful Gillian Stern, for her invaluable editorial insights. I trust you all.

There would be no book without the adults, children and young people whom I have tried to help over the years. They have been the beginning, the middle and the end of everything I have done. I owe it all to them, and to the colleagues and managers who have allowed me to go my eclectic way in the NHS and beyond. Sometimes with a little persuasion.

Thank you to the GPs and psychiatrists who have picked me up when I have been struggling with my own, recurrent depression. And to my family of origin, who did not understand but with whom I am reconciled in my head. You have been the inspiration to do it better in my own family and to help others to do so in theirs.

And most of all, my wife Mary. She has been my rock throughout, a yardstick for what is right or wrong, and an encouragement when I have wilted at the prospect of tackling yet another cause. She has refused to share the credit when things have gone right and willingly shared the stress when they have not. For this, my thanks, my apologies, and my love. As ever.

TEXT PERMISSIONS

Extract, p. 105, from 'Timothy Winters' by Charles Causley, reproduced with permission from *Collected Poems 1951–2000*, Macmillan, 2000

Extract, p. 290, from 'Days' by Philip Larkin, reproduced with permission from *The Whitsun Weddings*, Faber & Faber, 1964